T0188564

The Writer's Guide to
BEGINNINGS

WRITER'S DIGEST
BOOKS

Writer's Digest Books
An imprint of Penguin Random House LLC
penguinrandomhouse.com

Copyright © 2016 by Paula Munier

Printed in the United States of America
10 9 8 7 6 5 4

ISBN: 978-1-4403-4717-7

Edited by Cris Freese
Designed by Alexis Estoye

DEDICATION

For Gina

"Whatever you do, or dream you can, begin it.
Boldness has genius and power and magic in it."
—*Johann Wolfgang von Goethe*

TABLE *of* CONTENTS

FOREWORD

William Martin

───────────────── ⬡ ─────────────────

You don't have much time.

The clock starts as soon as a reader looks at the book and thinks about buying it, or an agent picks up the manuscript and wonders if this is the one they'll auction to every editor in town.

So put yourself in the mind of one of them, then count:

One one-thousand: Good title. Don't know the author but maybe—

Two one-thousand: What's it about?

Three one-thousand, four one-thousand: (With a glance at the flap copy or cover letter.) Hey, sounds interesting. Let's read a bit.

Leading to:

Five one-thousand, six one-thousand: "It was a dark and stormy night …" Nope. Heard it before. Next!

Or:

Five one-thousand. Six one-thousand: "It was the best of times, it was the worst of times." Wait … what? How can it be both at once? Let's read some more.

And ya got 'em … or not.

It can be that brutal.

Six seconds—or even sixty—is not much time to decide the fate of something that may have taken all your waking hours (and spoiled your sleep) for months … even years.

But the truth is that an editor or agent can always tell on the first page, often in the first paragraph, and sometimes in the first sentence, if you know what you're doing. Can you grab them right away? Make their skeptical eyes track to the bottom of the page? Get their itchy fingers to turn it? If not, well, manuscripts are overflowing the mail room and query e-mails are overwhelming the company servers. So there's plenty more where you came from.

Readers can be even tougher. They live in a world where one-hundred-and-forty-character sentence fragments pass for intelligent discourse. They can watch movies—actual big-time, full-length features, from *Casablanca* to *Paul Blart, Mall Cop*—on a device that fits right in their hand. This device also enables them to watch videos of cats and car crashes, or listen to music, or read random opinions from electronic "friends" scattered across the globe at any time of day or night. And it entices them with games, too, so that instead of reading about *three*-dimensional characters on a printed page, they can become *one*-dimensional characters in a three-dimensional cyberworld.

And you're working in a medium that a Spaniard named Cervantes invented five centuries ago. It's enough to make you feel like Don Quixote himself.

When readers open your book or turn on their devices and see your backlit text on their black-and-white screens, they're thinking one thing: "This better be good."

So how do you make it good?

Begin by reading a book about beginnings. Listen to Paula Munier. Her experiences as a writer, editor, and agent have taught her the most important truths that every writer—neophyte or old pro—needs to know. And you need to learn them.

But some of her truths are hard.

For starters, Paula can't teach you creativity. No one can. No one really knows where it comes from or why some have it and others, who yearn for it, don't. No one—not even you—can say how the ideas, observations, and memories swirling about in your head will coalesce into a coherent fictional idea. And no one can predict if your creativity will earn you "best of times" fame or a slow fade into that "dark and stormy night."

This leads to the second hard truth: No one can teach talent. Lots of people have the creativity to come up with a fresh plot hook or a cool character setup. But as the legendary detective novelist Robert B. Parker used to say, it's all in the execution. And execution reveals talent, that indefinable something that separates one writer from the rest, like a "third eye" that lets some see a story all the way through in a way that no one else has.

But here's the best and most important truth of all: You probably have a lot more talent than you think. If you are willing to sit at a desk, deny the distractions, and write until you're numb, you have one of the main components of talent, which is the discipline to draw it out of yourself. And when you tell a story, you are responding to one of the deepest impulses of the species. Human beings have been making sense of the world through storytelling since we could first make sense of anything. So the instinct's in you, too.

And Paula Munier can teach you the rock-solid principles and techniques that will reward your discipline and unleash your instinctive talent on all those agents, editors, and readers out there, just praying for a book to sweep them away.

E.L. Doctorow once said about beginning a novel, "You don't start with any artistic manifesto. You just do what works." This book, with incisive analysis and vivid examples, well-chosen quotes from great authors, sharp lists, and challenging exercises, will help you to discover what works best for you. It is a practical book for people who would make a living in the wildly impractical business of turning their fantasies into reality on the page.

Yes, Paula talks about the big ideas, the grand arcs, and the importance of the three-act structure in both story and scene. But she concentrates on the beginning, because the DNA of you as a writer and of your novel exists in those first sentences, in the expectations and questions they raise in the reader, in the answers they offer about you and your ability to deliver what I call the six Ps of page one: personality, punch, plot, place, pace, and promise.

Do you create a character who inhabits a believable world, who wants something, and whose desire—when met by opposition—will drive the story to ever greater levels of intensity? Do you deliver it in prose that snaps and crackles and somehow captures the mood of the story itself? Well, do you?

Writing a novel is damned hard business. That's the most basic truth. If it was easy, everyone would do it. So you can use all the help you can get. So listen to Paula. And listen to the giants she quotes, like F. Scott Fitzgerald, who once scrawled on the back of an envelope: "Action is character." It can't be said more clearly than that. And Paula will have you saying it to yourself on page one and repeating it all the way to the end.

As you struggle, remember that no matter what kind of software or hand held device competes with it, the novel is still the best form of virtual reality there is. All it needs are your well-chosen words and the imagination of a willing reader.

So what are you waiting for? Begin with *The Writer's Guide to Beginnings*. Then start writing. Grab those readers on the first page, and they may never let go.

INTRODUCTION

"The first page sells the book;
the last page sells the next book."
—*Publishing Proverb*

———————— ⬡ ————————

There is something magical about the beginning of a good story. Something profoundly moving about "Once upon a time ...," the classic opening that has resonated with readers for hundreds of years. If you've ever told a bedtime story to a child and tried to shorten it in the name of a good night's sleep, you've suffered the indignity of being told quite firmly to "start over *at the beginning*" because kids know that the best stories have beginnings too good to miss.

Beginnings are not only the door to the fictive world, they are the door to the publishing world—from agents and editors to the readers themselves. But this is a door that may shut as quickly as it opens. Agents and editors are notorious—myself included—for passing judgment on a manuscript based on only a few opening lines, paragraphs, or pages.

Readers are just as quick to judge. Consider this: The typical book buyer decides whether or not to buy a book in less than sixty seconds. The reader sees the cover and is drawn to it. Check (or click)! The reader notes the title and reads the jacket copy. Check (or click)! Then the reader opens the book to the first page and reads it. Sold (or not)!

Such is the power of a well-crafted story opening. Nail it, and you win yourself a sale, a reader, maybe even a career. Flub it, and you may lose yourself a sale, a reader, maybe even a career. As a writer, I've rewritten the beginnings of my own stories countless times, knowing that without a good beginning, no one will bother reading through to my mind-blowing ending. As an editor, I've driven writers crazy with my insistence that they get their beginnings just right because I know that good beginnings can equal good sales. And as an agent, I've passed on thousands of projects whose beginnings failed to capture my imagination—and sold the ones whose beginnings rocked their stories right into print.

Crafting a compelling opening isn't easy. The most successful stories grab the reader from word one and never let go. But that's just the beginning of what good beginnings do. The best beginnings are also rich in theme, voice, and nuance. They introduce the protagonist that readers will follow anywhere; they ground the story in setting and sow the seeds of plot points and subplots. Most important, beginnings are the harbingers of the exciting journey to come, hinting at the ending even as they shift the story into high gear, catapulting it into Act Two and sweeping the reader along for one hell of a ride.

In *The Writer's Guide to Beginnings*, you'll learn how to craft story openings that impress agents, engage editors, and captivate readers. Inspired by my popular First Ten Pages Boot Camp at Writer's Digest University, this one-of-a-kind primer reveals the secrets of creating beginnings that sell—no matter what your genre. Complete with exercises and prompts as well as examples from today's best-seller lists, *The Writer's Guide to Beginnings* provides all the tools and techniques you'll need to create the kind of beginning guaranteed to keep readers turning the pages.

So let's begin: Because if the beginning doesn't work, the rest of the story doesn't really matter.

CHAPTER ONE

IN THE BEGINNING WAS THE WORD

The Anatomy of a First Page

"At the beginning of everything is the word.
It is a miracle to which we owe the fact that we are human.
But at the same time it is a pitfall and a test,
a snare and a trial."
—*Vaclav Havel*

"The most difficult and complicated part of the writing process is the beginning." —*A.B. Yehoshua*

"Tell me a story."

These are words that have resonated with us from our very beginnings as a species. Story is part of what makes us human; in fact, storytelling is one of the few human traits that occurs in all cultures across our known history.

Since the dawn of man, we've gathered around the fire, telling stories to understand the world and our place in it, to process the past and prepare for the future, to entertain and soothe, and, ultimately, to pass on our collective knowledge and wisdom to the next generation. Storytelling is our rage against the darkness, lighting the way for our children and our children's children.

Our stories live on, to be told again and again and again. This timelessness of story is why storytellers play a sacred role in many cultures, as anointed elders who earn their place by capturing and holding the attention of their people with stories well told from the very first word.

When we answer that call to "tell me a story," we take on that sacred mantle of storyteller ourselves. So we need to start strong, too, just as our predecessors did. We need to tell our own stories well, from the very first word.

We have our work cut out for us. Unlike the storytellers of old, we do not command the attention of an audience gathered around the only source of light in the village to hear the only stories being told that evening by the only anointed storyteller in the tribe. We must compete with countless points of light, countless stories being told by countless storytellers, in books and at the movies and in our own living rooms—even on our phones.

The competition is fierce—and that's why your first words must be fierce as well.

"Those who tell the stories rule the world." —*Hopi Proverb*

FIERCE FIRST WORDS

The best story openings are fierce enough to grab the attention of readers, editors, and agents. This means keeping a lot of balls in the air. Skillful storytellers are master jugglers: They juggle voice, character, premise, setting, dialogue, conflict, point of view, style, and theme in an endless and seamless circle of story. They toss those story balls and knives and flamethrowers around with a fierceness we haven't quite experienced before. And thus we are compelled to read on.

A tall order.

Once I was in a writer's group where one of the writers was struggling with her opening. Margaret was a good storyteller, and while her story was solid, her opening did not work. Her first words were unworthy of the rest of her novel, and she knew it. She'd rewritten the first page a dozen times but remained unhappy with the results. She was stumped.

She stayed behind after everyone else had left, and we sat on my sofa and talked about the problem with the opening of her thriller.

"When in doubt," I said, "look to the masters." And I jumped up and went to my bookshelf, pulled down the first several thrillers I found, and stacked them on the coffee table.

We took turns reading aloud the first page of each novel. When we were finished, we looked at each other and grinned.

"Thanks," said Margaret. She went home and wrote a new opening. She published that book and several others since. (Check out *Under Fire*, *Under Oath*, and *Whitey on Trial* at www.margaretmclean.com.)

It worked for Margaret, and it will work for you. No matter what your genre, the quickest way to understand what constitutes a fierce beginning is to read the first words of several best-selling works. So let's pull seven stories off the shelf and take a hard look at the opening words.

Of course, the selections will be from my bookshelf since I am writing this book. Lucky for you, I have very eclectic tastes, so the odds are good that whatever genre you are writing will be represented somewhere below.

> All this happened, more or less. The war parts, anyway, are pretty much true. One guy I knew really *was* shot in Dresden for taking a teapot that wasn't his. Another guy I knew really *did* threaten to have his personal enemies killed by hired gunmen after the war. And so on. I've changed all the names.
>
> —*Slaughterhouse-Five*, by Kurt Vonnegut

> The first annoying thing is when I ask Dad what he thinks happened to Mom, he always says, "What's most important is for you to understand it's not your fault." You'll notice that wasn't even the question. When I press him, he says the second annoying thing, "The truth is complicated. There's no way one person can ever know everything about another person."
>
> Mom disappears into thin air two days before Christmas without telling me? Of course it's complicated. Just because it's complicated, just because you think you can't ever know everything about another person, it doesn't mean you can't try.
>
> It doesn't mean I can't try.
>
> —*Where'd You Go, Bernadette*, by Maria Semple

LOG ENTRY: SOL 6

I'm pretty much fucked.

That's my considered opinion.

Fucked.

Six days into what should be the greatest two months of my life, and it's turned into a nightmare.

I don't even know who'll read this. I guess someone will find it eventually. Maybe a hundred years from now.

For the record ... I didn't die on Sol 6. Certainly the rest of the crew thought I did, and I can't blame them. Maybe there'll be a day of national mourning for me, and my Wikipedia page will say, "Mark Watney is the only human being to have died on Mars."

—*The Martian*, by Andy Weir

I like to save things. Not important things like whales or people or the environment. Silly things. Porcelain bells, the kind you get at souvenir shops. Cookie cutters you'll never use, because who needs a cookie in the shape of a foot? Ribbons for my hair. Love letters. Of all the things I save, I guess you could say my love letters are my most prized possession.

I keep my letters in a teal hatbox my mom bought me from a vintage store downtown. They aren't love letters that someone else wrote for me; I don't have any of those. These are ones I've written. There's one for every boy I've ever loved—five in all.

—*To All the Boys I've Loved Before*, by Jenny Han

April 1962

Porto Vergogna, Italy

The dying actress arrived in his village the only way one could come directly—in a boat that motored into the cove, lurched past the rock jetty, and bumped against the end of the pier. She wavered a moment in the boat's stern, then extended a slender hand to grip the mahogany railing; with the other, she pressed a wide-brimmed hat against her head. All around her, shards of sunlight broke on the flickering waves.

Twenty meters away, Pasquale Tursi watched the arrival of the woman as if in a dream. Or rather, he would think later, a dream's opposite: a burst of clarity after a lifetime of sleep.

—*Beautiful Ruins*, by Jess Walter

The Writer's Guide to Beginnings

All the dying that summer began with the death of a child, a boy with golden hair and thick glasses, killed on the railroad tracks outside New Bremen, Minnesota, sliced into pieces by a thousand tons of steel speeding across the prairie toward South Dakota. His name was Bobby Cole. He was a sweet-looking kid and by that I mean he had eyes that seemed full of dreaming and he wore a half smile as if he was just about to understand something you'd spent an hour trying to explain. I should have known him better, been a better friend. He lived not far from my house and we were the same age. But he was two years behind me in school and might have been held back even more except for the kindness of certain teachers. He was a small kid, a simple child, no match at all for the diesel-fed drive of a Union Pacific locomotive.

—*Ordinary Grace*, by William Kent Krueger

"We should start back," Gared urged as the woods began to grow dark around them. "The wildlings are dead."

"Do the dead frighten you?" Ser Waymar Royce asked with just the hint of a smile.

Gared did not rise to the bait. He was an old man, past fifty, and he had seen the lordlings come and go. "Dead is dead," he said. "We have no business with the dead."

"Are they dead?" Royce asked softly. "What proof have we?"

"Will saw them," Gared said. "If he says they are dead, that's proof enough for me."

Will had known they would drag him into the quarrel sooner or later. He wished it had been later rather than sooner. "My mother told me that dead men sing no songs," he put in.

—*A Game of Thrones: Book One of A Song of Ice and Fire*, by George R.R. Martin

Each of these openings draws us in and compels us to read on. Each of these writers sets up the story, juggling voice, character, premise, setting, dialogue, conflict, point of view, style, and theme into that aforementioned seamless circle of story. Kurt Vonnegut does it in only fifty-seven words, but even the longest of these openings—the first paragraph of Krueger's *Ordinary Grace*—comes in at only 158 words. That's craftsmanship. Juggling at its best.

These are all smart writers who play to their strengths:

- Kurt Vonnegut relies on the uniqueness of his voice and the authority of his own experience to pull us into *Slaughterhouse-Five,* his psychedelic World War II classic about the absurdity of war.
- Maria Semple uses the irresistible premise of *Where'd You Go, Bernadette*—an abandoned child determined to find her mother in a world run by dissembling grown-ups—as hook, line, and sinker for us readers. And it works.
- Andy Weir serves up *The Martian*'s high-concept storyline—*Cast Away* on Mars—with style, and we fall in love with the profane astronaut recording what might be the rest of his brief life.
- Jenny Han opens with a lonely-hearted teenage girl who writes her crushes love letters and hides them in a hatbox—but we know that somehow, some day soon, those letters are going to find their way into the wrong hands. We are actively worried about her, and so we keep on turning the pages of *To All the Boys I've Loved Before.*
- Jess Walter gives us a picture-perfect setup for sweet suffering in *Beautiful Ruins*: a dying actress, a village by the sea, a handsome Italian (Walter doesn't actually say that he's handsome, but he must be; mustn't he?), and love at first sight—the kind of story no romantic can resist.
- William Kent Krueger goes for broke in his first paragraph of *Ordinary Grace*, telling us in elegiac prose that "All the dying that summer began with the death of a child"—and setting the stage for our young hero's wrenching coming of age in this elegant and evocative literary mystery.
- George R.R. Martin builds a world readers fall in love with in very few words in his opening to *A Game of Thrones*, which seduces us with wildlings and lordlings and boys in a darkening woods inhabited by the dead. We aren't sure yet what it all means, but we are compelled to find out.

The Writer's Guide to Beginnings

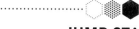

JUMP-START

What are your strengths? How might you use them to your best advantage in the opening of your story? If you're not sure, exchange first pages with a writer friend. (If you don't have any writer friends, it's time to make some, preferably some more experienced and more widely published than you.) Examine each other's story openings, and discuss how you each might better play to your respective strengths. Revise, and repeat.

Deconstructing the First Page

"In literature and in life we ultimately pursue, not conclusions, but beginnings." —*Sam Tanenhaus*

In the examples we've just seen, not only do the writers grab and keep our attention, they answer the questions every reader asks as a story begins—questions that need to be answered, if the reader is to relax and enjoy the ride.

Think of driving a new automobile for the first time. Sure, you've driven a car before; you consider yourself a good driver. Still, in order to relax and enjoy the ride, you need to know a few things about this specific vehicle before you hit the road on a long journey: What kind of car is it? Will it take you where you want to go? Does it have four-wheel drive, automatic transmission, and cruise control? Where are the headlights, the emergency brake, and the turn signals? How worn are the tires?

Before you drive on down the road, you adjust the seat and rearview mirror and check out the controls. You consult a map or turn on the GPS. You find the radio station you prefer or plug in your mp3 player. You put on your seatbelt, turn on the ignition, and look both ways before you pull out into the street. Only then do you hit the gas and go.

Readers approach a new story in the same way. Like drivers, they're going on a journey, too. But before they settle into the story, they need to know:

- What kind of story is this?
- What is the story really about?
- Who is telling the story?
- Which character should they care about most?
- Where and when does the story take place?
- How should they feel about what's happening?
- Why should they care what happens next?

Answer these questions, and your readers will relax and enjoy the ride of your story. They'll read your first fierce words and breathe a sigh of relief and pleasure—that same sigh of relief and pleasure you breathe every time you open to the first page of a new book by your favorite author. You believe you are in good hands because you've read this writer before and enjoyed the experience, and you're looking forward to repeating that reading experience. You read the first fierce words of this new book, and they confirm your belief that this is a writer who knows how to drive. This is a journey worth your time and money.

You, too, can write a fierce beginning worth your readers' time and money, a beginning that allows your readers to settle in for the long haul as they turn the pages, heading farther down the road and deeper into the journey.

Let's take a harder look at those questions because these are the questions that, left unanswered or answered insufficiently, can blow your chances of hooking agents and editors, as well as readers.

What Kind of Story Is This?

If you're writing science fiction, the story should read like science fiction. Andy Weir makes it perfectly clear on the first page of *The Martian* that he is writing science fiction when the main character tells us that people probably think he "is the only human being to have died on Mars."

NOTE: If you're thinking the title *The Martian* says it all, you're wrong. Readers (and agents, editors, publishers, and booksellers) hate it when the title sounds like one thing and the book turns out to be something else altogether. That's the sort of marketplace confusion that can derail a career. Your first words must reinforce the genre identity set by the title, or you'll lose the reader—and the sale.

Similarly, William Kent Krueger makes it clear in his first words that he's writing a crime novel: "All the dying that summer began with the death of a child ..." Jenny Han writes about teenage girls thinking about teenage boys—what else could it be but a young-adult novel? Jess Walter shows us a man falling in love with a woman far above his station, and we fall in love with another love story. George R.R. Martin drops us into a dark world full of strange creatures, and we know we're reading a fantasy. Maria Semple gives us a precocious kid who ignores her father's prevarications and decides to find her mother on her own in classic book-club-best-seller form. Even Kurt Vonnegut makes it clear we're about to read a story unlike any we've read before, a story that defies classification as we know it—memoir, science fiction, war story, literary fiction, or ... whatever it is, it's good.

FOR WANT OF A GENRE

I've learned the hard way that it's very hard to sell any story that doesn't fit neatly into a known category. I won't know where or how to sell it, the editor won't know how to pitch it to her publishing board, the publisher won't know how to market and/or promote it, the booksellers won't know where to shelve it, and the readers won't know where to find it.

"For want of a genre, the sale was lost ..."

As an agent, when I read a story opening that doesn't read like the genre the writer claims it to be, I pass—and fast—because I can only assume that the writer doesn't know his genre well enough to write a story that will appeal to that genre's readers.

Which means that I can't sell it.

Unless you're Kurt Vonnegut. But there's only one Kurt Vonnegut—and he's dead. May God rest his beautiful writer's soul.

If you're the *next* Kurt Vonnegut, then you probably don't need this book. Then again, maybe you do. Either way, I'd like to hear from you.

What Is the Story Really About?

Think about the last great book you read, the one you recommended to your best friend, your book club, or your writers' group. And when you did, your BFF/book clubber/writer asked, "What's it about?" The odds are good that you could answer in fifty words or less.

For me, that great book was *The Rosie Project* by Graeme Simsion. I recommended it to my friend Susan, who asked me: "What's it about?" And I said: "It's a romantic comedy about a genetics professor with Asperger's in Melbourne, Australia, who decides to use the scientific method to find himself the perfect wife."

But it just as easily could have been *The Martian*. In that case I would have said, "It's a science-fiction novel about an astronaut who gets stranded alone on Mars and how he tries to survive."

Or *Where'd You Go, Bernadette*: "It's a very funny novel about a girl in Seattle whose mother disappears right before Christmas and how she'll go to the ends of the earth—literally—to find her."

Or *Beautiful Ruins*: "It's a love story about an Italian guy from a remote coastal village who falls for a beautiful actress with a secret."

Or *To All the Boys I've Loved Before*: "It's a young-adult novel about a teenage girl yearning for love who writes secret letters to her crushes and then ..."

Or *Ordinary Grace*: "It's a mystery about a Minnesota boy named Frank whose friend is run over by a train and how his death and the ones that follow affect Frank, Frank's family, and the whole town."

Or *Slaughterhouse-Five*: "It's a wild story about an American POW in Dresden during World War II. A lot of other crazy stuff happens, too, but I don't want to ruin it for you."

Or *A Game of Thrones*: "It's like Tolkien's *Lord of the Rings* and the Wars of the Roses had a love child—a fantasy about wildlings and lordlings and power and death and dragons and everything, man, just everything." Okay, okay, so *A Game of Thrones* is the exception to this rule. As it turns out, *A Game of Thrones* is the exception to a lot of rules, which we'll learn more about in chapter five.

The point is, in most of these stories, the opening makes it very clear what the story is about. Readers want to know what they're reading; they want to know that it's their kind of story. They don't want to wander around in a story that doesn't know what it is. That's a story going nowhere.

I can't sell a story going nowhere. Since becoming an agent, I've learned that if I can't say what a story is about in 50 words or less, I can't sell it. And even when I can describe it, if it isn't clear what the story is about from the very opening of the story, I still can't sell it.

Who Is Telling the Story?

Consider the source. When you're writing a story, your point-of-view character is the source. So readers need to know right away who this POV character is. The POV character is often the protagonist. In five of our seven examples, the protagonist is telling the story from a first-person point of view.

First-person point of view is often the POV of choice for writers with a strong voice. I admit to being a sucker for a strong voice and thus a sucker for first-person point of view, which demands a strong voice. (**NOTE:** I am not alone in this. Agents, editors, and readers alike will follow a strong voice anywhere.)

In stories with multiple points of view, the POV character shifts from one character in one scene to another character in the next. In a mystery, say, the point of view may shift from hero to villain to victim and back again. Both *Beautiful Ruins* and *A Game of Thrones* are written in multiple third-person POV. Even so, the authors make it clear who's telling the story in the opening scene and in every scene thereafter.

We'll discuss the finer details of point of view in chapter five, but what you need to know now is this: Make it clear from the very beginning who is telling your story.

Which Character Should Readers Care About Most?

Readers always play favorites. They always prefer one character over all the others—and with any luck, that character is your protagonist. To put it another way, if you do your job right, the character that readers will care about most is your protagonist. They will fall in love with your heroine and follow her through hell and high water to "The End" (and beyond, should you be fortunate and skillful enough to create a series character that readers will pay to spend time with book after book).

The sooner you can make it perfectly clear who your heroine is and why readers should care about her, the better.

As readers, we can't help but care about an American prisoner of war stuck in Dresden during World War II (*Slaughterhouse-Five*), a forsaken child determined to find her mother (*Where'd You Go, Bernadette*), an astronaut marooned on Mars (*The Martian*), a teenage girl whose secret crushes won't stay secret for long (*To All the Boys I've Loved Before*), an Italian hotelkeeper destined for a doomed love (*Beautiful Ruins*), a boy whose friend is mysteriously killed by a train (*Ordinary Grace*), and a kid who's seen the dead wildlings for himself and wants to get the heck out of the dark woods, pronto (*A Game of Thrones*). These are all characters who (1) engage our sympathy and (2) find themselves in situations that command our attention.

Ask yourself why readers should care about your protagonist. What about your story opening will endear your readers to your hero? What about your heroine and/or her situation will evoke empathy on the part of the reader? What will resonate with readers?

One of the most common complaints I hear from editors when they pass on projects is this: "I just didn't fall in love with the protagonist." You want everyone who reviews your work—agents, editors, and readers—to fall in love with your hero. The sooner, the better. What you're aiming for in your story opening is love at first sight.

Where and When Does the Story Take Place?

Eudora Welty once said, "Every story would be another story, and unrecognizable as art, if it took up its characters and plot and happened somewhere else." Welty believed that "fiction depends for its life on place." The life of your story depends on place, too. That's why it's critical you ground your story in setting from the very beginning. Think of it as the establishing shot in a film.

Here are the opening settings in our examples:

- Dresden, Germany during World War II (*Slaughterhouse-Five*)
  NOTE: If you're thinking that the setting is really Ilium, New York, 1968 ... well, fair enough. But the narrator (who may be in Ilium and may or may not be Billy Pilgrim or even Vonnegut himself) is talking about the war, and his imprisonment in Slaughterhouse-Five. It's complicated (in theory, if not in the reading) but compelling.
- Seattle, Present Day, Christmastime (*Where'd You Go, Bernadette*)
- Mars, Sol 6, sometime in the future [2035, according to the readers geeky and obsessed enough to figure it out] (*The Martian*)
- Suburban Charlottesville, Virginia, Present Day (*To All the Boys I've Loved Before*)
- Porto Vergogna, Italy, April 1962 (*Beautiful Ruins*)
- New Bremen, Minnesota, Summer of 1961 (*Ordinary Grace*)
- The haunted forest, another time and space (*A Game of Thrones*)

Each writer's approach to setting is as different as the settings themselves. Most are settings that are new to readers, as most of us did not survive the firebombing of Dresden or visit the Ligurian coast in 1962 or spend the summer of 1961 in small-town Minnesota. None of us has braved the haunted forest beyond the Wall in the North or the alien landscape of Mars. That's why the authors who take us to these places spend more time on setting throughout their stories.

The only settings here that most of us might be familiar with are the city of Seattle and the insular suburban world of the American teenager. So there's little mention of setting in these short opening excerpts of *Where'd You Go, Bernadette* and *To All the Boys I've Loved Before.* But within just a few pages of the former, Maria Semple will begin her hilarious satirizing of Seattle's coffee and Microsoft culture and foreshadow the Antarctic setting that plays such a prominent role later in the story. In the latter, Jenny Han uses the bland homogenous suburban landscape of American adolescence—McMansions and malls, Costcos and drive-thrus, school libraries and gymnasium pools—as a backdrop to the colorful and chaotic emotions of puberty.

What is your setting? How do you ground your story in that setting? What about that setting is unique to that story, and how does that setting help shape your story? Taking readers somewhere they've never been before—be it Mars, Antarctica, or New Bremen—is always an attraction, to agents, editors, and readers alike. If you're sending readers on a journey to somewhere more familiar than Winterfell, then you'll need to show them your singular view of that familiar place—as Maria Semple does in her farcical take on Seattle—or use that familiarity to highlight contrast, as Jenny Han does while chronicling angst-ridden teenagers in the humdrum of suburbia.

Wherever you place your story and however you distinguish that place, you should aim for creating a setting so well-drawn that it becomes a character as compelling as any other in your story.

How Should Readers Feel About What's Happening?

Why do we love stories? Why do we read fiction and memoir? Sure, we want to be entertained; we want to learn about new people and places, but most of all, we want to feel something.

Art is meant to be cathartic—and your story is no different. The best stories are rollercoasters of emotion for the reader, who hopes to be soothed and scared, enlightened and misled, teased and thrilled, angered and delighted, agitated and becalmed, embraced and spurned, reassured and unnerved, saddened, maddened, gladdened, and ultimately, *moved.*

The sooner you can evoke emotion in your readers, the sooner you draw them into your story. Make 'em laugh, make 'em cry, make 'em scream in fear and joy and surprise.

The Writer's Guide to Beginnings

When the woods darken around Will in *A Game of Thrones*, we're afraid for him and what's to come. In *Ordinary Grace*, we share Frank's sympathy for his dead friend, his melancholy and bewilderment at the mysterious death, and his survivor's guilt. Lara Jean tells us about her secret love letters in *To All the Boys I've Loved Before*, and we remember the angst of our own teenage crushes and worry about what will happen to her when the letters are discovered. When Bee decides to find her mother in *Where'd You Go, Bernadette*, we feel the pain and confusion of her abandonment, and applaud her determination as we pray that she is not doomed to disappointment, for we have also suffered disappointment at the hands of our parents and we know how much it hurts. We watch Pasquale Tursi fall for the elusive and beautiful actress in *Beautiful Ruins*, and our hearts ache along with his. In *The Martian*, we feel as frustrated and frightened as Mark Watney when the weight of his impossible situation sinks in.

And when we read the tragicomic opening of *Slaughterhouse-Five*, as told by the narrator/Billy Pilgrim/Vonnegut, we feel like laughing and crying and screaming all at the same time.

So it goes.

Identify the emotion you need to evoke in your readers in your fierce first words. Evoke that emotion successfully, and you've engaged your readers—and the pull of that emotion will compel them on to the next page, and the next and the next.

"Good writing is supposed to evoke sensation in the reader— not the fact that it is raining—but the feeling of being rained upon." —*E.L. Doctorow*

Why Should Readers Care What Happens Next?

This is a bigger—and more complicated—question than you may think. This question has to do with: (1) the action happening as the story opens, (2) the premise of the story, and (3) the big idea of the story itself.

These three factors all play into how much your readers will care about what happens next. And if they don't care what happens next, they won't read on—and you've lost them, possibly forever.

Sometimes, all three factors are the same thing; sometimes they are very different things. Let's take a look at each in turn.

1. **THE ACTION HAPPENING AS THE STORY OPENS:** One of the main reasons that people stop reading is because nothing happens in those opening pages. Or at least nothing *interesting enough* happens. The engine of narrative thrust must begin as your story begins and keep running hard until your story ends. Narrative thrust is the tight construction of story, line by line, beat by beat, event by event, pushing the action forward—and the reader with it. A lack of narrative thrust is the most common reason I pass on manuscripts because, as an agent, I know that the basic formula of commercial fiction is this: *No narrative thrust equals no sale.* Without narrative thrust to drive your plot, you have a story going nowhere. And, at the risk of repeating myself, no one will buy a story going nowhere. (See chapter eight to learn about testing your story for narrative thrust.)

2. **THE PREMISE OF THE STORY:** Premise is the basis, or the starting point, of a plot. Without a strong premise, you can't get your story off to a good start. You're grounded before you've even begun—a shuttle with no rocket boosters—and the reader is grounded with you. Your premise needs to be compelling enough to blast your story shuttle right into outer space, deep into the unknown territory of your narrative, where readers long to go.

3. **THE BIG IDEA OF THE STORY:** This is the idea that sells the story to agents, editors, and readers. It's the hook, what sets it apart from the competition, what persuades those agents, editors, and readers to invest in this story instead of a story written by one of the best-selling authors they already know and love. The big idea is what everyone is looking for; give me (or any agent) a big idea, and I have a great pitch. And pitching is how I sell books. We'll talk more in chapter three about how to come up with a big idea, but for now, just know that the bigger the idea is and the sooner it shows up in your story, the better your chance of selling it.

In *Beautiful Ruins*, two of these three factors are the same. The story opens with innkeeper Pasquale Tursi watching, mesmerized, as a boat carrying a beautiful and mysterious American actress pulls into the cove at Porto Vergogna. Tursi is smitten, and as a result, the trajectory of his life is forever changed. That's the opening action and the premise, but the story itself is far more complicated, weaving storylines, spanning decades, and hopping continents in what the *New York Times* called a "high-wire feat of bravura storytelling." As Jess Walter says, *Beautiful Ruins* is "a story about fame and how we all endeavor now to live our lives like movie stars, like celebrities, each of us an eager inner publicist managing our careers and our romances and our fragile self-images (our Facebook pages and LinkedIn profiles)." Or as I would have pitched it: *Love Story* meets *La Dolce Vita*—complete with Elizabeth Taylor and Richard Burton. Big idea, indeed.

Yet in *A Game of Thrones,* all three of these factors are different. The story opens with Will and dead wildlings and ends with a lethal encounter with one of a deadly race of creatures known only as the Others. The premise of the novel, however, is revealed nearly fifty pages later, when Ned Stark is named the Hand of the King, setting off a struggle for power—*a game of thrones*—that will last five volumes and counting. And the big idea of *A Game of Thrones* is very big, colossal even: an epic fantasy that, as we've said, could best be described—and pitched—as "*Lord of the Rings* meets the Wars of the Roses."

Finally, in *The Martian*, all three of these factors are the same. The story opens with an astronaut alone on Mars, trying to figure out how he can survive. That's the action of the story opening, the premise, and the big idea.

What happens in your story opening? How does that relate to the premise of your story and the big idea that differentiates your story from all others?

IMPROMPTU

Consider these same questions from earlier in the chapter now in relation to your own story:

- What kind of story is this?
- What is the story really about?
- Who is telling the story?
- Which character should readers care about most?
- Where and when does the story take place?
- How should readers feel about what's happening?
- Why should readers care what happens next?

Set a timer for ten minutes, and write out the answer to each. If you can't do it in ten minutes, you don't know enough about your story yet.

PUTTING IT ALL TOGETHER

Now that we have discussed what strong story openings do to capture readers—the questions and answers that mark strong story openings— let's tackle the meat of the opening itself. In chapter two, we'll explore the most dramatic way to open a story and the mechanism by which you can achieve that drama.

"There is something delicious about writing the first words of a story. You never quite know where they'll take you." —*Beatrix Potter*

CHAPTER TWO

THE END IS WHERE WE START FROM

Scene One

"What we call the beginning is often the end.
And to make an end is to make a beginning."
—*T.S. Eliot*

"In the long run, I write novels. In the short run, I write scenes."
—*Timothy Hallinan*

The most important thing your opening needs to do is this: *Keep the reader reading.*

As someone who reads thousands of story openings every year—and no, I'm not exaggerating—I can tell you that surprisingly few keep the reader reading. At our agency, we ask writers to include the first ten pages of their stories in their query letters. We do that because we need to see the story itself—not just the pitch for the story.

I receive some ten-thousand queries a year. I also read the work of hundreds of writers I meet at conferences, workshops, boot camps, and of course, that of my own clients and friends, as well as best-selling authors. No matter how you do the math, that's a lot of story openings. More often than not, I do not keep reading. Here's why: I'm not engaged, entertained, or enlightened. I'm mostly bored. And so I put that story down and move on to the next. And the next. And the next.

When I first started at the agency and found myself overwhelmed by the sheer volume of the queries in my inbox—over a thousand during my very first week on the job—our founder, Gina Panettieri, told me not to stress over it.

"For every two-hundred queries you receive," Gina said, "you'll only find one or two story openings compelling enough to prompt you to request the rest of the manuscript."

As it turns out, Gina was right (about that and nearly everything else related to the job, she says with humility). I only request a handful of complete manuscripts every month. These are the ones that work, the ones that capture my attention and hold it, the ones that answer the questions we talked about in chapter one.

Just as important, the story openings good enough to stand out from the rest of the slush pile are those that avoid the common mistakes that sink the others. The most significant of which is this: *Nothing happens.*

Too many writers open with backstory or description or inner monologue—which means that nothing is happening. The opening falls flat on its face, felled by its own static weight. Or something is happening, but it's something that we've seen a million times before—and don't care to see again. Or something is happening, but it's drowning in minutiae. Or something is happening, but it's not fully dramatized.

Dramatization is the key. Drama is the stuff of storytelling—and it's what separates the boring beginnings from the compelling beginnings. Dramatize your opening, and you will fulfill the promise of "Once upon a time."

This means writing in scenes.

THE SCENE'S THE THING

The most efficient and effective way to begin a story is with a scene. Scenes are the units of storytelling, the pieces of continuous action that you string together to form your narrative. Writing in scenes is the best way to ensure that something happens, which prevents you from boring your readers—and keeps them reading.

Because if nothing's happening, it's not a scene.

A well-written scene accommodates all of the elements we've talked about: genre, action, character, setting, voice, emotion, etc. What's more, well-written scenes are the key to building and sustaining narrative thrust. Write a great opening scene, and you give your story the rocket boosters it needs to launch your beginning.

"[The Rosie Project is] structured as a romantic comedy and reads as a series of scenes. And it moves along pretty quickly."
—*Graeme Simsion*

TOP TEN (PLUS ONE!) REASONS YOUR STORY OPENING DOESN'T WORK

1. Not enough happens.
2. The story's genre is not clear.
3. It's not clear what the story is about.
4. It's not clear who the protagonist is.
5. There's nothing unique enough about the story to set it apart.
6. The story is not grounded in setting.
7. The protagonist is not likable or admirable and readers can't relate to him/her.
8. The story does not engage the reader's emotions.
9. It's all showing and no telling.
10. The story is not told in a strong voice.
11. There's no narrative thrust.

Let's take a look at some swell opening scenes. These are all stories in which the writer begins *in medias res*, that is, "into the middle of things." As an agent, I find that the easiest stories to sell are the ones with strong opening scenes. Gone are the days of the nineteenth-century novel, which could begin with elaborate descriptions of the landscape, long backstories of every character, and expansive discourse on the nature of philosophy and the meaning of life. In the 140-character world in which we live and write, we don't have much time to get our stories moving.

That doesn't mean every story has to start with car chases and explosions, but every story should start with compelling opening action. As we'll see in the following examples—which run the gamut from memoir and women's fiction to thriller and science fiction—action counts.

> When a high-powered rifle bullet hits living flesh it makes a distinctive—*pow-WHOP*—sound that is unmistakable even at tremendous distance. There is rarely an echo or fading reverberation or the tailing rumbling hum that is the sound of a miss. The guttural boom rolls over the terrain but stops sharply in a close-ended way, as if jerked back. A hit is blunt and solid like an airborne grunt. When the sound is heard and identified, it isn't easily forgotten.
>
> When Wyoming Game Warden Joe Pickett heard the sound, he was building a seven-foot elk fence on the perimeter of a rancher's haystack. He paused, his fencing pliers frozen in midtwirl. Then he stepped back, lowered his head, and listened. He slipped the pliers into the back pocket of his jeans and took off his straw cowboy hat to wipe his forehead with a bandanna. His red uniform shirt stuck to his chest, and he felt a single, warm trickle of sweat crawl down his spine into his Wranglers.
>
> —*Open Season,* by C.J. Box

In this first of the popular Joe Pickett series, C.J. Box opens with a bang—or rather, a "*pow-WHOP*"—that grabs the reader by the throat and doesn't let go. We meet our hero on his feet, working hard, and ready to follow that shot wherever it takes him—even if it makes him sweat. *And we're sweating for him.*

> Well, I have broken the toilet. I flushed, the water rose, then rose higher, too much. I stared at it, told it, "No!" slammed the lid down, then raised it back up again. Water still rising. Water still rising. I put the lid down, turned out the light, tiptoed out of the bathroom, across the hall, and into my bedroom, where I slid under my bed.
>
> Now I hear the water hitting the bathroom floor. It goes on and on. Niagara Falls, where the honeymooners go and do what they do. There is the heavy tread of his footsteps coming rapidly up the stairs. I hear him turn on the bathroom light and swear softly to himself. "Katie!" he yells. He comes into my room. I stop breathing. "Katherine!" I am

stone. I am off the planet, a star, lovely and unnamed. He goes into my sister's room. "What the hell did you do to the toilet?"

—*Durable Goods,* by Elizabeth Berg

In Elizabeth Berg's classic debut novel, we meet twelve-year-old Katie in full crisis mode. She clogs the toilet and then panics, sneaking out of the bathroom and into her bedroom. She's so scared of the grown-up who's heard the water overflowing and is coming up the stairs calling for her that she hides under the bed. *And we're scared for her.*

The trees were tall, but I was taller, standing above them on a steep mountain slope in northern California. Moments before, I'd removed my hiking boots and the left one had fallen into those trees, first catapulting into the air when my enormous backpack toppled onto it, then skittering across the gravelly trail and flying over the edge. It bounced off of a rocky outcropping several feet beneath me before disappearing into the forest canopy below, impossible to retrieve. I let out a stunned gasp, though I'd been in the wilderness thirty-eight days and by then I'd come to know that anything could happen and that everything would. But that doesn't mean I wasn't shocked when it did.

My boot was gone. Actually gone.

—*Wild: From Lost to Found on the Pacific Crest Trail,*
by Cheryl Strayed

Cheryl Strayed begins her best-selling account of her life-changing 1,100-mile trek along the Pacific Crest Trail thirty-eight days into the journey—*in medias res*—at the point where she loses a boot, the only thing between her and the rough ground she's traversing, exposing the most vulnerable and critical body part, the part hikers must protect above all others: the foot. Cheryl is alarmed by this turn of events. *And we're alarmed, too, by her predicament and her unshod foot.*

Maggie and Ira Moran had to go to a funeral in Deer Lick, Pennsylvania. Maggie's girlhood friend had lost her husband. Deer Lick lay on a narrow country road some ninety miles north of Baltimore, and the funeral was scheduled for ten-thirty Saturday morning; so Ira figured they should start around eight. This made him grumpy. (He was not an early-morning kind of man.) Also Saturday was his busiest day at work, and he had no one to cover for him. Also their car was in the body shop. It had needed extensive repairs and Saturday morning at opening time, eight o'clock exactly, was the soonest they could get it back. Ira said maybe they'd just better not go, but Maggie said they had to. She and Serena had been friends forever. Or nearly forever: forty-two years, beginning with Miss Kimmel's first grade.

They planned to wake up at seven, but Maggie must have set the alarm wrong and so they overslept. They had to dress in a hurry and rush through breakfast, making do with faucet coffee and cold cereal. Then Ira headed off for the store on foot to leave a note for his customers, and Maggie walked to the body shop. She was wearing her best dress—blue and white sprigged, with cape sleeves—and crisp black pumps, on account of the funeral.

—*Breathing Lessons*, by Anne Tyler

Anne Tyler's Pulitzer Prize-winning novel opens with long-married couple Ira and Maggie Moran late to a funeral ninety miles away, a journey that begins with the usual marital complaints—bad coffee, cold cereal, and a car in the shop—and promises to proceed downhill from there. Ira's worried about his customers. Maggie's worried about her grieving friend. *And we're worried about their marriage.*

Ria's mother had always been very fond of film stars. It was a matter of sadness to her that Clark Gable had died on the day Ria was born. Tyrone Power had died on the day Hilary had been born just two years earlier. But somehow that wasn't as bad. Hilary hadn't seen off the great king of cinema as Ria had. Ria could never see *Gone With the Wind* without feeling somehow guilty.

She told this to Ken Murray, the first boy who kissed her. She told him in the cinema. Just as he was kissing her, in fact.

"You're very boring," he said, trying to open her blouse.

"I'm not boring," Ria cried with some spirit. "Clark Gable is there on the screen and I've told you something interesting. A coincidence. It's not boring."

—*Tara Road,* by Maeve Binchy

In this opening scene, Maeve Binchy gives us Ria, a romantic teenage girl experiencing one of life's great rites of passage: her first kiss. But

The Writer's Guide to Beginnings

Ria's expectations are the stuff of cinema—and the boy's expectations are the stuff of testosterone. Ria is completely misunderstood by her supposed admirer, not to mention disappointed and somewhat disillusioned. *And we are disappointed for her as well—and worried that this misunderstanding/disappointment/disillusionment cycle might prove the first of many.*

"Marx has completely changed the way I view the world," declared the Pallières boy this morning, although ordinarily he says nary a word to me.

Antoine Pallières, prosperous heir to an old industrial dynasty, is the son of one of my eight employers. There he stood, the most recent eructation of the ruling corporate elite—a class that reproduces itself solely by means of virtuous and proper hiccups—beaming at his discovery, sharing it with me without thinking or ever dreaming for a moment that I might actually understand what he was referring to. How could the laboring classes understand Marx? Reading Marx is an arduous task, his style is lofty, the prose is subtle and the thesis complex.

And that is when I very nearly—foolishly—gave myself away.

"You ought to read *The German Ideology*," I told him. Little cretin in his conifer green duffle coat.

—*The Elegance of the Hedgehog,* by Muriel Barbery

Muriel Barbery opens her international bestseller with this quietly subversive encounter between middle-aged Parisian concierge Renée and young Antoine, whose wealthy family lives in the building. Renée reveals that she is not what she seems to be, not what she actively pretends to be, and she is dismayed that she has come so close to blowing her cover. *And we are dismayed as well, not just because she is so nearly found out but because she feels it necessary to hide who she really is and because we sense that there is more dissembling to come—and consequences to pay.*

"So, have you split up now?"

"Are you being funny?"

People quite often thought Marcus was being funny when he wasn't. He couldn't understand it. Asking his mum whether she'd split up with Roger was a perfectly sensible question, he thought: they'd had a big row, then they'd gone off into the kitchen to talk quietly, and after a little while they'd come out looking serious, and Roger had come over to him, shaken his hand and wished him luck at his new school, and then he'd gone.

"Why would I want to be funny?"

"Well, what does it look like to you?"

"It looks to me like you've split up. But I just wanted to make sure."

"We've split up."

"So he's gone?"

"Yes, Marcus, he's gone."

He didn't think he'd ever get used to this business. He had quite liked Roger, and the three of them had been out a few times; now, apparently, he'd never see him again. He didn't mind, but it was weird if you thought about it. He'd once shared a toilet with Roger, when they were both busting for a pee after a car journey. You'd think that if you'd peed with someone you ought to keep in touch with them somehow.

—*About a Boy,* by Nick Hornby

In this poignant beginning, we meet Marcus, a lonely boy baffled by the world of adult relationships. Marcus is questioning his mother, trying to understand what has happened between her and her latest boyfriend. Marcus is saddened and unnerved by Roger's abrupt departure because inevitably, his mother's loss is his loss as well. *And we're saddened and unnerved for Marcus, who must now face his new school without the buffer of Roger in his life.*

It was a pleasure to burn.

It was a special pleasure to see things eaten, to see things blackened and *changed.* With the brass nozzle in his fists, with this great python spitting its venomous kerosene upon the world, the blood pounded in his head, and his hands were the hands of some amazing conductor playing all the symphonies of blazing and burning to bring down the tatters and charcoal ruins of history. With his symbolic helmet numbered 451 on his stolid head, and his eyes all orange flame with the thought of what came next, he flicked the igniter and the house jumped up in a gorging fire that burned the evening sky red and yellow and black. He strode in a swarm of fireflies. He wanted above all, like the old joke, to shove a marshmallow on a stick in the furnace, while the flapping pigeon-winged books died on the porch and lawn of the house. While the books went up in sparkling whirls and blew away on a wind turned dark with burning.

Montag grinned the fierce grin of all men singed and driven back by flame.

—*Fahrenheit 451,* by Ray Bradbury

Ray Bradbury's classic futuristic story opens with firefighter Montag burning down a house full of books with a pleasure that borders on madness. *We are equally disgusted and intrigued by his behavior, and we read on to find out why he would do such a thing and who will stop him.*

1978

"Wake up, genius."

Rothstein didn't want to wake up. The dream was too good. It featured his first wife months before she became his first wife, seventeen and perfect from head to toe. Naked and shimmering. Both of them naked. He was nineteen, with grease under his fingernails, but she hadn't minded that, at least not then, because his head was full of dreams and that was what she cared about. She believed in the dreams even more than he did, and she was right to believe. In this dream she was laughing and reaching for the part of him that was easiest to grab. He tried to go deeper, but then a hand began shaking his shoulder, and the dream popped like a soap bubble.

He was no longer nineteen and living in a two-room New Jersey apartment, he was six months shy of his eightieth birthday and living on a farm in New Hampshire, where his will specified he should be buried. There were men in his bedroom. They were wearing ski masks, one red, one blue, and one canary-yellow. He saw this and tried to believe it was just another dream—the sweet one had slid into a nightmare, as they sometimes did—but then the hand let go of his arm, grabbed his shoulder, and tumbled him onto the floor. He struck his head and cried out.

—*Finders Keepers,* by Stephen King

Stephen King knows how to start a story—and this one is no exception. He gives us an old man dreaming of his youth and awakening to the nightmare of three masked men in his bedroom. He is sorry that his dream is over and scared of the men assaulting him. *We are both sorry and scared for him.*

> July
>
> When she saw the glint of the revolver barrel through the broken glass in the window, Hadley Knox thought, *I'm going to die for sixteen bucks an hour.* Sixteen bucks an hour, medical, and dental. She dove behind her squad car as the thing went off, a monstrous thunderclap that rolled on and on across green-gold fields of hay. The bullet smacked into the maple tree she had parked under with a meaty thud, showering her in wet, raw splinters.
>
> She could smell the stink of her own fear, a mixture of sweat trapped beneath her uniform and the bitter edge of cordite floating across the farmhouse yard.
>
> —*I Shall Not Want*, by Julia Spencer-Fleming

This crime novel opens with yet another cop under fire—but this is a cop whose ironic self-awareness never fails her, even when the bullets are flying. *She so badly wants to live, and we so badly want her to live, and we keep on reading in the hope that she does.*

In all of these examples—the longest of which is only 232 words—something happens. Sometimes it's as subtle as an intellectual sleight of hand, as in the concierge's conversation with the "little cretin" in *The Elegance of the Hedgehog*. Sometimes it's as brash as a bullet, as in the gunshots plaguing the game warden in *Open Season* and the cop in *I Shall Not Want*. But regardless, *something* happens, and it happens to *someone*, someone we find endearing, like Marcus, the boy querying his mother in *About a Boy*, Katie, the girl hiding under the bed in *Durable Goods*, and Ria, the dreamy-eyed teenager longing for true romance in *Tara Road*. Perhaps it happens to someone we find amusing, vulnerable, and all too human, like middle-aged marrieds Ira and Maggie Moran in *Breathing Lessons* or old Rothstein dreaming of lost loves in *Finders*

The Writer's Guide to Beginnings

Keepers. It might even happen to someone we find compelling but abhorrent, like Montag the book burner in *Fahrenheit 451.*

Something happens to someone, and that someone reacts. Then the reader reacts and keeps on reading. This is the engine of story. As the writer, it's your job to build the scenes, the units of action, that fuel the engine of your story. You make something happen to your characters, your characters react, and the reader reacts ... and turns the page. Repeat. Repeat. Repeat. All the way to "The End."

JUMP-START

Take a look at the first 250 words of your story. Examine it in light of the engine of story:

- **SOMETHING HAPPENS TO SOMEONE.** What happens in your story? To whom?
- **THAT SOMEONE REACTS.** What does that someone do?
- **THE READER REACTS.** How does the reader react? Are you sure? Give the opening to a few readers, and then ask them how they feel about what they've read. Did they react the way you intended?

NOTE: This is a good exercise for your writers' group. Exchange openings, and discuss the engine of each story.

THE STRUCTURE OF THE SCENE

We've been examining the very first paragraphs of the opening scenes of great stories. But scenes are units of action, as we've observed. Just as your story has a beginning, middle, and end, each scene in your story should follow that same structure. Likewise, there's an arc to each scene, just as there is an arc to your story. Crafting scenes with beginnings, middles, and ends is the way you build a story, beat by beat, scene by scene, and act by act.

Beginnings, Middles, Ends

"People have forgotten how to tell a story. Stories don't have a middle or an end anymore. They usually have a beginning that never stops beginning." —*Steven Spielberg*

Director Steven Spielberg knows how to begin a story. A storyteller of the first order, he knows how to grab the audience and hold its attention. Let's take a look at the opening scenes from three of his most successful films:

Jaws: Scene One

BEGINNING: A drunken teenage boy chases a girl named Chrissie along the beach. He's trying to catch up with her as she strips and runs into the ocean.

MIDDLE: Chrissie swims out towards the buoy and is pulled down into the water. She's screaming and thrashing and we can't see what's got her. Too drunk to stand, the boy falls down on the sand and passes out.

END: Chrissie manages to make it to the buoy, but she's pulled down again and this time, there's no escape from whatever has taken her. The boy dozes on the beach.

Watching this scene, we are pulled into the story kicking and screaming. We watch Chrissie disappear under the water, and we wonder who'll be next. This iconic scene is so terrifying that many who saw the film for the first time in theaters gave up going into the ocean forever. I myself avoided seeing the film for years because I was afraid that if I saw it, I'd never swim in the sea again.

Raiders of the Lost Ark: Scene One

BEGINNING: Indiana Jones is trekking through the jungle with Satipo, hunting for a golden idol. He consults the map and finds the cave.

MIDDLE: Once inside, Indy foils the spiders and booby traps and discovers the idol. He swaps a bag of sand for the idol—but the theft triggers a new series of booby traps. Satipo betrays Indy, steals the idol, and leaves Indy for dead. Indy uses a fraying vine to escape and goes after Satipo, who has fallen victim to one of the booby traps. Indy grabs the idol. A huge stone ball threatens to steamroll him, and he races out of the cave.

END: Upon exiting, Indy lands at the feet of rival archaeologist Belloq, who is backed by a large group of hostile natives. The Frenchman steals the idol, but Indy escapes the angry natives and makes it to his plane just in time.

This scene is one of the most entertaining scenes ever filmed, and it sets the stage for the rest of the serial-style action to come. The opening of *Raiders of the Lost Ark* is one of the many reasons this movie remains a crowd-pleaser. I for one am compelled to watch it whenever it's on—and it's on a lot—whether I want to or not.

E.T.: Scene One

BEGINNING: E.T. opens with a small alien wandering away from the area where his fellow aliens are collecting horticultural specimens from Earth to take back to their home planet.

MIDDLE: When a group of scientists discover the spaceship, the aliens prepare to leave. One alien stands at the stairs leading into the craft, waiting for E.T. However, the scientists close in, and the aliens close up their ship and take off into space, leaving E.T behind.

END: E.T. is left alone on Earth. He runs away from the scientists, toward the bright lights of suburbia.

From the very beginning, we fall in love with E.T., a little extraterrestrial abandoned on an unfriendly planet, just as we would any lost child. We want him to find his way home safely somehow, and are compelled to see him through his journey back to his own kind, come what may.

All of these beginnings have memorable opening scenes built on a strong structure. The beginnings, middles, and ends of each scene are clear and solid. We know what each story is about right from the very beginning: something deadly lurking just below the surface of the sea, an adventurer/archaeologist willing to risk everything for priceless treasure, an extraterrestrial lost on Earth. And we are hooked.

The End Is Where We Start From

IMPROMPTU

Seducing the Reader with Structure

Readers, like viewers, love structure; stories that are on solid ground allow readers to relax during the actual reading of the story. Structure gives your story, and every scene in it, ballast.

The Brilliant Ballast of *Eat, Pray, Love*

Perhaps the most beautifully structured story in recent memory is the blockbuster *Eat, Pray, Love* by Elizabeth Gilbert. In this memoir, a depressed American divorcée goes on a journey in search of the meaning of life—only to find herself. That's what her story is about.

The promise of the perfect scaffolding for this classic true tale of self-actualization is right there in the title: *Eat, Pray, Love.* The journey itself provides the storyline, divided into three acts:

BEGINNING/ACT ONE

Elizabeth learns to feed her body by eating her way through Italy. She sublimates her desire for Italy's handsome men and focuses on food. From the spaghetti alla carbonara and tiramisu in Rome to the margherita pizza with double mozzarella in Naples, she leaves no plate unclean. She comes to Italy, she says, "pinched and thin," and she leaves four months later "noticeably bigger" in every way.

MIDDLE/ACT TWO

Elizabeth learns to feed her soul by praying in India. She goes to an ashram, where she chants, meditates, and scrubs the temple floors, all in the quest for enlightenment. But what she finds there—after endless hours of chanting, meditating, and scrubbing—is that what she needs right now is not exactly enlightenment but the capacity to forgive herself and her ex-husband for their failed marriage. Her fellow seeker, an American named Richard, tells her to "find somebody new to love someday."

END/ACT THREE
Elizabeth learns to feed her heart by falling in love in Bali. She meets a lovely Brazilian man named Felipe and abandons her vow to remain celibate during her journey. She falls in love and learns to trust, not just in Felipe, but in herself. As Elizabeth says, the new "happy and balanced me" sails off into the sunset with Felipe.

Elizabeth Gilbert needs to learn to nurture herself, and she does it in three acts: Once upon a time there was a very unhappy woman who decided to eat, pray, and love herself back to life, and she lived happily ever after. (Well, at least until her next book.)

Scene One Breakdown
The opening scene of *Eat, Pray, Love* takes place in Italy, on the first lap of her journey.

BEGINNING/SCENE ONE
I wish Giovanni would kiss me.
Oh, but there are so many reasons why this would be a terrible idea. To begin with, Giovanni is ten years younger than I am, and—like most Italian guys in their twenties—he still lives with his mother. These facts alone make him an unlikely romantic partner for me, given that I am a professional American woman in my mid-thirties, who has just come through a failed marriage and a devastating, interminable divorce, followed immediately by a passionate love affair that ended in sickening heartbreak. ... This is why I have been alone for many months now. This is why, in fact, I have decided to spend this entire year in celibacy.

Elizabeth is in Italy—a place many people on this side of the pond associate with impetuous sexual alliances, rightly or wrongly—and while we know that *she knows* that she is a heartbreak waiting to happen, we are worried that she might succumb to Giovanni's charms nonetheless.

MIDDLE/SCENE ONE

Now we are at my door. … He gives me a warm hug. … we're pressed up against each other's bodies beneath this moonlight … and of course it would be a *terrible* mistake ….

The temptation is so great—the door, the hug, the moon. And we hope against hope that she will resist this terrible temptation because she insists that's what she needs to do, and we agree with her, given her recent romantic history. But we also know that given the same scenario, we might just surrender our self-imposed virtue ourselves.

END/SCENE ONE

I walk up the stairs to my fourth-floor apartment, all alone. … I shut the door behind me. … I am alone, I am all alone, I am completely alone….

Grasping this reality, I let go of my bag, drop to my knees and press my forehead against the floor. There, I offer up to the universe a fervent prayer of thanks.

Elizabeth has resisted the lure of the lovely Giovanni. She has kept her promise to herself. We are exhilarated and hopeful that she may actually succeed in her quest to abandon self-destructive behavior and become a healthier and happier person, but we also know that it is early in her journey and that she has a lot of miles—and men—ahead.

The opening scene in *Eat, Pray, Love* is full of conflict that echoes the main story questions of the book: Will Elizabeth learn to make better choices? Will she learn to treat her body, soul, and heart with kindness and compassion? And if she succeeds, how will her life change as a result?

Analyze the first scene in your story. Ask yourself the following questions:

- What is the conflict that drives the scene?
- How does that conflict echo the main story questions of the work?
- Can you break down the scene into beginning, middle, and end?
- How does each relate to the others?

The Circle of Story

If we look ahead to the end of the story, to the last scene in *Eat, Pray, Love*, we see Elizabeth in a very similar situation, on the cusp of another decision—another decision concerning a man. This time we know he's the right man for her and that she's earned the right to love again, but does she recognize the right man when she sees him? Does she have the courage to love again? Has her journey of self-actualization led her to a happier, healthier self?

In the best stories, the ending always circles back to the beginning. This circle of story is what separates the great storytellers from everyone else. If you know the end of your story already, then you can make sure that your opening scene echoes that last scene. But if you don't yet know where your story will end or if you are not sure how to close that circle of story, don't worry. We'll talk more about that in chapter seven.

Just keep in mind that the answer lies in whatever your story is about. As *Eat, Pray, Love* is about a woman's journey to love and wholeness, the beginning of the story is about her deciding to make that journey to love and wholeness in good faith, and the end of the story is about her deciding that she's completed that journey. She learned what she needed to learn about love and wholeness on the way and can now choose a more fulfilling life with the right man. Whatever your story is about, you can make the same kinds of connections.

"I write the last line, and then I write the line before that. I find myself writing backwards for a while, until I have a solid sense of how that ending sounds and feels. You have to know what your voice sounds like at the end of the story, because it tells you how to sound when you begin." —*John Irving*

SPEAKING OF THE END

In the most beautifully crafted stories, the last lines echo the fierce words of the opening lines:

Beach Music, by Pat Conroy

FIRST LINE(S):
In 1980, a year after my wife leapt to her death from the Silas Pearlman Bridge in Charleston, South Carolina, I moved to Italy to begin life anew, taking our small daughter with me.

LAST LINE(S):
Because she had promised it and because she had taught me to honor the eminence of magic in our frail human drama, I knew that Shyla was waiting for me, biding her time, looking forward to the dance that would last forever, in a house somewhere beneath the great bright sea.

The Rosie Project, by Graeme Simsion

FIRST LINE(S):
I may have found a solution to the Wife Problem. As with so many scientific breakthroughs, the answer was obvious in retrospect. But had it not been for a series of unscheduled events, it is unlikely I would have discovered it.

LAST LINE(S):
Had it not been for this unscheduled series of events, her daughter and I would not have fallen in love. And I would still be eating lobster every Tuesday night.
    Incredible.

The Invention of Wings, by Sue Monk Kidd

FIRST LINE(S):
There was a time in Africa the people could fly. Mauma told me this one night when I was ten years old. She said, "Handful, your granny-mauma saw it for herself. She say they flew over trees and clouds. She say they flew like blackbirds. When we came here, we left that magic behind."

LAST LINE(S):
When we left the mouth of the harbor, the wind swelled and the veils round us flapped, and I heard the blackbird wings. We rode onto the shining water, onto the far distance.

Cape Cod, by William Martin

FIRST LINE(S):

A.D. 1000

Strandings

Each year the whales went to the great bay. They followed the cold current south from seas where the ice never melted, south along coastlines of rock, past rivers and inlets, to the great bay that forever brimmed with life. Sometimes they stayed through a single tide, sometimes from one full moon to the next, and sometimes, for reasons that only the sea understood, the whales never left the great bay.

LAST LINE(S):

And the whales swam north, past the point that might once have been called Kiarlness, the sandpit that sheltered the *Mayflower* for six miserable weeks, north from the bay that brimmed with life, north along coastlines of rock, past rivers and inlets, north to the seas where the ice never melted, to the place where the glaciers shimmered, the great white mountains of ice, the shaping hands of God.

....

"I always rewrite the very beginning of a novel. I rewrite the beginning as I write the ending. ... So the style of the novel has a consistency." —*Joyce Carol Oates*

THE GOOD ENOUGH OPENING

By now you've taken a hard look at your beginning. You've analyzed the beginning, middle, and end of your opening scene. You know what that scene is about and how it relates to what your *story* is about.

The question is: Is that enough? Is the idea of your story strong enough to support a good opening scene, and even more important, is it strong enough to support an entire narrative? Can it succeed in today's challenging marketplace?

In truth, it doesn't matter how good your opening scene is if the idea on which your story is based is flawed, either in storytelling terms or marketing terms. As an agent, I see writers pour their hearts and souls into stories whose basic premise is too slight or too trite or too old-fashioned to attract agents, editors, or publishers, much less readers.

In chapter three, we'll talk about how to make sure your idea is strong enough, how to tweak it if it isn't, and how to ditch it altogether and come up with something new and improved. We'll also talk about how to rethink your opening scene so that you get the biggest possible blastoff for your story.

CHAPTER THREE

ONCE UPON
A TIME

Your Best Idea

"Imagination is the beginning of creation.
You imagine what you desire,
you will what you imagine, and
at last you create what you will."
—*George Bernard Shaw*

———————— ⬡ ————————

"Bring ideas in and entertain them royally, for one of them may
be the king." —*Mark Van Doren*

In Hollywood, they say that you're only as good as your last movie. Well,
there's a corollary in publishing: You're only as good as your last idea.

Ideas are the currency of publication. No matter what kind of writer
you are or what kind of format you're writing in—short form or long,
print or digital, fiction or nonfiction—if you want to get published, you
need good ideas to write. I have learned this the hard way with every
step in my career in publishing. I started off as a reporter writing for
newspapers and magazines. As a junior reporter, I learned very quickly
that if I wanted to see my byline on any really cool stories, I'd have to
come up with the story ideas myself. Otherwise I'd be stuck with the
ideas assigned by the editor, who gave all the best ideas to the senior
reporters. So I started pitching my own ideas for stories; I got so good
at it that eventually I became an editor myself, responsible for conceiv-
ing and assigning story ideas for the whole editorial staff.

Coming up with ideas for newspapers and magazines is fun and
relatively easy for a number of reasons. In the case of newspapers,

there's always news happening, and news needs reporting—from local happenings to local angles on national events. Magazines are targeted to a particular audience, and stories must play to that audience, whether it's a cooking magazine for foodies or a fashion magazine for teenagers; those parameters help generate ideas. Also, newspapers and magazines have shorter shelf lives and lots of stories in each issue, so the relative importance of individual story ideas is amortized over the course of the issue. The stories are short in comparison to books, and thus the supporting details for the main ideas don't have to be as strong—the profitability of the enterprise rarely depends on a single story. It's easier to keep the reader's attention for five hundred or even five thousand words than for five hundred pages, which is what you have to do when you are generating ideas for book-length work.

Story ideas for books are trickier. When I got my first job in book publishing, I was thrilled to think that they were going to pay me to sit around and make books all day. But at my first acquisitions meeting, I realized that the criteria for story ideas in this business were different—and complicated. Ideas for books have to be strong enough to:

1. stand apart in a crowded marketplace
2. sustain a book-length narrative
3. keep the reader's attention for hundreds of pages
4. attract a large, definable audience
5. justify a profitable price point
6. compete successfully against best-selling competition
7. appeal to reviewers, bloggers, and the like
8. support a long shelf life
9. lend themselves to follow-up titles
10. help build the author's brand

An idea for a book has a lot more riding on it than an idea for a news story or a magazine article. The investment on the part of everyone involved in the making of a book—from the writer to the agent, editor, designer, publisher, publicist, and more—is considerable. Failure is not an option.

And yet many books fail to find an audience. They fail to make a profit. They fail to build the reputation of the writer or the bottom line of the publisher.

"Ideas are like pizza dough, made to be tossed around."
—Anna Quindlen

That's why ideas are so important—and that's why everyone is always looking for "the next big idea." When I was in acquisitions, I often worked for independent publishers without the resources to compete with the Big Five for authors and projects. We were not at the top of agents' lists, so we often received their B-list authors and projects. If we wanted A-list books, we had to come up with A-list ideas ourselves and commission the writers to execute those ideas.

I got pretty good at coming up with ideas—ideas that became best-selling titles and series, too. From the *A Cup of Comfort* series and the *Everything* series to *WTF?*, *Train Your Brain*, cookbooks, coloring books, crime fiction, romance, YA, science fiction/fantasy, video-game strategy guides, college handbooks, and business bestsellers, I spent my days brainstorming ideas and then shepherding those ideas into print. That was, in effect, my job: to come up with ideas for books and then make those ideas into books. In one year alone, I came up with a thousand ideas for books, and I helped my staff come up with ideas as well. Together we'd brainstorm thousands of ideas in the hope of coming up with a couple hundred ideas good enough to print each year.

"The best way to have a good idea is to have a lot of ideas."
—Linus Pauling

It took a lot of brainstorming to generate the ideas that met the afore-mentioned criteria. In today's super-tough marketplace, those criteria are more important than ever. As an agent, I help my clients come up with ideas and tweak their own to meet those criteria. I also help them develop their ideas when they get stuck or when they struggle to best their idea from Book One upon sitting down to write Book Two ... or Three ... or Four.

TOP TEN REASONS IDEAS DON'T PASS PUB BOARD

Here are the top ten reasons a story idea does not pass muster:

1. The idea is too derivative.
2. It's an article, not a book.
3. It's a short story, not a book.
4. The idea is too niche to attract a large audience.
5. There's something too similar out there in the marketplace already.
6. There's something too similar on the publishing house's list already.
7. It's not an idea that people will pay good money for.
8. It's not an idea that will be easy to market and/or promote.
9. It's not an idea that will appeal to reviewers, bloggers, etc.
10. It's not an idea whose time has come.

Along the way I learned a lot of tips and tricks to help get the creative juices going. Let's take a look at some of these tricks and techniques, some of which are based on science, some of which are based on art, and some of which I stole from other writers and editors.

"If you can see a bandwagon, it's too late to get on." —*Lee Child*

BRAINSTORMING FOR STORY IDEAS

As we've seen, the best beginnings are based on strong story ideas that immediately set the book apart from all others of its ilk. If, having read this far you're getting a bad feeling that your story idea is not compelling or unique enough to hook agents or editors, much less readers, then this is the section I wrote just for you. Because all other things being equal, the lack of a strong story idea is the biggest problem I see in manuscripts by writers trying to break into the business—or break out of the midlist onto the best-seller list.

Some of these tricks and techniques may seem a little offbeat to you, but give them a try anyway. Many are aimed at seducing your

The Writer's Guide to Beginnings

subconscious, a critical if obstinate ally in your quest to tell a good story. So give me the benefit of the doubt regarding these tried-and-true brainstorming and idea-capturing methods.

Pay Attention

"You get ideas from daydreaming. You get ideas from being bored. You get ideas all the time. The only difference between writers and other people is we notice when we're doing it."
—Neil Gaiman

Paying attention is perhaps the most obvious and difficult way to generate ideas. Ideas are everywhere if you know where to look and remember to look there. In a world where we are continually bombarded by sounds and images, overstimulated by everything from traffic to texts, and distracted from the minute we open our eyes in the morning to the last flicker of the screen before our weary eyes finally surrender to sleep, the gentle art of observation often goes unpracticed. Yet observation is one of the writer's keenest tools—one that cannot be replicated by technology. It's on you to observe the world around you—people, places, and things, from local flora and fauna to conversations overheard on the subway. The world is the writer's oyster, so put that smartphone and those earbuds in your pocket; go out into the world, and take note(s).

JUMP-START

Go to your usual hangout—a coffee shop, diner, or bar. Spend the first ten minutes simply sitting and watching. Then spend the next ten minutes writing down everything you've observed as quickly as you can. Don't stop to think. Read it back, and notice what you noticed.

NOTE: This is a fun exercise to do with your writing group. Be sure to share your observations and compare notes.

A GOOD IDEA: MEDITATION

Meditation boosts your creativity, not only by teaching you how to pay attention and focus your mind but also by facilitating brainstorming. According to a Leiden University study, meditating for a half an hour before beginning a creative endeavor is beneficial because doing so enhances your divergent thinking skills (idea generation) as well as your convergent thinking skills (problem solving). Idea generation and problem solving are invaluable weapons in the storyteller's arsenal, as is the art of observation. Orna Ross and Alice Walker are among the many writers whose writing process incorporates meditation.

"Whenever people ask where I get my sick and twisted ideas from, I reply, 'Just open your eyes'." —*Mark Billingham*

Always Have a Notebook Nearby

"Ideas are elusive, slippery things. Best to keep a pad of paper and a pencil at your bedside so you can stab them during the night before they get away." —*Earl Nightingale*

Ideas can strike at any time—when you're in the shower, in line at the grocery store, drifting off for a nap. But like lightning, they come and go in a flash. So be ready to capture them. Keep a pen and a notebook in your pocket or purse, and failing that, you can always email yourself notes or use the voice recorder app on your phone. I have sticky notes and index cards all over the house. I even sneak a pencil and paper into yoga class because doing yoga, like meditating, often acts like an idea faucet. One downward dog and the faucet goes on—the ideas flow.

"Ideas aren't magical; the only tricky part is holding on to one long enough to get it written down." —*Lynn Abbey*

Take Stock of Your Writing Self

"Until you know who you are you can't write." —*Salman Rushdie*

Knowing who you are is critical to coming up with your own ideas. You are your own best source, and I'm not just talking about who you are as a person but who you are as a writer. It is your unique writer's fingerprint that can unlock your best ideas.

Here's a brainstorming exercise to help you explore the various aspects of your true writer's self. Using the bubble chart on the following page, take a piece of paper and jot down entries for the lists. Do it off the top of your head; don't think about it. When you're finished, think about what comes up in this process. Which resonate with you? What stories do they suggest to you? How might you combine them to create something new and different?

"There are no original ideas. There are only original people."
—*Barbara Grizzuti Harrison*

Mix It Up

"Creativity and insight almost always involve an experience of acute pattern recognition: the Eureka! moment in which we perceive the interconnection between disparate concepts or ideas to reveal something new." —*Jason Silva*

As we've seen, divergent thinking—defined as "developing in different directions"—helps us look at options that may never have occurred to us and thereby generates new ideas. Here's how that can work in terms of generating ideas for your story. Take a look at the top-ten lists you made during the bubble-chart exercise. Pick three of the lists—say, "Top Ten People You'd Like to Meet," "Top Ten Places You'd Like to Visit," and "Top Ten Hobbies/Interests." Write each item from each list on a separate slip of paper, and place them all in a hat. Pull several out at random, and use these elements to brainstorm as many story ideas as

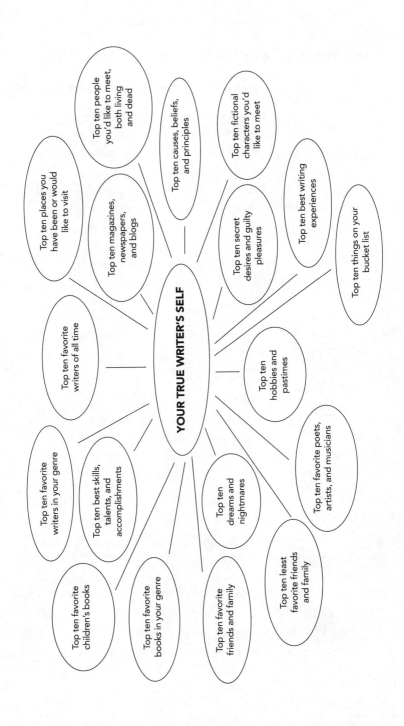

YOUR TRUE WRITER'S SELF

- Top ten people you'd like to meet, both living and dead
- Top ten causes, beliefs, and principles
- Top ten fictional characters you'd like to meet
- Top ten places you have been or would like to visit
- Top ten magazines, newspapers, and blogs
- Top ten secret desires and guilty pleasures
- Top ten best writing experiences
- Top ten things on your bucket list
- Top ten favorite writers of all time
- Top ten hobbies and pastimes
- Top ten favorite writers in your genre
- Top ten best skills, talents, and accomplishments
- Top ten dreams and nightmares
- Top ten favorite poets, artists, and musicians
- Top ten favorite children's books
- Top ten favorite books in your genre
- Top ten favorite friends and family
- Top ten least favorite friends and family

The Writer's Guide to Beginnings

possible. Go wild; think outside the box, the genre, and the planet. This is divergent thinking in action.

Do this over and over again with different lists from the bubble chart, and make up your own lists as well. You'll be training yourself in the art of divergent thinking, and you'll be rewarded with lots of new ideas.

JUMP-START

The next time you're with a group of writers, try this fun game that we often play at the New England Crime Bake, an annual conference for crime writers. Start with a prompt, whether ready-made or made up on the spot, such as: *Once upon a time there was a car salesman in Anchorage, Alaska, who found a dead body in a new Chevy.* Then go around the room, and have each writer add to the story. Don't stop until *The End.* You'll be pleased not only with how much creative fun this game is for all concerned but by the number of ideas for your own stories you'll generate in its wake.

"Ideas, like large rivers, never have just one source." —*Willy Ley*

Play Around

"For most people, creativity is a serious business. They forget the telling phrase 'the play of ideas' and think that they need to knuckle down and work more. Often, the reverse is true. They need to play." —*Julia Cameron*

It's impossible to be creative when you're miserable. So many of us are so busy and so stressed and so burdened with too much to do in too little time that we forget to play. We may not even value play much anymore. This is a kind of sabotage, a hindrance to our creativity, a betrayal of our writer's self. And there's only one cure: Play!

I'm a big fan of Julia Cameron's "Artist Dates." In her classic bestseller *The Artist's Way*, a must for every writer's bookshelf, she encourages us to "play artfully." The next time you find yourself stuck or stymied or simply too exhausted to think, call a *writer* friend and make an Artist's Date. An Artist's Date is anything that amuses the artist in you: concerts, art exhibits, films, readings, literary events, and pilgrimages, whatever feeds your writer's soul.

Whenever I find myself so buried in work that I start griping about it to anyone who'll listen, from my colleagues to my cat, I call my writer friend Susan and we bail out of our respective offices to go do something fun. Sometimes it's as highbrow as a visit to a new exhibit at the Museum of Fine Arts, and sometimes it's as lowbrow as coffee and cinnamon rolls at a bakery. (But our coffee klatsch conversation is—I assure you—*très distingué*.) We take our notebooks with us because we know good things come to those who play.

JUMP-START

Go on an Artist's Date with a writer friend. Repeat as needed, no less than once a month. Learn to play artfully.

"The creation of something new is not accomplished by the intellect but by the play-instinct acting from inner necessity. The creative mind plays with the objects it loves." —*Carl Jung*

Get Silly

"The best ideas come as jokes. Make your thinking as funny as possible." —*David Ogilvy*

Being funny is, by definition, a creative act. That's because humor often stems from making unexpected connections. The best punchline is a surprise—and we laugh at the novelty of the connection. Putting together familiar things in an unfamiliar way—that's idea generation.

The Writer's Guide to Beginnings

Whenever the ideas aren't flowing, use humor to get your juices flowing again. If you're stuck on your beginning, rewrite it as a funny scene. See the humor in something, and the whole world may open up around it. That's where the space is, the room you need to root around for a new approach.

JUMP-START

Spend the day with little kids. (If you don't have any kids or grand-kids, borrow some.) Make them laugh. Blow bubbles, play Twister, or pretend to be princesses and superheroes. Get silly. Notice how children play as if it were the most important work in the world. Because it is.

"Always write your ideas down, however silly or trivial they might seem. Keep a notebook with you at all times." —*Michael Morpurgo*

Keep an Idea Box

"I have four or five ideas that just keep floating around, and I want to kind of just let one—like a beautiful butterfly, let it land somewhere." —*Gillian Flynn*

This may seem simplistic, but this practice really works. Every writer should have a *physical* place, be it a box under the bed, a file cabinet in the corner, or a bulletin board on the wall, to keep anything and everything that might prove useful for a story someday. Maps, postcards, souvenirs, slogans, affirmations, news clippings, photos, illustrations, magazine articles—collect it all. Think of it as your secret treasure, and whenever you find yourself at a loss for a good idea, rummage through it.

I have an idea box, but I rarely go through it. *Out of sight, out of mind*—that's truer for me than it should be. Recognizing this about myself, I've designed a better way to display images and ideas that resonate with me. Instead, I have covered the fronts of two cabinet doors with cork. Door #1 is my Plot Door, where I pin the index cards I use to plot my work in progress—a scene for each card. On Door #2, I tack reminders of elements I might use in a story someday: photos of interesting places, snippets of dialogue, pictures of people who'd make good characters, sticky notes (right now there's one that says, "Read more John Cheever"), artwork that somehow evokes the themes that preoccupy me, etc. Every time I look at it, I can almost feel my little grey cells start firing.

Granted, my approach is that of a Luddite. If you're an early-adopter type, use technology to jump-start your creativity. Some writers swear by Scrivener; others use Pinterest. Find what works for you, and get your own synapses firing.

JUMP-START

If you don't have an idea box, create one. If you have one, go through it and jot down ideas that come to you as you consider each item. Don't stop until you have at least a dozen ideas.

"Ideas are like rabbits. You get a couple and learn how to handle them, and pretty soon you have a dozen." —*John Steinbeck*

Research for Fun

"It's easy to come up with new ideas; the hard part is letting go of what worked for you two years ago but will soon be out-of-date." —*Roger von Oech*

When all else fails, research. Research, which is just a form of focused reading for fun and profit, is one of the best ways to generate ideas in a hurry. Pick an element of your story—a time period, a setting, your hero's occupation, whatever—and research it. Go online, hit the library, or spend an afternoon in your favorite bookstore. Dive into the details, and come up with a slew of new ideas for your story.

I am a sucker for research. It's really one of my favorite parts of the writing process. For this book, for example, I spent an inordinate amount of time researching recent *New York Times* best-selling novels, the movies of Steven Spielberg, and the ways in which walking benefits the brain. I also devoted hours to finding just the right writers' quotes to begin and end sections, and when the book designers complain that too many quotes complicate the book's layout (as they inevitably do), I'll fight for every last one because I know that we writers love to hear what other writers have to say about the process. Best of all, I read all kinds of stories to discover the ones that served as the best examples of good beginnings. In the process, ideas for this book filled my head and the page before me. What's more, ideas for new books pop up as well—and I write them down, quick. Give yourself permission to research for fun, and see where it takes you.

JUMP-START

Do a deep dive on a subject that interests you, a subject unrelated to your story. Spend a couple of hours investigating every possible aspect of your chosen topic. Be alert for details that could inform your story. How can you marry the ideas you've run across in this research to your work in progress? Brainstorm as many possibilities as you can.

"The imagination needs moodling—long, inefficient, happy idling, dawdling, and puttering." —*Brenda Ueland*

Hang Out with Other Creative People

"As you navigate through the rest of your life, be open to collaboration. Other people and other people's ideas are often better than your own. Find a group of people who challenge and inspire you; spend a lot of time with them, and it will change your life." —*Amy Poehler*

Writing is supposed to be a solitary profession, but the truth is that smart writers hang out with smarter writers. Hemingway did it; heck, he and all his famous cohorts hung out in Paris, and they had a good time, learned from each other, and got a lot of good writing done. Dorothy Parker, James Thurber, and company drank and joked at the Algonquin; Virginia Woolf had high tea with her Bloomsbury pals.

Cross-pollination is good for your brain and your ideas. Find your tribe. If you don't know any other writers, then join the local chapter of your genre association, take a writing class at your local college, or attend a book-club meeting at your local independent bookstore. I've done all of those things and more, and my writing life—and my writing—has been all the better for it.

JUMP-START

Comedians are famous for working together and fueling each other's creative fires. (And they *are* writers, after all.) Form your own artist's troupe, and get together on a regular basis. This is not a writers' group *per se*; the aim is to talk shop, go out to dinner, watch movies, and hang out. Just make sure that you are in good company—that is, with people who are smarter, more prolific, and more widely published than you are.

"A good writer possesses not only his own spirit but also the spirit of his friends." —*Friedrich Nietzsche*

Take a Walk

"If you are seeking creative ideas, go out walking. Angels whisper to a man when he goes for a walk." —*Raymond Inmon*

Walking has long been touted as the writer's best medicine. Visionaries from Henry David Thoreau to Steve Jobs attributed their creativity to their daily habit of long walks. Thoreau mostly walked alone, but Jobs was famous for his walking meetings (a practice that Mark Zuckerberg has apparently adopted as well). In fact, the list of writers who walk is too long to include here, but you can count Joyce Carol Oates, Julia Cameron, and Jean-Jacques Rousseau among their company.

They're on to something. Stanford researchers have found that creativity jumps 60 percent when you walk. That is, if you get up off your butt and take a walk, your creative output will increase by 60 percent. It doesn't matter whether you're strolling through the park or trudging along a treadmill, the mere act of walking stimulates idea generation.

What's more: Take a forty-minute walk three times a week, and your hippocampus—the region of the brain that forms, stores, and organizes memories—will actually grow, according to a recent University of Pittsburgh study.

So take a walk already. If you don't like walking, get over it or get a dog. Dogs love to walk, and their enthusiasm will make a believer out of you, as will all those ideas that flood your brain as you stride forward.

JUMP-START

Take a walk. End of story. Or a *new beginning!*

"I only went out for a walk and finally concluded to stay out till sundown, for going out, I found, was really going in." —*John Muir*

Exercise Regularly

"I get so many big ideas while I'm running and such clarity while I'm lifting weights. And staying fit keeps me happy and positive."
—*Robin S. Sharma*

Walking is one thing; vigorous exercise is another. Yet both are good for your writer's brain. As Susan Reynolds says in her fabulous book *Fire Up Your Writing Brain*, exercise has positive effects on our brainpower. Neuroscientists look for changes in the levels of oxygen in the blood when they study brain activity. Here's what they've found: Jogging for even five minutes increases the blood flow to your brain. All that oxygen is good for your brain: The more active your brain is; the more oxygen you use, which floods your brain with oxygen. It's a cycle that's great for generating ideas.

If you really want to boost your brainpower, keep up that jogging or any vigorous exercise for at least thirty minutes, and you'll improve your brain's very plasticity, according to a recent study by the University of Adelaide in Australia. And as you might imagine, a flexible brain is a writer's best friend.

JUMP-START

Regular exercise leads to thicker and denser white matter in the brain, according to a recent University of Illinois at Urbana-Champaign study. White matter is known as "the subway of the brain" for its ability to connect the various areas of grey matter in the cerebrum. This means a better memory, a longer attention span, and greater cognitive efficiency. So incorporate into your schedule thirty minutes of cardio, three times a week. Your brain and your writing will be better for it.

"True enjoyment comes from activity of the mind and exercise of the body; the two are ever united." —*Wilhelm von Humboldt*

Stand Up; Sit Down; Write, Write, Write!

"Writing and travel broaden your ass, if not your mind, and I like to write standing up." —*Ernest Hemingway*

If you think that I'm writing this just so I can throw in that swell ass quote from Hemingway, well, you're only half right. The truth is that sitting is the new smoking—bad for your body and your brain. Sitting disease, a term coined to describe our increasingly sedentary lifestyle, is associated with thirty-four chronic diseases and conditions, according to the Mayo Clinic. Spend more time on your feet and more time off your butt, and you can add at least two more years to your life and improve your brain's functioning.

Like most writers, I sit too much, but I've done two things that have cut my sitting time in half: (1) I have a standing desk, and I love it. I can stand, fidget, do yoga stretches, even dance when the right song comes along on my mp3 player. I do some of my writing at the desk, but mostly I use it when I'm doing research, talking on the phone, and video-chatting with clients. (2) I got an Apple Watch, which tells me when I've been sitting for an hour nonstop and prompts me to get up and move around. According to the National Health and Nutrition Examination Survey, we need to get up and walk around for at least two minutes every hour—and doing so may lower the risk of premature death by 33 percent (and of course, helps us brainstorm). So when my Apple Watch tells me to stand up, I stand up and walk around, but you don't need an Apple Watch for this; there are Fitbits, timers, and more.

Remember, even if you exercise regularly, it's not enough to counteract the detrimental effects of sitting too much and/or too long. So stand up for your writing!

"I am writing this at my standing desk; my standing desk is against the window, and the window offers a pleasant prospect over the lime trees and sun-bathed Saale hills."
—*Friedrich Nietzsche*

Relaxing Fuels Your Creativity

" … a writer of fiction … lives in a world of fear. Each new day demands new ideas, and he can never be sure whether he is going to come up with them or not." —*Roald Dahl*

When it comes to creativity, stress is the enemy. According to a recent study by Harvard, we're far more creative when we're in a positive frame of mind. Conversely, we're far less likely to generate new ideas and solve problems in new ways when we're feeling the negative emotions of stress, including anger, frustration, fear and/or sadness.

This would come as no surprise to my father, the Colonel, a Norman Vincent Peale acolyte who's been preaching to me the gospel of PMA—positive mental attitude—all my life. I've always teased him about it, but apparently in this, as with most things, he's right.

To come up with great ideas, you need to relax … right into positivity. The best part about this creativity/relaxation link is that when you're too stressed to be creative, simply doing something creative can reduce your stress. This is one of those revitalizing cycles—as opposed to vicious cycles—that we can use to our advantage as storytellers.

JUMP-START

The next time you are feeling too stressed to think about your writing, do something creative to relax. It doesn't have to be writing: Do woodworking, knit a scarf, play an instrument, color a mandala, sing a song, paint a picture, or dance around the house. Then get yourself to your desk, and write away!

Do Something Else

"Some of the best ideas I get seem to happen when I'm doing mindless manual labor or exercise. I'm not sure how that happens, but it leaves me free for remarkable ideas to occur." —*Chuck Palahniuk*

Agatha Christie, whose diabolically clever ideas for mysteries still engross audiences nearly a hundred years later, used to say that the best time to plot a novel was while washing the dishes. At more than two billion—yes, you read that right—copies sold, Christie is ranked by the Guinness Book of World Records as the best-selling novelist of all time. Which is enough to make me consider giving up my dishwasher permanently. Almost.

The point is that sometimes the best thing to do when you think you'll never have another good idea again is to abandon your desk and do something else entirely. Preferably something that occupies your conscious mind, letting your subconscious mind out to play. Chores are good—mopping the floor, folding the laundry, polishing the silver, chopping wood, weeding the garden, ironing shirts, raking leaves—and they offer the added benefit of providing a sense of accomplishment and an orderly environment in which the chaos of your own creativity can hold court. Just be prepared to stop mid-chore to run to your desk and capture all the great ideas prompted by that homely art of housekeeping.

JUMP-START

The next time you get stuck, wash the dishes, sweep the porch, or change the sheets. Do not listen to music, watch television, or distract yourself; just do the chore, and let yourself fall into that meditative state. You'll be well rewarded—and not just by clean sheets.

"Your best ideas, those eureka moments that turn the world upside-down, seldom come when you're juggling emails, rushing to meet the 5 P.M. deadline, or straining to make your voice heard in a high-stress meeting. They come when you're walking the dog, soaking in the bath, or swinging in a hammock."
—*Carl Honoré*

Go to Sleep

"Brainstorming, for me, takes place in my bed at night between the time I turn out my lights and I finally fall asleep. It is not a very violent storm, but what's happening is I am just thinking about different ideas and maybe things I've seen that day that I think might make a good story." —*Chris Van Allsburg*

Okay, I admit it. This one may be my personal favorite. I think of sleeping as a delicious addiction, one that, as Fran Lebowitz says, is "both pleasant and safe to use." Ever since college, where I dismayed my fellow co-eds by disdaining the practice of pulling all-nighters before exams and insisting on going to bed early instead, I've understood the value of a good night's sleep. I knew I tested better when I was well-rested. In truth, I do everything better when I am well-rested. My inability to complete a sensible sentence in my addled, sleep-deprived head during my early child-rearing years as a new mom attests to this fact.

The good news is that science agrees with me. According to a study by Harvard Medical School, imagining problems you want to solve before you go to sleep can help you dream novel solutions to those problems. This is putting your subconscious to work for you, and you don't even have to be awake to do it. That is my kind of brainstorming.

Here's how it works: Dreams come from a more highly functioning part of the brain known as the anterior cingulate cortex (ACC). Research conducted by the University of Pittsburgh Medical Center revealed that the ACC grows very active during REM sleep. Because we're in a different biochemical state when we're dreaming, we can literally dream our way out of being stuck.

Even a nap can help. In an experiment at the University of Lübeck in Germany, students were taught how to solve a complicated and time-consuming mathematics problem. When they came back some eight hours later to be retested, the students who slept during the break proved twice as likely to figure out a simpler way to solve the math problem than those who did not nap. So when in doubt, go to sleep. Works for me.

The Writer's Guide to Beginnings

JUMP-START

Tonight, think about your story idea before you go to sleep. Ask your subconscious to come up with a way to improve on your story idea. See what happens, and keep a pen and notebook right by the bed so you can capture your thoughts immediately upon waking, before they slip away into that Neverland between sleep and wakefulness.

"I've dreamt in my life dreams that have stayed with me ever after and changed my ideas: They've gone through and through me, like wine through water, and altered the color of my mind."
—*Emily Brontë*

Let the Sun Shine In

"Live in the sunshine, swim the sea, drink the wild air's salubrity...."
—*Ralph Waldo Emerson*

No, I'm not completely crazy. I told you some of these ideas would be a little offbeat. But this one—get some sun!—has its roots in solid science. As reported in the *Creative Research Journal*, research conducted by Washington State University indicated that doing creative work in nature boosts creativity levels. The key is to work in areas high in direct sunlight and natural wood, as opposed to areas of drywall and plastic. I know this works because I wrote most of my first book on the beach in Monterey. When I was running *Good Times,* an alternative weekly newspaper in Santa Cruz, California, I'd organize our weekly editorial meetings. We discussed story ideas for the next issue at a little breakfast place in Capitola, right on the water. I did the same thing when I transitioned to the book business: When I was running acquisitions for a publishing house, I used to conduct brainstorming meetings in my own backyard, on a wide deck that fronts a lovely lake. Just getting out of the office and into the light did wonders for our idea list, and the editorial staff loved it. The next time you want to fire up your writing brain, go outside and get some Vitamin D. You know it's good for you—and your ideas.

JUMP-START

When you need a new idea, go to the nearest park and write or host your next writers' group meeting outside in your garden. Better yet, go on a writer's retreat somewhere where the sun's shining. As I write this, it's late January and the lake is frozen under a grey sky, but I'm contemplating next month, when I'll spend a week in St. Augustine at a writer's retreat run by Michael Neff under the auspices of the Algonkian Writer Conferences. Heaven!

"Some old-fashioned things like fresh air and sunshine are hard to beat. In our mad rush for progress and modern improvements, let's be sure we take along with us all the old-fashioned things worthwhile." —*Laura Ingalls Wilder*

Be Happy

"To be creative means to be in love with life. You can be creative only if you love life enough that you want to enhance its beauty; you want to bring a little more music to it, a little more poetry to it, a little more dance to it." —*Osho*

We've already talked about the power of PMA—uh, thanks, Dad—but being positive is only part of being happy. To be truly happy, you need to go deeper than a positive outlook. You need to believe that you are leading a meaningful life (or, failing that, a life at least worth living). Fortunately for writers, writing is a way of creating meaning out of what for many can feel like an existential void. That void is a source of sorrow, and sadness, like stress, is the enemy of creativity.

Unhappiness impedes the creation of new ideas, according to researchers at Penn State University. People suffering from even a mild case of the blues tend to hold back, wary of making mistakes and cautious to the point of inhibiting creative work. Moreover, people in sunny moods outperform those in sad or neutral moods in all kinds of divergent thinking, from word association to story ideas. Seriously.

Happiness is not just good for your personal life; it's good for your professional life as well, not to mention your writer's soul. So don't worry; be happy, and keep writing.

JUMP-START

Get out a pen and paper, and set a timer for ten minutes. Spend that period of time writing down everything that makes you happy. Do this quickly and without thinking about it.

The results may surprise you, and even if they don't—because on some level we all know what makes us happy—then you may be surprised at how little of your life is devoted to those people, places, and things that make you happy. Vow to change that. Going forward, devote an hour a day to something that makes you happy. You and your writer's soul will be glad you did.

"A harmless hilarity and a buoyant cheerfulness are not infrequent concomitants of genius, and we are never more deceived than when we mistake gravity for greatness, solemnity for science, and pomposity for erudition." —*Charles Caleb Colton*

FINDING YOUR BEST IDEA

"Ideas can be life-changing. Sometimes all you need to open the door is just one more good idea." —*Jim Rohn*

Okay, now that you're attentive, self-aware, eclectic, playful, active, fit, well-rested, sociable, relaxed, happy, and living in the light, it's time to put on your thinking cap and come up with an idea that will propel you right onto the best-seller list. Or tweak the one you have to up the odds of publication.

If you're thinking that it's about time, well, the reason we've spent so much time on the best ways to enhance your ability to come up with new ideas is because as an agent, I know how challenging—if not impossible—it can be to sell weak or derivative ideas. No matter how well-written the story, if the idea upon which the story is based is one we've all seen too many times before, it's very tough to sell in today's market. Frankly, I've given up trying.

What I'm looking for is the next big idea, and I am not alone in that. Everyone involved in books is looking for that, from the agents, editors, and publishers to the readers themselves.

It breaks my hard agent's heart to meet so many writers who have spent years revising and polishing stories that have no chance of being sold, simply because they were ill-conceived from the get-go. I'd like to spare as many of you as possible from this indignity.

As it says in Ecclesiastes 1:9, "There is nothing new under the sun." But what can make *nothing new* into *something new* is what you, as the writer, bring to your story. How will you show us something old in a new way or something new in an old way? How will you play the old songs with new instruments or play new songs with the old instruments? How will you twist the old story conventions into new forms or twist new story conventions into the old forms?

This is the creative leap beyond one plus one equals two, to one plus one equals *infinity and beyond.*

These creative leaps are what bestsellers are all about:

- In *Gone Girl,* Gillian Flynn takes the disappearing-spouse trope to a new level in a story that could be described as "Harlan Coben meets *The War of the Roses.*"
- In *Harry Potter and the Sorcerer's Stone,* J.K. Rowling reimagines the English public school as an educational institution for wizards.
- Andy Weir was not the first writer to show us Mars or even people on Mars, but in *The Martian,* he shows us the hard science behind what it would take for an astronaut stranded on Mars to survive.
- In *Dorothy Must Die,* Danielle Paige recasts the children's classic *The Wonderful Wizard of Oz* as a dark and edgy young-adult novel

with echoes of *The Hunger Games*, the Harry Potter series, and *The Chronicles of Narnia.*

- In *A Thousand Acres*, Jane Smiley sets Shakespeare's *King Lear* on a farm in twentieth-century Iowa—with devastating results for the family who lives there.
- In the adventure novel *Watership Down*, Richard Adams tells a classic hero's journey story as outlined by mythologist Joseph Campbell while borrowing from Homer's *The Odyssey* and Virgil's *The Aeneid*—with rabbits!
- In *My Sister's Keeper*, Jodi Picoult refashions a story ripped from the headlines about a couple who has a baby in the hope that the baby's bone marrow can save her dying sister's life.
- In *East of Eden*, John Steinbeck rewrites the Bible story of Cain and Abel—a brutal retelling complete with a depraved version of Eve.
- In *Middlesex*, Jeffrey Eugenides tells a family saga of three generations of Greeks, centering on intersex protagonist Callie/Cal.
- In the satirical novel *Catch-22*, Joseph Heller takes his experiences as a bombardier during World War II and transforms them into a bitingly hilarious commentary on the bureaucracy of the military and the absurdity of war.

In each of these examples, the writer takes an idea we've seen before and remakes it. Whether it's a story based on the Bible or hermaphroditism or the Second World War, the author has made the story his own. You need to make your story your own, and you start by refining your story idea.

Start with a Title

"I don't have goals when writing books, apart from getting to the end. I have rather vague ideas about how I want things to feel; I'm big on ambience. I have a title, a beginning, and a probable ending and go from there." —*Kate Atkinson*

When I was in the newspaper business, I learned to write headlines. There's an art to coming up with a good headline, just as there's an art to coming up with a good title. In fact, the process is much the same. Both require the quirky ability to (1) get to the essence of the story, (2) identify the aspect of the story that will most appeal to readers, and (3) communicate that essence in as few, direct, and judicious words as possible. At many newspapers, writing headlines is a job left to the editor, rather than the reporters writing the stories themselves, because the headlines are considered too important to leave to "mere" reporters.

In learning to write headlines, I also learned that the best way to write a story was to come up with the headline first. By forcing myself to write the headline, I identified what the story was about, and then I could write the story fairly easily.

The same holds true for book titles. As an acquisitions editor, I knew that the right title could sell a book on the spot. I worried over titles; with the right title, it was much easier to convince the publishing board to approve the project. As an agent, I won't shop anything until it's got a title I know will work.

I know you've heard that titles don't matter, that publishers change them anyway, but the reason they change them is because most titles suck. You should worry over your title, just as you worry about your story idea, and do it now, before you even start writing.

What's in a Title?

The best titles are often those that sum up the big idea of the story:

- *Moneyball*, by Michael Lewis
- *Eat, Pray, Love*, by Elizabeth Gilbert
- *East of Eden*, by John Steinbeck
- *Jurassic Park*, by Michael Crichton
- *Jaws*, by Peter Benchley
- *The Exorcist*, by William Peter Blatty
- *Sophie's Choice*, by William Styron
- *How Stella Got Her Groove Back*, by Terry McMillan
- *The Five People You Meet in Heaven*, by Mitch Albom
- *The Help*, by Kathryn Stockett

- *The Devil Wears Prada*, by Lauren Weisberger
- *Pet Sematary*, by Stephen King
- *The Horse Whisperer*, by Nicholas Evans
- *And Then There Were None*, by Agatha Christie
- *The Godfather*, by Mario Puzo
- *Dork Diaries 1: Tales from a Not-So-Fabulous Life*, by Rachel Rene Russell
- *Orange Is the New Black*, by Piper Kerman
- *Room*, by Emma Donoghue
- *The Martian*, by Andy Weir
- *Middlesex*, by Jeffrey Eugenides
- *The Cold Dish*, by Craig Johnson
- *A Passage to India*, by E.M. Forster
- *Memoirs of a Geisha*, by Arthur Golden
- *Where the Wild Things Are*, by Maurice Sendak

You should try to sum up the big idea of your story. In chapter one, you pondered what your story was about. In chapter two, you identified how that story idea might relate to the opening scene of your story. Now try to pare that story idea down to just a few words. If you can't or if those few words are boring, dated, derivative, or obscure, you still have work to do. You still need to work on differentiating your story from the competition.

"It's no secret that I like using phrases for my titles that might have a double or deeper meaning." —*Craig Johnson*

YOUR BEST DIFFERENTIATOR

Remember the Your True Writer's Self bubble chart exercise you completed earlier? Get those top-ten lists out; they'll be your guides as you figure out Your Best Idea.

NOTE: If you haven't done the bubble chart, then do it now. I know you don't want to, but consider it insurance against writing ideas you can't sell.

These lists are your ticket to your best differentiator. If you have yet to identify what makes your story special, then take a look at these lists. Continue mixing and matching and mashing up the elements of your story with these lists, and see what you can come up with. You may find it helpful to take a look at how some best-selling writers came up with their story ideas.

> "It is a novel about being careful and about that not being enough."
>
> —John Irving, on *The World According to Garp*

In John Irving's classic novel, terrible things happen to his characters, often at random. Irving says that becoming a family man when he married and had children truly scared him; he was always worried about what might happen to his kids. He played on those fears in *The World According to Garp.*

> "Some of the story is taken from my real life, but all of the story is taken from my real heart. I have experienced every emotion that I put onto these pages."
>
> —Tayari Jones, on *Silver Sparrow*

With *Silver Sparrow,* Tayari Jones was inspired by her personal obsession with the two half-sisters she knew little about as a child to write a novel about the effects of a bigamist's lifestyle on his two families. Jones' father was no bigamist, but her history gave the novel a poignant authenticity it would not have had otherwise. Your personal history may prove fertile ground as well.

> "I was living in Massachusetts, sitting at my desk one day writing a nonfiction snippet about how it felt to move so often, about what it was like being an army brat. That little section, which is in the novel, was so full of feeling for me [that] I knew there was a lot of material to be mined. So I began writing a novel."
>
> —Elizabeth Berg, on *Durable Goods*

In *Durable Goods,* Berg draws on her army-brat childhood to pen a story about an army brat less fortunate than she. As an army brat myself,

I can tell you that she writes so insightfully about what it's like for girls to grow up in the military life that this book remains one of my all-time-favorite novels. That said, Berg's impulse to write the story came from a nonfiction piece she'd written about moving a lot when you're a kid. If you've written nonfiction, look to that material as a rich source for your fiction and a possible differentiator.

> "I heard stories of cities on fire, teenagers who were whipped for giving starving Jewish people bread on their way to concentration camps, and people huddled in bomb shelters .... But I also had a story about a book thief set in my hometown of Sydney. I just brought the two ideas together .... "
>
> —Markus Zusak, on *The Book Thief*

Zusak married an unlikely pair of ideas—an Australian book thief and the Holocaust—to create one of the most haunting novels in recent memory. Take a look at those lists from the bubble chart, and try marrying unlikely pairs of your own.

> "About a decade ago, while visiting my in-laws in North Dakota, I came across a nonfiction book printed by the Fort Seward Historical Society called *Century of Stories: Jamestown and Stutsman County, 1883–1983*. In it was an article titled 'They called it "Orphan Train"'—and it proved there was a home for many children on the prairie. My husband's grandfather Frank Robertson and his siblings featured prominently in the story. This was news to me—I'd never heard of the orphan trains."
>
> —Christina Baker Kline, on *Orphan Train*

As Baker Kline points out, her blockbuster *Orphan Train* has its roots in a lucky accident, her finding a story about her husband's family in a book she'd otherwise never have picked up. She seized on that mention of the orphan trains—and the rest is best-seller history. This goes to prove that ideas are everywhere—even at your in-laws'—if you are paying attention.

> "Quite simply, this story was inspired by the nightly news. As the war in Iraq went on, I watched the stories—night after night—[of] our

troops lost or wounded in battle and the stories of their families left behind, waiting for them to return. … I began to wonder what it must be like to go off to war and leave your children behind. I can't imagine anything that would be more terrifying and difficult. I realized that I had never read that story, and I wanted to. I wanted to explore the idea of a woman torn between love and honor. So I decided to write it."

—Kristin Hannah, on *Home Front*

In *Home Front*, Hannah gives us the story she says that she wants to read, the story she's not seen before: war, only written from the side of the deployed woman soldier forced to leave her children behind. The title, *Home Front*, plays on this reversal. This is an idea whose time had come, and she recognized it. The next time you watch the news, think about how you might turn the events of the day into story ideas—and which of those ideas might be ideas whose time has come.

"While this is a work of fiction, it was initially inspired by a moment described in Jane Howard's 1984 biography *Margaret Mead: A Life* and my subsequent reading of anything I could locate about anthropologists Margaret Mead, Reo Fortune, and Gregory Bateson and their few months together in 1933 on the Sepik River of what was then called the Territory of New Guinea. I have borrowed from the lives and experiences of these three people but have told a different story."

—Lily King, on *Euphoria*

This fascinating novel dramatizes the lives and lusts of three gifted anthropologists whose passionate love triangle is as dramatic as anything they're documenting in New Guinea. Like most writers, King is a voracious reader, and that reading led her to this story. Reading nonfiction can be particularly useful in this regard; be sure to include nonfiction in your own reading, and when you are struck by a fact or figure, follow it wherever it may lead, as King did.

"From the moment I decided to write about Sarah Grimké, I felt compelled to also create the story of an enslaved character, giving her a life and a voice that could be entwined with Sarah's. I felt I couldn't write the novel otherwise, that both of their worlds would have to be represented here. Then I came upon a tantalizing detail. As a girl, Sarah was given a young slave named Hetty to be her waiting maid. According to Sarah, they became close. Defying the laws of South Carolina and her own jurist father who had helped to write those laws, Sarah taught Hetty to read, for which they were both severely punished. There, however, ends the short narrative of Hetty. ... I would try to bring Hetty to life again."

—Sue Monk Kidd, on *The Invention of Wings*

The Invention of Wings is told through two points of view—that of young Sarah and her slave maid, Hetty—and it's that juxtaposition that makes this story so powerful. Research led Monk Kidd to Hetty, and she took it from there to the best-seller list. When you're researching your story idea, be alert to the details that can make all the difference. Don't be married to the facts if you're writing fiction; let the facts be a springboard to your best story idea.

"I was initially inspired by my first visit to Masada, a spiritual experience so intense and moving [that] I felt as though the lives that had been led there two thousand years earlier were utterly fresh and relevant. The tragic events of the past and the extraordinary sacrifices that were made in this fortress seemed to be present all around me. It was as if those who had lived there and died there had passed by only hours before."

—Alice Hoffman, on *The Dovekeepers*

Travel can be a writer's best friend. In this case, a trip to the ancient fort triggered a deep desire in Hoffman to tell the story of the voices that spoke to her when she visited that sacred place. Further research led her to the writings of the historian Josephus, who claimed that two women and five children had survived the siege by hiding in the water system. Hoffman decided to write their story, and the magnificent novel *The Dovekeepers* was the result. The next time you take a trip to a new place, pay attention to the voices you hear there, and imagine the stories you could write about them. Your best story idea may be waiting for you, right there on vacation.

"This novel is for my grandparents Clarence and Ruth Huling, who would have been married for seventy years on June 19, 2013. This book was meant to be published in honor of their anniversary."

—Elin Hilderbrand, on *Beautiful Day*

For Hilderbrand, a best-selling author of women's fiction, her grandparents' long and happy marriage proved the impetus for *Beautiful Day*, a moving novel about weddings, marriages, and families. She wanted to honor their long union, and she did. How might you honor the people and places in your life? What story ideas might help you do that?

"As a Canadian, I was raised on lore of the famous Dionne quintuplets, born in Callander, Ontario, in 1934. They were a phenomenon and a sensation. Many of you might have recognized them in my Ouellet Quints, and the truth is, the fictional Ouellets were certainly inspired by the Dionne girls. But in researching *How the Light Gets In*, I was careful not to delve into the real lives of the Dionne quintuplets.... That freed me up to create whatever life I wanted and needed for *my* Quints."

—Louise Penny, on *How the Light Gets In*

Louise Penny's Inspector Gamache mystery novels are bestsellers—and *How the Light Gets In* is no exception. Much has been written about the famous Dionne quintuplets, but leave it to the ingenious Penny to write their doppelgangers into a crime novel. Who are the real people and what are the real events that might make their way, altered or not, into your story? What fascinations that haunt your dreams might haunt your story? Look to those top ten lists, and brainstorm. And remember: These connections to real people and events are often selling points for your story.

"I try not to be timid about what 'happens' in a novel. One good thing about my journalism career was that I saw amazing, outrageous, unlikely things happen all the time."

—Jess Walter, on *Beautiful Ruins*

In Walter's novel, all kinds of amazing, outrageous, unlikely things happen—some of them involving Elizabeth Taylor and Richard Burton, no less. But he makes it work, and you can, too. The first novel I ever published was a commissioned young-adult novel for HarperCollins. To win the contract, I had to create an outline for the story, a story that I had yet to write. I'd never plotted a novel before, so it took me several tries to get that outline right. And each time the editor said to me, "Go bigger; go bigger!" So don't be afraid to go big when it comes to story ideas: Go big, or go back.

> "I never think of an entire book at once. I always just start with a very small idea. In *Holes,* I just began with the setting, a juvenile correctional facility located in the Texas desert. Then I slowly make up the story and rewrite it several times, and each time I rewrite it, I get new ideas and change the old ideas around."
>
> —Louis Sachar, on *Holes*

Sachar says that his "juvenile correctional facility located in the Texas desert" is a small idea, but anyone who knows his work knows that *Holes* is one of the funniest and most original stories ever set in the Lone Star State. As we've seen, setting can inspire great story ideas, and the limitations of the landscape can play into the plot. They certainly play into Sachar's plot in *Holes.* Play around with settings for your story idea, and brainstorm ways in which those settings could play into the plot to give your story a strong differentiator.

These examples reveal the many differentiators that can set a story apart and how various elements, such as setting, point of view, historical events, real people and imagined characters, personal history, arcane facts, and obscure sources can be used and/or combined to create strong story ideas that will capture the reader's imagination.

YOUR BEST GENRE

Sometimes writers have story ideas that could be strong if they would only factor in one of the most critical factors in publishing today: genre. We've discussed the importance of knowing what kind of story you're telling and how to communicate that classification from word one. Now consider the genre that might best serve as the receptacle for your story idea.

To give you an idea of how versatile a good story idea can be, let's take a look at Jane Austen's *Pride and Prejudice*. This classic was published in 1813, more than two hundred years ago, and remains as popular as ever. The appeal of this novel is so enduring that it has spawned a cottage industry of sequels, mash-ups, hybrids, imitators, and more. On Goodreads alone, there are 277 works (and counting) listed as "inspired by *Pride and Prejudice*."

Here's a small sampling of the myriad ways in which the original story idea—the unlikely pairing of Elizabeth Bennet and Mr. Darcy—has been tweaked and stretched and twisted into many different forms:

- **THE ORIGINAL:** *Pride and Prejudice*, by Jane Austen
- **"SEQUEL":** *Mr. Darcy Takes a Wife*, by Linda Berdoll
- **CONTEMPORARY FICTION:** *The Jane Austen Book Club*, by Karen Joy Fowler
- **CONTEMPORARY ROMANCE:** *Bridget Jones's Diary*, by Helen Fielding
- **PARANORMAL ROMANCE:** *Mr. Darcy, Vampyre*, by Amanda Grange
- **WESTERN:** *Pemberley Ranch*, by Jack Caldwell
- **ADVENTURE:** *Pirates and Prejudice*, by Kara Louise
- **GOTHIC ROMANCE:** *Pemberley Shades*, by D.A. Bonavia-Hunt
- **SPY NOVEL:** *Spies and Prejudice*, by Talia Vance
- **YOUNG-ADULT FICTION:** *Prom and Prejudice*, by Elizabeth Eulberg
- **MYSTERY:** *Death Comes to Pemberley*, by P.D. James
- **HORROR:** *Pride and Prejudice and Zombies*, by Seth Grahame-Smith
- **TIME TRAVEL ROMANCE:** *Seducing Mr. Darcy*, by Gwyn Cready
- **GHOST STORY:** *Haunting Mr. Darcy*, by KaraLynne Mackrory
- **MANGA:** *Manga Classics: Pride and Prejudice*, by Stacy King, PoTse, and Jane Austen
- **STEAMPUNK:** *Steampunk Darcy*, by Monica Fairview
- **EROTICA:** *Pride and Prejudice: The Wild and Wanton Edition*, by Jane Austen and Michelle M. Pillow

As this list demonstrates, with a little imagination you can adapt any story idea to any genre, and in so doing, you may very well create a stronger, more compelling, more unique story idea. So, even if you are convinced it's a total waste of time, play with your story idea and change it to fit at least half a dozen different genres. *Especially* if you think it's a total waste of time. This is an exercise that may reap enormous benefits if you are flexible and open-minded enough to try it.

IMPROMPTU

Take one of those story ideas that you've adapted for a different genre, and write an opening scene for that story. Take your time with it, and give it your best shot. Now compare it to the one you've written for your original story idea. Which is better? Why? What can you steal from one to improve the other? Which is more likely to grab the reader by the throat? Which would be more likely to attract an agent/interest an editor/find an audience? Why?

NOTE: This is a good exercise for your writers' group, too—and one guaranteed to provoke an interesting debate.

"New ideas pass through three periods: 1) It can't be done. 2) It probably can be done, but it's not worth doing. 3) I knew it was a good idea all along!" —*Arthur C. Clarke*

YOUR BEST OPENING

As we said in the beginning of this section, in publishing parlance, you're only as good as your last idea. But with the tools and techniques we've discussed here, you've got what you need to brainstorm good story ideas—and your next one should be a winner. What's more, you've learned how to examine your story idea from all angles, all aspects, and even all genres.

Now you're ready to apply these principles to the story opening itself. Back to the beginning …

"I think one of the keys to better writing is releasing all of your ideas and to not be afraid. Dream big. This could be the greatest novel in the world …." —*Adora Svitak*

The Writer's Guide to Beginnings

CHAPTER FOUR

THE EDGE OF
THE BEGINNING

Where to Begin

"Sometimes when you think you are done,
it is just the edge of beginning....
It is beyond the point when you think you are done
that often something strong comes out."
—*Natalie Goldberg*

"Ideas excite me, and as soon as I get excited, the adrenaline gets going, and the next thing I know, I'm borrowing energy from the ideas themselves." —*Ray Bradbury*

Ray Bradbury is correct, as usual: You know that you've hit on the right story idea when that idea energizes you. That energy is your key to completing the marathon that is writing any full-length work. Use that energy well, and it will sustain you throughout the process. Squander it, and your story will falter and maybe stall out altogether, forever grounded.

You start, as we all must, at the beginning. As we've seen, the best story openings are those that capitalize on the energy of the right story idea. Take a look at your current opening. Where's the energy? Where's the juice? Where's the momentum?

THE SCENE ONE FAIL-SAFE STARTER-KIT

There are a number of tricks to making sure that you get your story off to a hot, hotter, hottest start, no matter what your genre. I know, I know, all of you people out there who are writing literary fiction are thinking, "I don't need a hot start to my story." Well, think again. Even beginnings for literary stories must aim for, at minimum, a slow burn.

I live in the Northeast, where winters can be brutal. (As I'm writing this, New York City is digging out of some two feet of snow.) When I moved here a dozen years ago after nearly twenty years in balmy California, I learned that the secret to staying warm as the thermometer plunges is to keep the fires burning on all fronts. I discovered the cozy beauty of cashmere sweaters, fingerless gloves, and glowing woodstoves. But I also learned that sometimes you have to break down and leave the house. Go begin a journey, even if it's only to the grocery store—which means venturing out into sub-zero temperatures to a frigid vehicle that may or may not start. It was a cold prospect I dreaded, until I happened upon two spectacular tools: remote car starters and heated car seats.

With a remote car starter, you can start your car from inside your warm house, wait until your automobile is revved up and ready to go, and then slip into a warm seat in a warm vehicle with a warm engine and hit the road. This is a beautiful thing.

You want to do the same thing with your story. Every reader starts a story cold, and you want to warm the reader up to your story as quickly as possible. You want the reader to slip into a warm seat in a hot story with a blazing beginning and take off for parts known only to you, the writer.

The good news: There are literary equivalents to remote car starters and heated car seats. Let's take a look at these, one by one.

"Ideas are easy. It's the execution of ideas that really separates the sheep from the goats." —*Sue Grafton*

Start with the Scene that Introduces Your Story Idea

As we've seen, this is the easiest and most efficient way to get your story off to its hottest start. So if it's at all possible to begin this way, you should, just as Peter Benchley did in the first scene of his classic horror novel, *Jaws*.

Yes, the terrifying film was based on the equally terrifying *New York Times* bestseller by Benchley. The details of the novel's opening scene and the film's opening scene differ—the couple in the book are a man and a woman sharing a beach house rather than a couple of teenagers at a beach party—but the action is the same: The woman goes for her last swim in the sea while her drunken companion passes out. And there we have it, the big story idea of *Jaws*: a monster great white shark terrorizes a seaside resort town.

Growing up, Benchley spent his summers on the island of Nantucket and became fascinated with sharks at an early age. He attributes his idea for the novel to a newspaper article he read about a "fisherman who harpooned a 4,500-pound great white shark off Long Island" and two seminal works about department-store heir Peter Gimbel's expedition to "find and film a great white shark," the film *Blue Water, White Death* and Peter Matthiessen's book *Blue Meridian*. The confluence of a childhood fascination with sharks, his continuing casual research into the subject, and three stories in three different mediums—newspaper, film, and book—all led Benchley to the big idea that became *Jaws*.

"Actually ideas are everywhere. It's the paperwork, that is, sitting down and thinking them into a coherent story, trying to find just the right words, that can and usually does get to be labor." —*Fred Saberhagen*

Start with the Scene that Foreshadows the Story Idea

If you truly believe that it is not possible to start your story by introducing the story idea, then you can do the next best thing: Start with a scene that foreshadows the story idea. According to Merriam-Webster, a foreshadowing is "something believed to be a sign or warning of a future event." For our purposes here, a foreshadowing is an opening scene that prefigures your story idea.

The most famous example of this might be the opening of Shakespeare's *Macbeth*, in which the three witches appear as a bad omen, especially for Macbeth.

MACBETH: ACT I, SCENE I

An open place. Thunder and lightning.

Enter three Witches.

FIRST WITCH: When shall we three meet again
In thunder, lightning, or in rain?

SECOND WITCH: When the hurly-burly's done,
When the battle's lost and won.

THIRD WITCH: That will be ere the set of sun.

FIRST WITCH: Where the place?

SECOND WITCH: Upon the heath.

THIRD WITCH: There to meet with Macbeth.

FIRST WITCH: I come, Graymalkin!

ALL: Paddock calls—anon!
Fair is foul, and foul is fair:
Hover through the fog and filthy air.

[Witches vanish.]

Many fairy tales begin this way as well. In Charles Perrault's *Sleeping Beauty*, a king and queen who'd waited years for a child celebrate their new baby princess's christening with a celebration. They invite the seven fairies of the kingdom to the feast. But an eighth fairy shows up, one long thought dead, and she curses the baby.

> The old Fairy's turn coming next, with a head shaking more with spite than age, she said, that the Princess should have her hand pierced with a spindle, and die of the wound. This terrible gift made the whole company tremble, and everybody fell a-crying.
>
> At this very instant the young Fairy came out from behind the hangings, and spake these words aloud:
>
> "Be reassured, O King and Queen; your daughter shall not die of this disaster: it is true, I have no power to undo entirely what my elder has done. The Princess shall indeed pierce her hand with a spindle; but instead of dying, she shall only fall into a profound sleep, which shall last a hundred years...."

The Writer's Guide to Beginnings

This is the scene that foreshadows the day when, fifteen years later, the princess does indeed prick her finger and fall into a long sleep … and, well, you know the rest.

To use a more contemporary example, consider the tender and funny *New York Times* bestseller *The Storied Life of A.J. Fikry*. In the opening scene, thirty-one-year-old book saleswoman Amelia Loman is stepping off the ferry to Alice Island, on her way to her first meeting with A.J. Fikry, owner of Island Books. She takes a call from Boyd, her latest "online dating failure," determined to let him down gently; only he's insulting, apologetic, and finally, weepy. Finally, she tells him that it would never work out because he's "not much of a reader." She hangs up and remembers her mother's warning that "novels have ruined Amelia for real men." And as she nearly walks right past the purple Victorian cottage that is Island Books, Amelia worries that her mother might be right.

In this scene, the foreshadowing is subtle but clear: Amelia needs a man who reads, and she's about to meet one who may seem unsuitable in nearly every other way save that one … but still, the possibility for romance is there. **NOTE:** This moving novel is a book lover's delight—if you haven't read it, you should because it's not only a great read but also a crash course in the business of book publishing. Not to mention that Fikry's hilariously genuine rant on books he will and won't sell in his independent bookshop is worth the price of the book alone.

Start with the Scene that Sets Up the Story Idea

We've seen this one a million times. Think of the opening scene of the original *Star Wars*, in which Princess Leia hides the plans for the Death Star in R2-D2, setting up the story idea, which is about how farm boy Luke Skywalker becomes a Jedi Knight, learns to trust the Force, and destroys the Death Star.

In murder mysteries, the opening scene is often the murder itself, setting up the main action of the story, which is the sleuth's search for the killer. For example: Tony Hillerman's *Hunting Badger* opens with an armed robbery at the Ute Casino, in which the bad guys kill the casino's security boss and wound a deputy sheriff moonlighting as a casino guard. The next scene opens with series hero Sergeant Jim Chee of the Navajo Tribal Police back from vacation and hoping the FBI are right when they say the fugitives are long gone—only to be dragged into the investigation when his fellow officer Bernie Manuelito asks him to help clear the wounded sheriff, who's suspected of being the inside man on the heist. *And the game is afoot.*

Other stories may begin this way as well. In Jeannette Walls's shattering memoir *The Glass Castle*, she opens with a scene that begins with the unforgettable line, "I was sitting in a taxi, wondering if I had overdressed for the evening, when I looked out the window and saw Mom rooting through a Dumpster." She goes on to describe this encounter with her mother, setting up the rest of the novel, which tells the unsettling story of her harrowing childhood, beginning at the age of three.

"If you say in the first chapter that there is a rifle hanging on the wall, in the second or third chapter, it absolutely must go off. If it's not going to be fired, it shouldn't be hanging there."
—*Anton Chekhov*

Too Much, Too Soon

Even when you've got an opening scene that either sets up, foreshadows, or introduces your big story idea, that scene can still fail to capture the reader's attention. One of the main reasons so many opening scenes fail is because the writer tries to tell too much about the story too soon.

Tell is the critical word here. The writer is telling—rather than showing—us the story. Many scenes are overburdened with backstory, description, and the characters' inner monologue, which leaves little room for the action that should be driving the story forward.

Remember: What the readers need to know to read the story is not what you needed to know to write it. Because the beginning is usually the first part of the story that you commit to paper, you are just getting to know your characters, setting, plot, and themes. You're exploring your characters' voices and histories, your setting's idiosyncrasies, your plot's twists and turns and detours and dead ends, your themes' nuances and expressions. You're thinking on paper, stretching your way into your story, and that stretching is a critical part of the writing process, but just as stretching before you run is paramount, it's not part of the run itself. It's preparation.

So you need to go through and trim the parts of your opening that are obscuring the action so you can get to your big story idea sooner. You need to prune back your writing so that the inherent drama of your story idea is highlighted.

If you're finding it difficult to edit your work, then try this trick. Print out your opening pages, and go through them, marking up the text in different colors to distinguish between backstory, description, and inner monologue. If you prefer to do this on the computer, you can use the "text highlight color" function in Microsoft Word to mark up your story.

- **BACKSTORY** Backstory is wherever you talk about what happened in the past, before the present action of your opening scene began— childhood memories, past relationships, etc. Mark these lines/paragraphs/sections in blue.
- **DESCRIPTION** These are the lines/paragraphs/sections where you describe your setting, expound on theme, detail backstory, etc. Mark these lines in pink.
- **INNER MONOLOGUE** These are the parts where you record your character's thoughts and feelings. Mark them in yellow, and underline the sections in which your character is alone as well.

I know that you're tempted to skip this exercise. But don't. Once you finish marking up your hard copy or highlighting your file, you only have to flip or scroll through it to know where you should edit your opening scene. This is one of the most useful exercises you'll ever do and the one my students, clients, and writing friends always most applaud me for. **NOTE:** There are variations on this exercise that can prove equally useful; we'll discuss those in chapter eight.

TURN TO PAGE FIFTY

For many writers, this warmup part of the writing process lasts about fifty pages (or around the 12,500- to 18,750-word mark). That's why I say to writers whose openings are slow, boring, obtuse, or otherwise unengaging: What happens on page fifty of your story?

Page fifty is where many stories truly begin. Turn to page fifty in your story, and see what's happening there. What's your protagonist up to? How does that relate to your story idea? Don't be surprised if this is where your story really begins. And don't be reluctant to toss out those first forty-nine pages of stretching if that's what it takes to get your run off to a good start.

"What lasts in the reader's mind is not the phrase but the effect the phrase created: laughter, tears, pain, joy. If the phrase is not affecting the reader, what's it doing there? Make it do its job, or cut it without mercy or remorse." —*Isaac Asimov*

PACING/EMOTION/NARRATIVE THRUST

As we've seen, to keep the reader reading, you need to engage that reader, and that requires using all of the tools and techniques at your command. That is, you must juggle all of the elements of fiction—action and dialogue, character and conflict, voice and point of view, setting and theme—while fueling your story with enough narrative thrust to keep up the pace. Most important, you need to make the reader care deeply enough about your hero and his predicament to want to find out what happens next.

Beware the Chunk

Many beginning writers are lousy jugglers. Indeed, a lot of beginning writers don't even try to juggle the many elements of fiction all at once. They simply throw one ball at a time up in the air and catch it. They

The Writer's Guide to Beginnings

write a chunk of description, toss it, and catch it. Then they write another chunk that's all backstory, toss that one up in the air, and catch that chunk. One by one, they toss up chunks of dialogue, inner monologue, description, and setting into the air.

This is not juggling. This is playing catch with yourself—a relatively easy task that requires very little craft. Juggling, on the other hand, requires great craftsmanship. Keeping all those different balls in the air is a very tricky business, and the very best jugglers don't just juggle balls; they juggle knives, plates, and even flaming torches.

You need to be a master juggler, dazzling the reader with your ability to keep all those elements in the air in one continuous stream of story. *New York Times* best-selling thriller writer Harlan Coben is a master juggler. Let's look at the opening line of his bestseller *Promise Me* and see how he keeps his knives, plates, and flaming torches in the air.

> The missing girl [*character, description, backstory, suspense, the reader is worried already*]—there had been unceasing news reports, always flashing to that achingly ordinary school portrait of the vanished teen, you know the one, with the rainbow-swirl background, the girl's hair too straight, her smile too self-conscious, then a quick cut to the worried parents on the front lawn, microphones surrounding them, Mom silently tearful, Dad reading a statement with quivering lip [*backstory, character, setting, description, inner monologue, suspense, conflict, the reader's lip is quivering, too*]—that girl, that *missing* girl, had just walked past Edna Skylar [*action, character, conflict, suspense, the reader is relieved and intrigued at the same time*].

Now that's juggling—and that's just the *first line* of Coben's story.

Juggle This!

Good storytelling is a juggling act that you must sustain line by line, scene by scene, and act by act. We've examined many story openings here thus far, but now, let's take a close look at an entire opening scene. We'll consider the process by which it was conceived and examine it line by line.

A CASE STUDY: *SPARE THESE STONES*

My first published novel, now long out of print, was a young-adult mystery novel called *Emerald's Desire*, published by Harper in 1995. I've always wanted to write another mystery, but somehow I wrote nearly everything else. I suffered through a couple of false starts, but ultimately I never got around to finishing another crime story. In fact, I was busy plotting a women's fiction story when a number of random things converged in the divergent thinking function of my brain, compelling me to write a mystery:

1. At the New England Crime Bake, one of my favorite editors asked me why I didn't write mysteries if I loved them so much.
2. I volunteered at Leo Maloney's fundraiser for the Mission K9 Rescue, a nonprofit organization devoted to rescuing, rehabilitating, and finding forever homes for retired military working dogs.
3. I met a number of swell working dogs and their handlers from the military and law enforcement.
4. I corresponded with the lovely, dedicated women who ran the nonprofit organization, one of whom had been a dog handler in the military.
5. I became obsessed with military working dogs and read everything I could about them.
6. I was reading up on Shakespeare and came across a line from his epitaph, "spares these stones," in reference to a grave and bones.
7. I adopted another dog, an abandoned, adorable Newfie-retriever mix from Alabama named Bear.
8. I went to Las Vegas and hiked up Mount Charleston with my family.
9. I went to Vermont and trekked around the Lye Brook Wilderness.
10. I ran across the story of a teenage boy out hunting with his grandfather, who found a newborn baby wrapped in a towel in the woods.

All of a sudden I had a story idea, one I knew that could sustain a book-length narrative—and my own sputtering attention span—and I *had* to write it. Let's take a look at the opening scene of my work-in-progress, *Spare These Stones*, and break it down into the elements (and reader's reactions) that help make it work. Look for the comments in italics found in the brackets.

Spare These Stones [*title in keeping with the genre*]
By Paula Munier

"Good friend for Jesus' sake forbeare,
To dig the dust enclosed here.
Blessed be the man that spares these stones,
And cursed be he that moves my bones."

—William Shakespeare (epitaph) [*builds on title and speaks to theme*]

The woods were blessedly cool, even in July [*setting, character, reader wonders why "blessedly," why does the narrator hate heat?*]. The northern hardwoods of the Southern Green Mountains were in full summer leafing, towering birches and beeches and maples draping the forest in shade [*time, place, setting*]. After several years in the desolate white heat of the Afghanistan desert, Elvis and I loved the gelid greens and blues and silvers of the trees [*character, backstory, the reader sympathizes with the characters and is intrigued by Elvis*]. We welcomed the soft sweep of moss and lichens and pine needles beneath our feet, the warble of wrens and the skittering of squirrels, the crisp scent of mountain air breathed in and out, in and out, in and out [*setting, character, description, the reader worries that this calm may be shattered*].

This was our happy place [*setting, suspense, the reader is getting a terrible feeling it won't be a happy place for long*]. The place where we could leave the hot, whirling sands of war behind us [*setting, character, backstory, suspense, conflict*]. After that last deployment, the one where I got shot and Elvis got depressed, we'd both been sent home [*backstory, character, conflict, the reader's sympathy and anxiety grows*]. It took me a year to track down the Belgian shepherd—think German shepherd, only sleeker and smarter—and another three months to talk the private contractor into letting me adopt him [*character, backstory, inner monologue, add admiration to the reader's feelings about the character*]. But in the end, Elvis and I prevailed—and entered retirement together [*character, backstory*]. Two former military police—one thirty-three-year-old two-legged female Vermonter with an exit wound scar blighting her once perfect ass and one handsome six-year-old four-legged male Malinois with canine PTSD—reclaiming our minds and bodies and souls in the backwoods, one hike at a time [*character, description, voice, setting, the reader is pulling for both of these wounded warriors now*]. U.S. Army Sergeant Mercy Carr and Military Working Dog Elvis reporting for permanent R&R [*character, backstory, suspense, now the reader is frightened for Mercy and Elvis because the reader knows that something is going to happen to ruin their R&R*].

Today was the Fourth of July [*time, setting, irony the reader won't miss*]. The holiday I once loved most [*character, backstory, inner monologue*]. But now Elvis and I spent every Independence Day independent of the trappings of civilization [*character, setting, the reader sympathizes*]. We didn't like fireworks much anymore [*character, backstory, the reader understands why*]. Sounded too much like Afghanistan on a bad day [*the reader can only imagine and does*]. Elvis and I worked explosives there; he'd sniff them out, and I'd call in the EOD team [*character, backstory*]. On good days, it was just that simple [*character, setting, backstory, the reader worries about the bad days*]. On bad days, it was all noise and blood and death [*character, backstory, conflict, description, setting, the reader's worst fears realized*].

Here in the Lye Brook Wilderness, all the sounds we heard were made by nature, not by man [*setting, description, foreshadowing*], save for the crunch of my old boots on the overgrown path and the *whoosh!* of Elvis as he bounded ahead of me, blazing the trail with no thought of IEDs [*action, character, description, foreshadowing*]. At least I hoped Elvis had no thought of IEDs here [*character, inner monologue, the reader hopes so, too*].

Deep in the timberland there was no past, no future. Only now [*setting, theme*]. The terrain grew rougher, steeper, tougher [*setting*]. I adjusted my pack, which at only 20 pounds barely registered on my body, once burdened by nearly 100 pounds of gear, including body armor, flak, weaponry, and an IV for Elvis if he got dehydrated in the desert [*action, backstory, description*].

All I carried now was a leash, lunch, and drinking water for me and Elvis, compass, hiking GPS, flashlight, lighter, power pack, sunscreen, bug spray, first-aid kit, duct tape, and extra batteries [*character, description*]. My keys, wallet, and smartphone were distributed among the many pockets in my cargo pants, along with my Swiss Army knife, dog treats, and Elvis's "rabbit," the indispensable squeaky Kong toy critical to his training and his joie de vivre [*character, description*]. One squeak and I had his full attention every time [*character*]. He lived for these squeaks, which signaled successful completion of the task at hand—from sit, down, and stay to alerting to explosive devices [*character, description, backstory*].

Not that Elvis was working now [*description*]. He was just playing, diving into the scrub, scampering over downed trees, racing up the rocky trail only to circle back to check my progress [*action, setting*]. A downpour the night before had left muddy puddles in its wake, and my boots were streaked with dirt [*description, setting*]. As was Elvis, his fawn fur stippled with dark splotches of sludge [*description, character*].

I kept my eyes on the slick, stone-ridden path, and my mind off my future, which loomed ahead of me with no clear goal in sight [*action, inner monologue*]. Unlike this trail we hiked, which led along the bed of a former logging railroad, rising before me along a steady 20 percent incline for some two-and-a-half miles up to Lye Brook Falls [*description, setting*]. The falls were among the tallest in Vermont, cascading down 160 feet [*description, setting*].

We'd hiked about two-thirds of the way so far [*action*]. I'd brought Elvis up here before; we both liked the trail, as much for its solitude as its scenery, provided you set off early enough [*character, description, setting*]. We began at dawn and so often had the trail to ourselves, even on glorious summer mornings like this [*action, setting, foreshadowing*]. Of course, this being the Fourth, most New Englanders were not hiking the wilderness; they were celebrating with family and friends at town parades and neighborhood barbecues and bonfires on the beach, a national fracas of hot dogs and beer and fireworks Elvis and I were content to miss [*setting, description, voice*].

Elvis plunged through a swollen stream and disappeared into a thicket of small spruce [*action*]. I saw no reason to follow him; I preferred my feet dry [*voice*]. I tramped on, dodging the worst of the mud and careful not to slip on the wet stones [*setting, description, action*].

After about half a mile, Elvis had still not returned [*conflict, suspense, the reader is worried*]. This was more than unusual; it was unprecedented [*suspense, inner monologue, backstory, the reader is very worried*]. Elvis's job had always been to walk in front of me, scouting ahead and alerting to danger [*character, backstory*]. The only dangers here were the ubiquitous clouds of biting black flies—and the occasional bear [*suspense, conflict, bears!?!*]. I whistled and waited [*action, conflict, suspense, the reader is waiting, too*]. Elvis darted out of the scrub onto the path [*action, the reader is relieved*]. He skidded to a stop right in front of me and jangled his head [*action*]. In his mouth he held what looked like one of his rabbits [*action*]. But it wasn't a doggie squeaky toy [*action, suspense, reader's curiosity mounts*].

"Drop it." I held out my hand [*dialogue, action*].

Elvis obliged, releasing the canary-yellow object into my open palm, his bright eyes on me and his new plaything [*action, good dog!*]. I held it up and examined it in the light filtering through the trees [*action*].

"I think it's a baby teether," I told Elvis [*dialogue*]. About 5 inches long, the teether was shaped like a plastic daisy with a thick stem, the better for a baby's grip, and a flower-shaped lion's head blooming at the top [*description*]. Apart from Elvis's drool, the little lion toy was clean, so it wasn't something that had been abandoned in the woods for long [*inner monologue*]. I bent over towards Elvis, holding the teether out to him. "Where did you get this?" [*dialogue, action, foreshadowing*]

Elvis pushed at my hand with a cold nose and whined [*action, conflict*]. With another quick yelp, he leapt back into the underbrush [*action, conflict, suspense*]. I tucked the baby toy into one of my cargo pockets and followed the dog, as he obviously meant me to do [*action, conflict*]. I cursed under my breath as I sank into a marshy patch, mud seeping into the tops of my boots as I stomped through the mire after Elvis [*action, conflict*]. Sometimes Elvis behaved erratically as a result of his PTSD [*character, conflict, suspense*]. Most of the time, I could anticipate his triggers: slamming doors, thunderstorms, fireworks [*character, conflict*]. But at other times, his triggers eluded me and were known only to Elvis: scents, sounds, and situations that went unnoticed by my human senses and were only ascertained by his superior canine senses [*character, suspense, description*]. But baby toys had never been among them [*suspense*].

Elvis led the way to a stream that paralleled the trail, a rushing of water over a bed of rocks [*action, setting*]. He jumped, clearing the 6-foot wide current easily [*action, setting*]. I splashed after him, not willing to risk breaking a leg or twisting an ankle in a poorly landed leap [action, conflict]. The cold water came up to my knees, and I was grateful it was July, or the water would have been even colder [action, conflict]. Elvis waited for me, his ears perked and his dark eyes on me [action, suspense, the reader worries about where the dog is taking Mercy].

I clambered out of the brook and stumbled over the stones into a thick copse of young birch trees [action, setting]. There Elvis sat down on his haunches in the middle of a large blowdown area littered with tree limbs [action, setting].

"What you got there, buddy?" I squatted down next to him [dialogue, action]. Elvis looked at me, dark eyes lively, ready for his reward—his own toy or a treat or both [character, action, suspense].

But he could not earn his reward until I could figure out what he'd found [inner monologue, conflict, suspense, the reader wonders what the dog has found]. Like all military working dogs, Elvis was trained as a patrol dog, to guard checkpoints and gates, detect intruders, secure bases, apprehend suspects, and attack on command [character, description]. But beyond that, MWDs were specialists; they were trained to sniff out drugs or cadavers or explosives [description, suspense, the reader is worried about possible bodies or bombs]. Elvis was an explosive-detection dog, trained to find weapons and to detect a number of explosive odors [description, character, suspense, the reader is very worried about explosives now]. When he was alerted to a scent, that scent was typically gunmetal, detonating cord, smokeless powder, dynamite, nitroglycerin, TNT, or RDX, a chemical compound often found in plastic explosives [action, character, description, suspense].

Elvis looked at me as if to say, "Okay, my job here is done. Where's my rabbit?" [dialogue, action, character]

I looked at the ground in front of his paws [action]. The forest floor was thick with detritus—dead leaves and twigs and pine needles— as well as mushrooms and moss and ferns and what looked like poison oak [description, setting]. No evidence of trespass here [action, description]. No evidence of explosives [action, description]. And no evidence of a baby to go with the baby toy, either [action, description, suspense, where's that baby?].

On the other hand, Elvis had an excellent track record—and the best nose of any dog I'd met, either in training or in Afghanistan [*description, character*]. He'd never been wrong before [*character, backstory*]. What were the odds he was wrong now [*inner monologue, suspense*]?

"Good boy," I said, scratching that favorite spot between his pointed ears [*dialogue, action*]. I slipped a treat out of my pocket and held it in my open palm, and Elvis licked it up [*action, the reader is happy for Elvis*].

"Stay," I said [*dialogue*].

Why Elvis would alert to a scent here in the Vermont woods was unclear to me [*inner monologue, suspense, conflict*]. If we were on a mission, we'd call in the Explosive Ordnance Disposal (EOD) team, responsible for bomb disposal [*description, inner monologue*]. We never touched anything; the EOD guys took it from there [*description, backstory*]. But here in the Lye Brook Wilderness, half a world away from the Middle East, I wasn't sure what to do [*inner monologue, suspense, conflict, setting*]. There was no EOD team trailing us; we weren't wearing flak or body armor [*inner monologue*]. I wasn't even sure Elvis had alerted to explosives [*inner monologue, suspense, conflict*]. Who would plant explosives in a national forest [*inner monologue, suspense, conflict, foreshadowing, the reader is scared for Mercy and Elvis*]?

Or maybe they were just fireworks [*inner monologue, the reader is relieved*]. It was the Fourth of July, after all [*time*]. Apart from sparklers, fireworks were illegal in Vermont [*description*]. Even supervised public fireworks displays required a permit [*description*]. But who would bother to bury fireworks in the woods—and even if someone had done so, you'd think they would have dug up them up by now for the holiday [*inner monologue, suspense, description*].

I slipped my pack off my shoulders and retrieved the duct tape [*action, the reader wonders what she's doing with the duct tape*]. I used the duct tape to rope off a crescent around Elvis and the target area, using birch saplings as posts [*action, suspense, the reader applauds Mercy's actions and hopes she doesn't set off any explosives*].

I pulled my cell phone out of my pocket and turned it on [*action, the reader wonders who she's calling*]. No bars [*action, suspense, conflict*]. No dial tone [*action, suspense, conflict*]. Coverage was spotty here [*suspense, conflict, the reader wishes Mercy could make her call*]. One bar [*action, suspense, conflict*]. Dial tone [*action, suspense, relief on the part of the reader*]. Quickly I dialed 911 and hoped that I'd get through [*action, suspense, conflict*]. But the connection died just as quickly [*action, suspense, conflict, the reader is dismayed*].

Elvis and I would have to head for higher ground and a stronger signal [*action*].

"Come on, Elvis." I headed over to the edge of the clearing, Elvis bounding ahead of me, disappearing into the brush [*dialogue, action*]. That's when I heard it [*action, suspense, conflict, the reader is beginning to panic*]. A thin cry. Followed by another. And another, growing in volume with each wail [*action, suspense, conflict, the reader's panic increases*]. Sounded like my mother's cat Alice back in Quincy, meowing for breakfast [*description, suspense*].

But I knew that was no cat [*voice, inner monologue, reader knows it's no cat as well*].

Elvis bellowed, accompanied by a burst of bawling [*action, suspense, conflict*]. I broke through the leatherleaf and bog laurel and came into a small glade [*action, conflict, setting*]. There in the middle sat a squalling baby in a blue backpack-style infant carrier [*action, conflict, setting, relief on the part of the reader that the baby is found*].

A baby girl, if her pink cap and long-sleeved onesie were any indication [*description*]. A red-faced, cherub-cheeked baby girl, her chubby arms and legs flailing against an assault of black flies [*description, action, suspense, conflict*].

I hurried over and fell to my knees in front of the pack, swatting away at the swarm [*action, conflict, suspense*]. The baby appeared to be about six months old, but that was hardly an educated guess [*description*]. Everything I knew about babies was based on my sister's toddler, Tommy, whose infancy I'd mostly missed [*description, backstory, inner monologue*].

This baby seemed okay, but her little neck and face and fingers were dotted with angry red marks left by the mean bites of black flies [*description, conflict, the reader worries about the baby's health and hopes Mercy will do something about those flies*]. I reached for my pack and the bug spray but then thought better of it. Nothing with DEET in it could be any good for babies [*action, conflict, suspense, description*].

She kept on screaming, and Elvis kept barking [*action, conflict, suspense*].

"Quiet," I ordered, but only the dog obeyed [*dialogue, action, voice, the reader is anxious for the baby*]. I looked around, but there was no mom in sight [*action, conflict, suspense, the reader is worried about the baby's mother, too*]. So I unbuckled the straps on the carrier and pulled the child out of it [*action*]. She lifted her small head up at me, and I stared into round sky-blue eyes rimmed in tears [*action, description*]. I took her in my arms and stood up [*action*]. I held her against my chest, then backed up to a tree to steady myself as I pulled the ends of my hoodie together and zipped it up around her as protection against the flies [*action, conflict*]. I bounced her up and down until her sobs subsided [*action*]. Within minutes she was asleep [*action, description, relief on the part of the reader*].

"Now, what?" I looked at Elvis, but he just stood there looking back at me, head cocked, ears up, waiting for our next move [*dialogue, action, suspense, conflict*]. Whatever that might be [*inner monologue, voice*].

One of the rules of the universe should be: Wherever there's a baby, there's a mother close by [*voice, inner monologue, the reader agrees*]. But I'd seen plenty of babies without mothers over in Afghanistan [*inner monologue, backstory*]. I just didn't expect to come across one here at home, in the Lye Brook Wilderness [*suspense, conflict, setting*].

"Where's your mother?" I asked the sleeping child [*dialogue, action, suspense, conflict*].

Maybe she'd gone off behind some bushes to pee [*inner monologue, the reader hopes this is the case*].

"Hello," I called. "Hello" [*dialogue, action*].

No answer. I kept on calling and bouncing [*action, conflict, suspense*]. The baby gurgled into my shoulder [*action*]. Maybe her mother had fallen or hurt herself somehow [*inner monologue, suspense, conflict*]. I walked around the clearing, eyes on the ground [*action*]. The leaves and detritus on the forest floor were disturbed around the backpack, but then both Elvis and I had been there [*description*].

I could see the trail we'd left behind as we'd barreled into the clearing from the south [*action, setting*]. But leading out in the opposite direction, I saw broken branches and rustled leaves and

The Writer's Guide to Beginnings

faint boot prints tamped in the mud [*action, suspense, description, the reader is excited*]. Elvis and I followed the trail out of the glade into a denser area of forest thick with maples and beeches in full leaf [*action, setting, suspense*]. We hiked for several minutes through the wood [*action*]. The traces ended abruptly at a rollicking stream some 10 yards wide [*setting, description, disappointment on the part of the reader*]. Too far to see across, too far to jump, and too far to ford across holding a baby [*inner monologue, description*]. I yelled again [*action*]. Elvis barked [*action*]. We both listened for the sounds of humans, but all I heard were the sounds of the water and the trees and the creatures that truly belonged here [*action, suspense, setting*]. The baby stirred against my chest [*action*]. She'd be hungry soon and tired and cold and wet and all those things that made babies uncomfortable [*description, foreshadowing*]. Not to mention those mean black-fly bites [*poor baby*]. I was torn: I wanted to find her mother or whoever brought her out here [*inner monologue, conflict*]. But I knew the baby needed more care than I could provide deep in the woods [*inner monologue, conflict, suspense*].

"We're going back," I told Elvis, and together we retraced our steps to the baby carrier [*dialogue, action*]. I carefully unzipped my hoodie and strapped the dozing child into the carrier [*action*]. Then I slipped off my small pack—thank God I was traveling light—and hooked it to the baby backpack [*action*]. I squatted down on my haunches and pulled the infant carrier onto my shoulders and pulled myself up to my feet [*action*]. The fit was good [*description*]. Not as heavy as my pack in Afghanistan but not exactly light, either [*description, backstory*]. And my pack in Afghanistan didn't squirm [*action, conflict, voice*].

"She's waking up," I told Elvis. "Let's go home" [*dialogue, the reader is glad that Mercy and Elvis are leaving the woods*].

We walked back to the Lye Brook Falls Trail, where I hoped my cell phone would work [*action*]. I wasn't exactly comfortable taking the baby, not knowing where her mother was [*inner monologue, suspense, conflict*]. But I couldn't leave her there, as someone else had obviously done [*inner monologue, suspense, conflict*]. How anyone could do such a thing was beyond me [*inner monologue, suspense, conflict*]. But I'd seen firsthand that people were capable of all manner of cruelty [*inner monologue, backstory*]. I just tried not to think about it these days [*inner monologue, character, backstory, conflict*].

Elvis set the pace, leading the way home [*action*]. You never had to tell him twice to go where his bowl and bed were [*character, description*]. I stepped carefully to avoid jostling my precious cargo, who apparently was napping again [*action*].

If my cell didn't work, we'd hike down the trailhead [*inner monologue, setting*]. The sun was climbing in the sky now, so there should have been more people out on the trail [*setting, description*]. We passed the area I'd roped off with duct tape, and I thought about taking it down [*setting, action, inner monologue*]. But Elvis had alerted for explosives there, or maybe that's where he found the baby teether [*description, setting, inner monologue*]. I didn't know why he'd designated that spot [*inner monologue, suspense, the reader is wondering about this, too*]. Maybe he was just confused, his PTSD kicking in [*inner monologue, conflict, backstory*]. But PTSD or no PTSD, I would never bet against Elvis and his nose [*character, inner monologue*]. I left the tape alone and kept on walking [*action*]. Elvis vaulted ahead, leading our way out of the forest [*action*].

When we reached the trail, I marked the spot where we'd gone into the woods with tape [*action, setting*]. I figured the authorities would want to know where we found the baby [*inner monologue, suspense*]. They could follow our path easily since we'd left a stream of muddy tracks and broken twigs and brush in our wake [*description, setting, suspense, the reader is wondering what law enforcement might find*].

I pulled my phone from my pocket [*action*]. Two bars [*action, suspense*]. Worth a shot [*inner monologue, voice*]. I dialed 911 and held my breath [*action, suspense, the reader is holding her breath, too*]. The call rang through on the third try [*action*]. I spoke to the dispatcher and had just enough time to say that I'd found a baby alone in the Lye Brook Wilderness when we got cut off [*action, suspense, conflict, the reader is frustrated*]. She called me back and told me she'd informed the authorities and that I should stay put until the game warden arrived [*action*].

"Roger that," I said, and promptly lost service again [*dialogue, action, suspense, conflict*]. I sighed, pocketed my phone, and sat down

The Writer's Guide to Beginnings

next to Elvis [*action*]. I shrugged off the baby carrier and tented my hoodie over it to keep away the bugs [*action, description*]. The baby slept on [*action*].

A cloud of black flies settled on me and Elvis [*description, action, conflict*]. Swatting them away with one hand, I pulled the bug spray out of my pack with the other [*action*]. Time to reapply, for both of us [*inner monologue*].

We could have a long wait ahead of us, and the black flies seemed to know it [*inner monologue, voice, conflict, the reader hopes that the game warden shows up soon*].

In this opening scene of *Spare These Stones*, you can see how the story idea is introduced and how that idea might be pitched: "*The Winter's Tale* meets C.J. Box" in *Spare These Stones*, in which retired Army Sergeant Mercy Carr and her retired Military Working Dog Elvis find a baby girl abandoned in the Southern Vermont woods and vow to find her mother, no matter what it takes.

You can also see the juggling act of elements that supports the cycle of *something happens to someone, someone reacts, and the reader reacts.*

Ask yourself how your opening scene reads. Consider how you:

1. handle your story idea
2. juggle the elements of fiction
3. engage the reader's emotions.

What can you do better?

JUMP-START

Go through your opening scene, and identify where you introduce, set up, or foreshadow the story idea. Mark up your scene line by line as we have done here, identifying the elements that appear as you go. Make sure that you are not writing in chunks but rather juggling the elements and reader reactions in a smooth and continuous arc of story.

NOTE: This is a good exercise to do with your writers' group.

KNOW YOUR ELEMENTS

Now you know where your story juice is, and you know what your first scene should do—and can do!—to get your story off to a blazing start. You've examined your first scene in terms of your story idea, the elements of fiction, and the reader's emotional response.

But to truly master the juggling act that is storytelling, you need to refine your understanding of the elements of fiction. In chapter five, we'll take a look at each of these elements in turn and give you a set of guidelines that can help you make your story the best it can be.

"What moves those of genius, what inspires their work is not new ideas but their obsession with the idea that what has already been said is still not enough." —*Eugène Delacroix*

CHAPTER FIVE

THE BEGINNINGS
RULEBOOK I

The Risk-Proof Beginning

"The beginning is the most important part of the work."
—*Plato*

"Always dream and shoot higher than you know you can do. Don't bother just to be better than your contemporaries or predecessors. Try to be better than yourself." —*William Faulkner*

Publishing has always been a risky business. But in today's volatile landscape, the publishing business is riskier than ever. And getting published can be tougher than ever, especially if you're a debut author and your aim is to be published by a traditional publisher.

There are only so many spots on a publishing house's list, and most of those spots are already taken by established writers. To make that list, you need to be better than your best, starting at the very beginning of your story. To make sure that you're putting your best story opening forward, you need to risk-proof your beginning.

In the thousands of story openings I read each year, I often see writers taking risks that effectively eliminate them from the competition, no matter how good their story ideas are. These risks involve questionable choices regarding the elements of fiction; many writers make these poor choices out of ignorance or arrogance or simply a gross misunderstanding of the marketplace.

As a debut author—or an author trying to break into a new genre or make the leap from a small publisher to a bigger one—you can only afford to take so many risks. In fact, the fewer risks you take, the better. And if you must take a risk, then you need to amortize that risk.

Start by conducting a risk assessment of your story. To do this, follow along with me as I share with you the rules regarding the elements of fiction, which you break at your peril. In this chapter, we'll look at the intricacies of the softer and subtler elements: voice, point of view, character, and setting. In the next chapter, we'll tackle the sharper elements of action, conflict, dialogue, and theme.

We begin with voice, the storyteller's instrument.

VOICE

"I thought I was clever enough to write as well as these people, and I didn't realize that there is something called originality and your own voice." —*Amy Tan*

A strong and original voice is a beautiful thing that can make your career as a writer. Just look at writers as diverse as J.D. Salinger and Anne Lamott, John Irving and Nick Hornby, and Jane Austen and Elizabeth George. Their unique voices played a starring role in their success. Strong voices—whether funny or brooding, satirical or lyrical, elegant or elegiac—are a critical selling point for writers and can make the difference when it comes to getting published.

That said, just as all strengths can be weaknesses if you rely on them too much and/or too often, a strong and original voice can be a weakness as well. Many writers fall in love with the sound of their own voice and rely on it to the detriment of other elements. They fail to realize that voice is the sound of the story, not the story itself.

If you consider voice one of your strengths, then you must ensure that you are using it to your best advantage. Go through your opening scene, and make sure that you:

- **SHOW; DON'T TELL.** Writers with a strong voice are especially prone to telling, rather than showing, their stories. This can be particularly true in the opening pages of the story. Break yourself of this bad habit, which can sabotage your efforts to get published.
- **EMPLOY ALL OF THE ELEMENTS OF FICTION.** Action, conflict, setting, dialogue, description, theme, etc.—all of these elements should be well-represented in your writing.
- **ELIMINATE CHUNKS OF NAVEL-GAZING, EDITORIALIZING, OR PROSELYTIZING.** Let your story speak for itself; don't drown your drama in pointless inner monologue.

Aim to use that strong voice of yours to enhance the action, reveal character, and, most of all, keep the reader engaged, as in the following examples of opening scenes marked by their writers' original voices.

> Tyler gets me a job as a waiter, after that Tyler's pushing a gun in my mouth and saying, the first step to eternal life is you have to die. For a long time though, Tyler and I were best friends. People are always asking, did I know about Tyler Durden.
>
> The barrel of the gun pressed against the back of my throat, Tyler says, "We really won't die."
>
> —*Fight Club,* by Chuck Palahniuk

> Hampton Court Palace, Spring 1543
>
> He stands before me, as broad as an ancient oak, his face like a full moon caught high in the topmost branches, the rolls of creased flesh upturned with goodwill. He leans, and it is as if the tree might topple on me. I stand my ground but I think—surely he's not going to kneel, as another man knelt at my feet, just yesterday, and covered my hands with kisses? But if this mountain of a man ever got down, he would have to be hauled up with ropes, like an ox stuck in a ditch; and besides, he kneels to no one.
>
> I think, he can't kiss me on the mouth, not here in the long room with musicians at one end and everyone passing by. Surely that can't happen in this mannered court, surely this big moon face will not come down on mine. I stare up at the man who my mother and all her

friends once adored as the handsomest in England, the king who every girl dreamed of, and I whisper a prayer that he did not say the words he just said. Absurdly, I pray that I misheard him.

—*The Taming of the Queen,* by Philippa Gregory

It began the usual way, in the bathroom of the Lassimo Hotel. Sasha was adjusting her yellow eye shadow in the mirror when she noticed a bag on the floor beside the sink that must have belonged to the woman whose peeing she could faintly hear through the vaultlike door of a toilet stall. Inside the rim of the bag, barely visible, was a wallet made of pale green leather. It was easy for Sasha to recognize, looking back, that the peeing woman's blind trust had provoked her: *We live in a city where people will steal the hair off your head if you give them half a chance, but you leave your stuff lying in plain sight and expect it to be waiting for you when you come back?* It made her want to teach the woman a lesson. But this wish only camouflaged the deeper feeling Sasha always had: that fat, tender wallet, offering itself to her hand—it seemed so dull, so life-as-usual to just leave it there rather than seize the moment, accept the challenge, take the leap, fly the coop, throw caution to the wind, live dangerously ("I get it," Coz, her therapist, said), and *take* the fucking thing.

—*A Visit from the Goon Squad,* by Jennifer Egan

Each of these novels opens with a compelling scene told in a strong and original voice—whether the narrator's disturbing showdown with Tyler or the distraught young widow Kateryn Parr dreading the inevitable kiss from King Henry VIII or Sasha contemplating stealing a woman's wallet in the ladies' room of the Lassimo Hotel.

These examples show how to make the most of an engaging voice, invigorating your story opening rather than slowing it down. Make sure your voice does the same thing for your beginning.

POINT OF VIEW

"It doubles your perception to write from the point of view of someone you're not. —*Michael Ondaatje*

The Writer's Guide to Beginnings

Point of view (POV) is a tricky bastard. All other things being equal, point-of-view issues have kept more writers I know from selling their work than anything else. So many people get point of view wrong, more than virtually any other element of storytelling. Worse, they often resist fixing it even when they know they're doing it wrong. Sometimes this is because they don't know how to fix it, and sometimes it's sheer stubbornness on their part. But it's a stubbornness born of hubris, and we all know what happens to characters suffering from an excess of hubris. (If you're not sure what happens, just reread your Greek tragedies.)

Point of view is one of the most complicated aspects of writing fiction and one of the easiest to screw up. And when you do, you'll be dismissed as an amateur right there in your opening scene. That's because point of view serves as a kind of litmus test for agents and editors; if you get it wrong, they will assume that you have not mastered your craft. And they'd be right.

When it comes to point of view, your best bet is to follow the rules. If you don't, the odds that you will fail are high, so high that I, for one, will no longer work with any writers unwilling or unable to address point-of-view issues in their stories. Every time I've made an exception—usually due the writer's insistence that I shop the manuscript despite the point-of-view problems—I have been unable to sell the story, *even when everything else in the story works.* I don't get paid until the story sells and the writer gets paid, so no sale for the writer spells no commission for me. *To wit:* I have wasted my time, energy, and expertise on a writer who refuses to acknowledge the problems with point of view. Now, that's hubris. Worse, that's a good book that didn't get published because the writer was too stubborn to revisit point of view.

Pardon my rant, which was a long way of saying that this is one risk you should think twice about taking, at least with your first novel. That said, writers who have mastered their craft have earned the right to break the rules. But you need to learn those rules first.

POV Rule #1

Your best bets are first-person point of view or third-person-limited point of view.

First person invites the reader directly into the head of the "I" narrator and as such is the most intimate point of view.

> Call me Ishmael. Some years ago—never mind how long precisely—having little or no money in my purse, and nothing particular to interest me on shore, I thought I would sail about a little and see the watery part of the world.
>
> —*Moby-Dick*, by Herman Melville

> Through my binoculars, I could see this nice forty-something-foot cabin cruiser anchored a few hundred yards offshore. There were two thirtyish couples aboard, having a merry old time, sunbathing, banging down brews and whatever. The women had on teensey-weensey little bottoms and no tops, and one of the guys was standing on the bow, and he slipped off his trunks and stood there a minute hanging hog, then jumped in the bay and swam around the boat. What a great country. I put down my binoculars and popped a Budweiser.
>
> —*Plum Island*, by Nelson DeMille

Third-person limited invites the reader into the head of the "he/she" character, as in:

> Richard Chapman presumed there would be a stripper at his brother Philip's bachelor party. Perhaps if he had actually thought about it, he might even have expected two. Sure, in sitcoms the stripper always arrived alone, but he knew that in real life strippers often came in pairs. How else could there be a little pretend (or not pretend) girl-on-girl action on the living room carpet? Besides, he worked in mergers and acquisitions, he understood the exigencies of commerce as well as anyone: two strippers meant you could have two gentlemen squirming at once.
>
> —*The Guest Room*, by Chris Bohjalian

> "Get that light out of my face! And get behind the tape. All of you. *Now*." Detective Jake Brogan pointed his own flashlight at the pack of

reporters, its cold glow highlighting one news-greedy face after another in the October darkness. He recognized television. Radio. That kid from the paper. *How the hell did they get here so fast?* The whiffle of a chopper, one of theirs, hovered over the riverbank, its spotlights illuminating the unmistakable—another long night on the job. And a Monday-morning visit to a grieving family. If they could figure out who this victim was.

—*The Other Woman*, by Hank Phillippi Ryan

POV Rule #2

Choose your point of view character(s) carefully.

Generally speaking, your point-of-view character should be your protagonist. Readers want to be in the head of their favorite character, which, as we've seen, should be your protagonist. (Unless your protagonist would be more appealing to readers though the eyes of another character—as the arrogant Sherlock Holmes is more appealing as seen through the eyes of his friend Dr. Watson. But this is rare.)

Sometimes point of view is what distinguishes the story and sets it apart from its competition. Think of *The Lovely Bones* by Alice Sebold, a heartbreaking thriller written from the point of view of Susie Salmon, a fourteen-year-old dead girl who was raped and murdered by a neighbor and now lives in heaven. Or *Room* by Emma Donoghue, written from the point of view of Jack, a five-year-old boy unknowingly held prisoner with his mother in a tiny space that constitutes their entire world. In Spencer Quinn's best-selling Chet and Bernie mystery series, each novel is written from the point of view of Chet, the dog who aids the private eye in his investigations. In Garth Stein's *The Art of Racing in the Rain*, the ailing mutt Enzo tells the story of his race-car driver human and a family torn apart by tragedy.

I know, I know, I hated the thought of reading stories from the points of view of dead girls and dying dogs, too, but I read all of these books and loved them, along with millions of other people. I fell in love with Susie Salmon and little Jack, although I admit I avoided their stories for the longest time because I knew that their stories would haunt me. And they do, to this day.

I fell in love with Chet and Enzo, too, and not just because I'm a dog person but because each canine voice was pitch perfect and the stories they told from their respective canine voices were compelling.

Point of view is problematic enough when you're writing from an adult human's point of view, when that's what you are. Writing from the point of view of a little boy or a dead teenage girl is wicked difficult; only experienced storytellers who've mastered their craft should attempt this. If I had a dollar for every awful story I've read where the writer tried and failed—badly—to write from the point of view of an animal or an alien or an adolescent, I'd be on the next plane to Paris. So think twice before you try this at home.

"When I write from the point of view of a child or a young person, I am trying to tell the truth as an adult voice sometimes cannot. We are so often wrapped in the garment of trying to reassure ourselves that we are not afraid." —*Michael Cadnum*

POV Rule #3

If you choose first person, then you must use that POV alone throughout the story.

I know that you see this rule broken all the time—most notably by Gillian Flynn in her megahit *Gone Girl*—but trust me, you don't want to go there, especially if this is your first story. You'll seriously handicap your opportunity to sell your work if you use multiple first-person points of view. Agents and editors mistrust multiple first-person points of view for good reason: With all those different "I" characters, it's difficult to keep track of which "I" is which.

This requires a very high level of craft to pull off properly. Don't risk it. I've had a few clients who failed to sell their work until I made them aware of this point-of-view issue. They fixed the problem, and I sold their work.

The Writer's Guide to Beginnings

POV Rule #4

If you choose third-person limited point of view, do not use more than six POVs per story. This is called multiple third-person limited POV.

We know that readers like to be in the head of the hero, so you need to stay in that hero's point of view most of the time. That said, you may need to use other point-of-view characters; in a mystery, for example, the points of view often include that of the victim and the villain, as well as the sleuth protagonist. Some novels feature dual protagonists; for example, both Hank Phillippi Ryan and Julia Spencer-Fleming use his-and-hers POVs in their mystery series. And you find novels with ensemble casts where the POV switches from chapter to chapter among the principals; in William Kent Krueger's Cork O'Connor novels, the author often includes chapters written from the point of view of Cork's nearest and dearest, who have become as beloved in readers' hearts as Cork himself. Whenever you change points of view, readers must shift their attention from the character they love—your heroine—to characters they don't love quite so much or may even loathe. So the fewer POV characters in your story, the better, and never risk more than six points of view per book. Yes, I know you see this rule broken all the time, most notably by George R.R. Martin in *A Game of Thrones*. But he's a master, and he knows how to break the rules (and we'll see just how he does it under the heading Breaking the POV Rules).

POV Rule #5

When writing in third-person limited point of view, don't jump from head to head.

You are not playing tennis here; you don't want your readers snapping back and forth from one character's head to another like they're at Wimbledon. Not to mention that editors hate it. The general rule of thumb when writing multiple third-person limited point of view is to stick to one POV per scene. This will help you avoid "jumping head syndrome."

POV Rule #6

Avoid using third-person-omniscient point of view.

Seriously. It should go without saying that you should not even think about using third-person-omniscient point of view, which is the author playing God and speaking directly to the reader, as is often seen in science fiction, fantasy, British mysteries, European fiction, nineteenth-century novels, and the like. Other writers—particularly those from the United Kingdom, Europe, and/or those originally published abroad—jump around from one character's head to another in the same scene all the time and get away with it. American editors view omniscient point of view as hopelessly outdated, so if you are shopping your work to American publishers in today's marketplace, don't do it.

Breaking the POV Rules: *A Game of Thrones*

When *Writers Digest* publisher Phil Sexton first asked me to write this book on story openings, I was skeptical at first. How could I come up with 75,000 words on beginnings? Sure, I'd been doing the Scene One: First Ten Pages Boot Camps for *Writers Digest* successfully for a couple of years, but I still was not entirely convinced I could manage it.

And then I talked to a client of mine, a wonderfully talented novelist who writes historical fiction. She'd written an extraordinary story that I loved, but she'd used several points of view, far more than the allotted six points of view that we've talked about here. I knew that so many points of view would make it a lot harder—if not impossible—to sell. I told her that, but she told me that other writers had pulled it off, notably William Faulkner in his classic *As I Lay Dying* and George R.R. Martin in his blockbuster *A Game of Thrones*.

First things first: Faulkner.

Seriously.

Sure, he's a genius, but you should know that whenever a writer invokes the "F" word, I tend to panic. And I'm not alone in that; most editors and agents would react the same way. (And I say that based on an informal, if admittedly anecdotal, survey of my colleagues.)

I panic because there's only one Faulkner, and he's one of the most obtuse writers of the twentieth century. This does not bode well for my marketing plan for any project, much less historical fiction, which often errs on the far side of pedantic anyway.

And if you're thinking, "What a Philistine," well, hello, I'm an agent and my job is to sell my clients' books. That said, I owed my client a sensible and thoughtful response. To that end, I reread the opening of *As I Lay Dying*, which confirmed my belief that this was a high-wire POV act only Faulkner could pull off successfully.

On the other hand, my client's story opening provided an uneven and unclear reading experience because, among other things, her opening was written in multiple first-person points of view, and these point-of-view switches came too often and too quickly—around every five hundred to one thousand words.

This muddled the story—and confused the reader. As an agent, I've found that it's hard as hell to sell confusion. What resonates with readers today is *clarity*.

To be fair, I also reread the first fifty pages of *A Game of Thrones* (which in the mass-market edition runs about twenty thousand words). I'd always remembered Faulkner as a challenging read for the reasons discussed, but I didn't remember any such issues with *A Game of Thrones*. And I was curious to see what my client was talking about regarding point of view in George R.R. Martin's bestseller.

As I suspected, my memory served me well. The opening of *A Game of Thrones* is *not* a choppy reading experience. You can sum up the reason for this in one word: *clarity*. And it's evident in the opening of *A Game of Thrones*. Martin uses multiple points of views, too, but he is very clever about it. Let's take a look at how Martin manages to break the rules—brilliantly!—when he:

1. sticks to third-person point of view (rather than first-person), which is much easier for the reader to follow, thanks to the blessing of pronouns and names
2. spends a significant portion of time with each point-of-view character before he switches to another character's point of view,

which allows readers to invest more heavily in each character and that respective character's thread of the story tapestry

3. chooses *very likable* point-of-view characters in very challenging situations
4. gives us great action, which keeps readers engaged even when they'd prefer to stay with the previous point-of-view character
5. provides clear links from one point-of-view character in one chapter to the next point-of-view character in the next chapter

A Game of Thrones Opening Breakdown

Let's break down the beginning of this compelling epic fantasy, piece by piece, point of view by point of view:

PROLOGUE

4,400 words

Will's third-person-limited point of view

Will, young man of the Night's Watch in the North, riding with Gared and Ser Waymar Royce, encounters the Others, and witnesses their attack on Royce (and his rising again!).

BRAN

3,600 words

Bran's third-person-limited point of view

Seven-year-old Bran sees his father Lord Ned Stark behead Gared (from the *Prologue*). Afterward they come across orphaned direwolf pups. (Beheadings and puppies! What's not to like?)

CATELYN

2,800 words

Catelyn's third-person-limited point of view

Catelyn, Bran's mother and Ned Stark's wife (from the Bran chapter), tells her husband that King Robert, who was married to her late sister, is coming from King's Landing to pay them a visit. (This is not good news!)

DAENERYS

4,600 words

Daenerys's third-person-limited point of view

Thirteen-year-old exiled princess Daenerys meets Khal Drogo, the rich and powerful barbarian leader of a great army, to whom her cruel brother Viserys has betrothed her in the hope of returning to King's Landing (from the Catelyn chapter) and recapturing his kingdom. (Thirteen! Married! Barbarian! Not to mention all the talk about dragons.)

EDDARD

4,400 words

Lord Eddard "Ned" Stark's third-person-limited point of view

Ned Stark of Winterfell entertains his former brother-in-law and comrade-in-arms King Robert from King's Landing, who asks him to come south to be the Hand of the King, a dangerous death-wish of a job (referencing all previous chapters in one way or another). An offer he can't refuse!

There are important lessons here. When you decide to take the risk of using multiple-first-person points of view or using more than six points of view even when writing in third-person limited point of view, know that you are making a decision that will undoubtedly complicate and hinder the selling of your work. If you make that risky choice, be sure that you amortize that risk by:

1. choosing your point-of-view characters carefully, with an eye towards likability
2. staying with each point-of-view character long enough for the reader to care about that character and invest in his or her particular perspective of the story
3. putting those point-of-view characters in very challenging situations, emotionally, mentally, physically, spiritually, and/or otherwise
4. giving the reader great action
5. providing very clear links from one point-of-view scene/chapter/section to the next

Stay with your likable point-of-view characters long enough for readers to get to know them, empathize with them, care about them, and/or invest in them. Plan your point-of-view switches carefully; don't let them come too soon and too fast, as that makes for a choppy reading experience.

Readers always want to get back to their favorite character, so they have to be invested enough in that character to wade through the other characters' point-of-view sections. This is why you need great action and clear links between points of view throughout so the reader understands why each moment is relevant to their favorite character's story.

Martin does this by giving us a young man, a child, the child's mother, the child's father, and a thirteen-year-old princess bride—all characters with whom we can sympathize, all in challenging, dangerous, and even poignant situations. And he keeps us with each point-of-view character long enough for us to get to know him or her and care what happens to him or her and his or her family or community (if he or she has one). So we keep on reading, without resenting the author for making us spend time with new point-of-view characters.

"One of the most beautiful things about *A Game of Thrones* is it's told from so many different points of view, and these characters can convince you that what they're doing is right. But they're only showing you a bit of the picture, and when you see it from another character's point of view, you may switch allegiances." —*Richard Madden*

This is what you need to do. If you can manage this magic trick, then you can keep these points of view. But providing a compelling reading experience while presenting all of these different points of view is the work of a master magician and best left to the Penns and Tellers of the writing world. If this is your first rodeo, you might want to reconsider your strategy.

As we've seen, using a plethora of points of view and having such different voices from one point of view to another can make for a choppy reading experience. Martin avoids this by (1) using third-person point of view instead of first-person, and (2) using the same authorial voice even as he switches from one point of view character to another. That said, using a very distinct voice in your story can be one of its greatest achievements, but that means that you have to work extra hard to make the point-of-view shifts flow smoothly enough to carry the reader along.

"You could tell *The Handmaid's Tale* from a male point of view. People have mistakenly felt that the women are oppressed, but power tends to organize itself in a pyramid. I could pick a male narrator from somewhere in that pyramid. It would be interesting." —*Margaret Atwood*

CHARACTER

"Character is king. There are probably fewer than six books every century remembered specifically for their plots. People remember characters." —*Lee Child*

Introducing your characters in the best light is one of the most important things you must accomplish in your beginning. All readers— agents, editors, publishers among them—are looking for the next Harry Potter, Jo March, Mr. Darcy, Lisbeth Salander, Easy Rawlins, Bridget Jones, T.S. Garp, Carrie Bradshaw, Hamlet and Viola and Puck, Cinderella, Hercule Poirot, Stephanie Plum, Rooster Cogburn, Jane Eyre, Tyrion Lannister, Scarlett O'Hara, James Bond, Scout Finch, Holden Caulfield, Katniss Everdeen, Jack Reacher, Celie and Pip and Alice, Old Yeller and Eeyore and Moby-Dick ... well, you get the picture.

Readers want protagonists they can love and antagonists they can love to hate. They want their heroes and villains alike surrounded by a strong supporting cast of characters, a community that populates the plot and brings the story to life. Let's take a look at the different ways that several beloved characters were introduced to readers.

Scarlett O'Hara was not beautiful, but men seldom realized it when caught by her charm as the Tarleton twins were. In her face were too sharply blended the delicate features of her mother, a Coast aristocrat of French descent, and the heavy ones of her florid Irish father. But it was an arresting face, pointed of chin, square of jaw. Her eyes were pale green without a touch of hazel, starred with bristly black lashes and slightly tilted at the ends. Above them, her thick black brows slanted upward, cutting a startling oblique line in her magnolia-white skin— that skin so prized by Southern women and so carefully guarded with bonnets, veils and mittens against hot Georgia suns.

—*Gone with the Wind,* by Margaret Mitchell

In the very first line of *Gone with the Wind,* Margaret Mitchell establishes Scarlett O'Hara's unique charm, born less of beauty than of vitality and determination. We see her flirting with the Tartleton twins, all Southern-belle coquette on the outside and all vitality and determination on the inside—the very qualities that that will see her through the burning of Atlanta and the love of Rhett Butler, among other challenges. Despite Scarlett's many faults, she's a survivor in a sea of lost causes, and readers love a survivor.

I was arrested in Eno's Diner. At twelve o'clock. I was eating eggs and drinking coffee. A late breakfast, not lunch. I was wet and tired after a long walk in heavy rain. All the way from the highway to the edge of town.

—*Killing Floor,* by Lee Child

In creating Jack Reacher, Lee Child said he aimed to give readers a tough and uncompromising hero who "always wins." In these opening lines of the first Reacher novel, we meet a guy so confident that he's more concerned about his breakfast than about getting arrested. This is a guy we can root for, even if he doesn't need us to.

"Bob Barnes says they got a dead body out on BLM land. He's on line one."
She might have knocked, but I didn't hear it because I was watching the geese. I watch the geese a lot in the fall, when the days get shorter and the ice traces the rocky edges of Clear Creek.

—*The Cold Dish,* by Craig Johnson

In this first novel of his popular Walt Longmire series, Johnson introduces us to a complicated and philosophical sheriff whose eyes are on the horizon watching birds fly when they aren't on the criminals in Absaroka County. We are intrigued and impressed. And do note that Johnson dropped a body in the very first line of the very first page. Now that's how to open a mystery.

> We called him Old Yeller. The name had a sort of double meaning. One part meant that his short hair was a dingy yellow, a color that we called "yeller" in those days. The other meant that when he opened his head, the sound he let out came closer to being a yell than a bark.
>
> I remember like yesterday how he strayed in out of nowhere to our log cabin on Birdsong Creek. He made me so mad at first that I wanted to kill him. Then, later, when I had to kill him, it was like having to shoot some of my own folks. That's how much I'd come to think of the big yeller dog.
>
> —*Old Yeller*, by Fred Gipson

Anyone who's read *Old Yeller* (or seen the Disney film based on the book) without crying is either made of stone or hates dogs (which, at least to dog lovers, is about the same thing). Here in the very opening lines of his classic story, Gipson makes us love this "dingy yellow" dog and tells us he's going to die at the hands of the boy who loves him. And we love him more.

> I could smell him—or rather the booze on his breath—before he even opened the door, but my sense of smell is pretty good, probably better than yours. The key scratched against the lock, finally found the slot. The door opened and in, with a little stumble, came Bernie Little, founder and part owner (his ex-wife, Leda, walked off with the rest) of the Little Detective Agency. I'd seen him look worse, but not often.
>
> —*Dog On It*, by Spencer Quinn

Another bestseller, another dog, another opening. Only this time, the dog is our narrator, and he's funny and smart and far superior in olfactory prowess to humans. We love that the canine Chet is the brains behind the Little Detective Agency—and, we suspect, the brawn as well—and we love Chet. We'll go where his nose leads us. *Woof, woof.*

> Emma Woodhouse, handsome, clever, and rich, with a comfortable home and happy disposition, seemed to unite some of the best blessings of existence; and had lived nearly twenty-one years in the world with very little to distress or vex her.
>
> She was the youngest of the two daughters of a most affectionate, indulgent father; and had, in consequence of her sister's marriage, been mistress of his house from a very early period. Her mother had died too long ago for her to have more than an indistinct remembrance of her caresses; and her place had been supplied by an excellent woman as governess, who had fallen little short of a mother in affection.
>
> —*Emma*, by Jane Austen

Readers have been falling in love with Jane Austen's characters for more than two hundred years. And here's why. From the very first line of *Emma*, we like this pretty young woman of privilege because we know that if Austen says that there has thus far been "very little to distress or vex her," that's about to change. And we know that Emma will have to change, too—if she is to win the heart of the ever noble Mr. Knightley.

> Once upon a time there was a young psychiatrist called Hector who was not very satisfied with himself.
>
> Hector was not very satisfied with himself, even though he looked just like a real psychiatrist: he wore little round glasses that made him look intellectual; he knew how to listen to people sympathetically, saying "mmm"; he even had a little moustache, which he twirled when he was thinking very hard.
>
> —*Hector and the Search for Happiness*, by François Lelord

A psychiatrist who is not very satisfied with himself? We're hooked already because this is a shrink character we have rarely seen before, if ever—one that plays against the stereotypes built on the likes of Freud and Jung. We can picture Hector meeting with patients in his office, twirling his little moustache, worrying about his adequacies and inadequacies as a psychiatrist and as a man. And we are ready to tag along on his search for happiness, hoping for the best.

> April 9, 1995
>
> The Oregon Coast
>
> If I have learned anything in this long life of mine, it is this: In love we find out who we want to be; in war we find out who we are. Today's young people want to know everything about everyone. They think talking about a problem will solve it. I come from a quieter generation. We understand the value of forgetting, the lure of reinvention.
>
> Lately, though, I find myself thinking about the war and my past, about the people I lost.
>
> Lost.
>
> —*The Nightingale*, by Kristin Hannah

In these opening lines of Hannah's bestselling historical novel, we meet the narrator of this story, and I won't say more than that, as revealing the identity of that narrator might prove a spoiler. In just these few lines, we suspect that the narrator has wisdom—learned the hard way—to impart and a good story to tell, perhaps even a heartbreaking story. And we want to hear it.

"Live through your characters. Let your characters live through you. Then you will love what you write, and others will, too."
—*Amanda Emerson*

Your Protagonist

"The main question in drama, the way I was taught, is always: 'What does the protagonist want?' That's what drama is. It comes down to that. It's not about theme; it's not about ideas; it's not about setting but what the protagonist wants."
—*David Mamet*

Your protagonist is the most important character in your story. All writers know this to be true, yet there are a number of issues that plague the protagonists in many of the story openings I see. Let's take a look at these issues, one by one:

The protagonist comes across as unlikable.

Your hero needs to be likable, if not altogether lovable. I know this may fly in the face of [insert favorite anti-hero here], but even our favorite rebels and rogues have a certain charm. No reader wants to spend 350 pages or more with an unlikable character any more than you'd want to be stuck with someone unlikable on a long car ride. (Remember that painful cross-country drive with that moron from college? Do you really want to pay for a similar experience?) Your protagonist must be someone you wouldn't mind being stuck with on a long car ride.

The protagonist is incompetent.

If your heroine isn't particularly likable, she should at least be competent. Sherlock Holmes is an arrogant drug addict, but he's so good at what he does that we forgive all just to be in the company of his genius.

The protagonist is passive.

Far too many protagonists are passive, rather than proactive. They don't do anything, especially in the beginning of the story. We want to meet our protagonist *in media res*, that is, in the middle of doing something interesting. We can't follow a character through a story if that character is not going anywhere.

The protagonist thinks too much.

Even heroes thinking great thoughts are not heroes unless they act. Heroes and heroines are, by definition, men and women of action. So have them step onto the stage of your story *ready to act*.

The protagonist is asleep.

Literally. Far too many stories begin with the heroine flat on her back, asleep, dreaming. This is no way to introduce your protagonist, no matter how good the dream is. Writers tell me all the time, "But it's such a *good* dream/vision/whatever." It doesn't matter; readers know the difference between dreams and real life. They want to see the heroine in her real life, facing real obstacles and challenges, overcoming great odds and growing in mind, body, and spirit as a result.

The protagonist is alone doing nothing.

Perhaps the deadliest mistake a writer can make in a story opening is to present the heroine solo, alone on the story stage, doing nothing but dreaming or ruminating about her life, past, present, or future. Again, this is not the way to introduce your protagonist. In fact, you should be very discerning about scenes in which your hero is alone, not just in the beginning of your story but throughout it as well. If your hero is alone, he'd better be doing something darn interesting, like robbing a bank, building a bomb, or charming a snake.

The protagonist does not drive the action.

The heroine must not only act, but her action must drive the story. You've given her the leading role; let her take her part and run with it; let her play her part for all it's worth. **NOTE:** This is one of the most common criticisms I hear from editors, that the protagonist does not drive the action of the story from beginning to end.

"The principle I always go on in writing a novel is to think of the characters in terms of actors in a play. I say to myself, if a big name were playing this part and if he found that after a strong first act he had practically nothing to do in the second act, he would walk out. Now, then, can I twist the story so as to give him plenty to do all the way through?" —*P.G. Wodehouse*

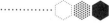

WRITERS ON HEROES, HEROINES, AND THE NATURE OF HEROISM

"Great heroes need great sorrows and burdens, or half their greatness goes unnoticed. It is all part of the fairy tale."
—Peter S. Beagle

"Over time, it's occurred to me that my protagonists all originate in some aspect of myself that I find myself questioning or feeling uncomfortable about."
—Julia Glass

"You have to go out of your way as a suspense novelist to find situations where the protagonists are somewhat helpless and in real danger.
—Nelson DeMille

"With the crime novels, it's delightful to have protagonists I can revisit in book after book. It's like having a fictitious family."
—John Banville

"Alpha heroes, even uberalpha heroes, still win readers' hearts. I like a masterful hero myself, but I also enjoy the idea that sometimes the heroine can be in charge."
—Emma Holly

"I had the feeling that focusing on objects and telling a story through them would make my protagonists different from those in Western novels—more real, more quintessentially of Istanbul."
—Orhan Pamuk

"Characters stretching their legs in some calm haven generally don't make for interesting protagonists."
—Darin Strauss

"I read the Harry Potter books as I was writing my own books, and I love them, but I don't think Harry was very much like I was as a kid. He's always brave, and he's perfect in a lot of ways."
—Jeff Kinney

"I'm not at all interested in the brave who fight against the odds and win. I am interested in those who accept their lot, as that is what many people in the world are doing. They do their best in ghastly conditions."
—Kazuo Ishiguro

"I've found in the past that the more closely I identify with the heroine, the less completely she emerges as a person. So from the first novel, I've been learning techniques to distance myself from the characters so that they are not me and I don't try to protect them in ways that aren't good for the story."
—Beth Gutcheon

"I'm not nearly as outrageously brave as many of my rascals that I write. But I think the rascal spirit must reside in me somewhere."
—Christopher Moore

" [A] hero is someone who has given his or her life to something bigger than oneself."
—Joseph Campbell

"My own heroes are the dreamers, those men and women who tried to make the world a better place than when they found it, whether in small ways or great ones. Some succeeded; some failed; most had mixed results ... but it is the effort that's heroic, as I see it. Win or lose, I admire those who fight the good fight."
—George R.R. Martin

"See, heroes never die. John Wayne isn't dead, Elvis isn't dead. Otherwise you don't have a hero. You can't kill a hero. That's why I never let him get older."
—Mickey Spillane

"There is perhaps no more rewarding romance heroine than she who is not expected to find love. The archetype comes in many disguises—the wallflower, the spinster, the governess, the single mom—but always with one sad claim: Love is not in her cards."
—Sarah MacLean

"I got tired of books where the boy is a bit thick and the girl's very clever. ... Why can't they be like the girls and boys that I know personally, who are equally funny and equally cross? Who get things equally wrong and are equally brave? And make the same mistakes?"
—Patrick Ness

"The life of the hero of the tale is, at the outset, overshadowed by bitter and hopeless struggles; one doubts that the little swineherd will ever be able to vanquish the awful Dragon with the twelve heads. And yet ... truth and courage prevail, and the youngest and most neglected son of the family, of the nation, of mankind, chops off all twelve heads of the Dragon, to the delight of our anxious hearts. This exultant victory, towards which the hero of the tale always strives, is the hope and trust of the peasantry and of all oppressed peoples. This hope helps them bear the burden of their destiny."
—Gyula Illyés

"My favorite literary heroine is Jo March. It is hard to overstate what she meant to a small, plain girl called Jo, who had a hot temper and a burning ambition to be a writer."
—J.K. Rowling

"I wanted to create a heroine that was flawed. I wanted her to be a real person. She's selfish; she's childish; she's immature and because I'm doing a three-book arc, I really played that up in the first book. I wanted the reader to be annoyed with her at times."
—Amber Benson

"Show me a hero, and I'll write you a tragedy."
—F. Scott Fitzgerald

"A good novel tells us the truth about its hero, but a bad novel tells us the truth about its author."
—G.K. Chesterton

....

Your Antagonist

"You don't really understand an antagonist until you understand why he's a protagonist in his own version of the world."
—*John Rogers*

If the protagonist is the most important character in your story, your antagonist should be willing to fight for the same distinction. In sports, playing a tough competitor helps you up your game, and your hero needs a powerful opponent to up his game as well. Too many antagonists are poorly drawn—cardboard villains who do not pose a threat worthy of your protagonist or your story. Create a complex and well-rounded villain; pit your protagonist against Hannibal Lecter, Medea, Count Dracula, Annie Wilkes, Norman Bates, Nurse Ratched, Mr. Dark, Lady Macbeth, Lord Voldemort, Cruella de Vil, or Iago. Give us a great villain, and put him to work bedeviling the protagonist right there in the beginning of your story.

Your antagonist is the second most important character in your story. All writers know this to be true, yet there are a number of issues that plague the antagonists in many of the story openings I see. Let's take a look at these issues, one by one.

The antagonist comes across as one-dimensional.

Your villain needs to be a hero in his own mind, as we all are the stars of our own stories. You want a villain who is more than just bad; you want a villain who is a contradiction—charming but lethal, smart but neurotic, devoted to his dogs even as he murders his mother. Just as important, you want to paint the portrait of your antagonist with fine strokes of many colors, rather than broad strokes of black and white.

Think of the manipulative and malicious Cersei Lannister, whom we first see through her brother Tyrion's eyes in *A Game of Thrones*.

> His sister peered at him with the same expression of faint distaste she had worn since the day he was born.

Here we can see that Cersei feels superior to her brother and most everyone else, a disdain that foreshadows her unkindness toward him and others.

The antagonist is stupid.

If your antagonist is an idiot, he's certainly not a worthy enough adversary for your hero. Many writers make the bad guys in their stories—especially in crime stories—so stupid that their capture seems inevitable, no challenge for the good guys at all. Better to make your antagonist smart, savvy, and sophisticated as Thomas Harris does in *The Silence of the Lambs* when he sends his heroine, Clarice Starling, to the Baltimore State Hospital for the Criminally Insane to talk to the elegant cannibal.

> Dr. Hannibal Lecter himself reclined on his bunk, perusing the Italian edition of *Vogue*. He held the loose pages in his right hand and put them beside him one by one with his left. Dr. Lecter has six fingers on his left hand.

This is a worldly man of taste and refinement, with a highly developed aesthetic and six fingers on his left hand. This Dickensian detail freaks us—and Clarice—out. We know it's a sign of aberrations to come.

The antagonist drops out of the story too soon.

Unlike many writers' unfortunate tendency to give their protagonists too little to do in the beginning of the story, many writers make the opposite mistake with their antagonists. The villains are very busy in the opening pages, deceiving their spouses and embezzling their employers and stabbing their rivals in their sleep, but then the villains may drop out of the story as the writers focus on the actions and reactions of the hero. This is fine; just don't lose sight of your villain altogether. Remember: Your antagonist does not cease to exist when your hero takes center stage. In fact, the busier your villain is when he's offstage, the better. Your antagonist should continue to plot against your protagonist throughout your story, just as the treacherous Iago does in Shakespeare's *Othello*, putting his plan in motion and seeing it through.

> Thus do I ever make my fool my purse;
> For I mine own gained knowledge should profane
> If I would time expend with such a snipe
> But for my sport and profit. I hate the Moor,
> And it is thought abroad that 'twixt my sheets
> He's done my office. I know not if 't be true,
> Yet I, for mere suspicion in that kind,
> Will do as if for surety. He holds me well:
> The better shall my purpose work on him.
> Cassio's a proper man: Let me see now,
> To get his place and to plume up my will
> In double knavery. How? How? Let's see.
> After some time, to abuse Othello's ear
> That he is too familiar with his wife.
> He hath a person and a smooth dispose
> To be suspected, framed to make women false.
> The Moor is of a free and open nature
> That thinks men honest that but seem to be so,
> And will as tenderly be led by the nose
> As asses are.
> I have 't. It is engendered. Hell and night
> Must bring this monstrous birth to the world's light.

The antagonist does not receive his just desserts.

The antagonist must throw down the gauntlet before the hero and fight hard and dirty, going for blood—but still earn eventual defeat. The shark must die in Peter Benchley's *Jaws*, Hilly must eat Minny's chocolate pie in Kathryn Stockett's *The Help*, Buffalo Bill must be stopped before he kills again in Thomas Harris's *The Silence of the Lambs*. From the very beginning, readers should see the storm clouds approaching and sense the drama of the thunder claps and lightning bolts to come. They should understand that this is the antagonist's handiwork, even if, as in a murder mystery, they don't know exactly who the villain is quite yet. They should be able to imagine that the time will come when the villain is defeated—even if they can't imagine how the villain will meet his well-deserved end. And they should be just as determined that the antagonist will receive his just desserts as the protagonist is, just as we are determined that Annie Wilkes should receive her comeuppance right there in the opening pages of Stephen King's *Misery* as we read about the protagonist, a writer named Paul.

> He discovered three things almost simultaneously, about ten days after having emerged from the dark cloud. The first was that Annie Wilkes had a great deal of Novril (she had, in fact, a great many drugs of all kinds). The second was that he was hooked on Novril. The third was that Annie Wilkes was dangerously crazy.

JUMP-START

When you create your antagonists, you need to go looking for the light … and the dark. As we've seen, the most compelling villains are those made up of every shade of gray—from charcoal to cloud. To make sure your antagonists are well-developed, fill out the following bubble chart and use it to design the most worthy of adversaries.

NOTE: Of course, this will work for your other characters as well, including your protagonist.

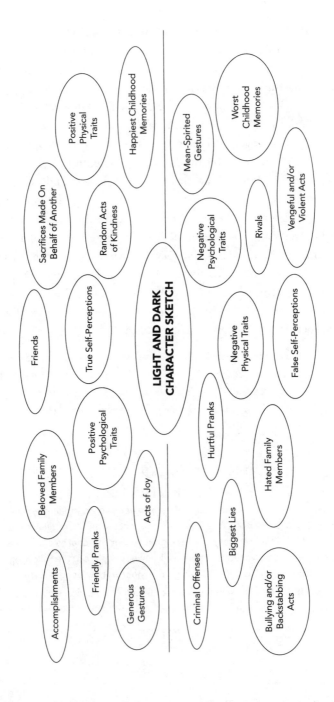

LIGHT AND DARK CHARACTER SKETCH

Positive Physical Traits

Happiest Childhood Memories

Mean-Spirited Gestures

Worst Childhood Memories

Sacrifices Made On Behalf of Another

Random Acts of Kindness

Vengeful and/or Violent Acts

Negative Psychological Traits

Rivals

Friends

True Self-Perceptions

Negative Physical Traits

False Self-Perceptions

Beloved Family Members

Positive Psychological Traits

Hurtful Pranks

Hated Family Members

Accomplishments

Friendly Pranks

Acts of Joy

Biggest Lies

Generous Gestures

Criminal Offenses

Bullying and/or Backstabbing Acts

The Writer's Guide to Beginnings

WRITERS ON VILLAINS AND VILLAINY

"The villain is the architect of the plot; make sure the villain is worthy of the hero."
—Cara Black

"Nobody is a villain in their own story. We're all the heroes of our own stories."
—George R.R. Martin

"Evil is relative—and what I mean by that is that our villains are as complex, as deep, and as compelling as any of our heroes. Every antagonist in the DC Universe has a unique darkness, desire, and drive."
—Geoff Johns

"People are much more complicated in real life, but my characters are as subtle and nuanced as I can make them. But if you say my characters are too black and white, you've missed the point. Villains are meant to be black-hearted in popular novels. If you say I have a grey-hearted villain, then I've failed."
—Ken Follett

"The battleline between good and evil runs through the heart of every man."
—Aleksandr Solzhenitsyn

"I like not fair terms and a villain's mind."
—William Shakespeare

"More and more these days, what I find myself doing in my stories is making a representation of goodness and a representation of evil and then having those two run at each other full-speed, like a couple of peewee football players, to see what happens. Who stays standing? Whose helmet goes flying off?"
—George Saunders

"Who is to say who is the villain and who is the hero? Probably the dictionary."
—Joss Whedon

"So once I thought of the villain with a sense of humor, I began to think of a name, and the name 'The Joker' immediately came to mind. There was the association with the Joker in the deck of

cards, and I probably yelled literally, 'Eureka!' because I knew I had the name and the image at the same time."
—Jerry Robinson

"The same energy of character which renders a man a daring villain would have rendered him useful in society, had that society been well organized."
—Mary Wollstonecraft

"I firmly believe that a story is only as good as the villain."
—Clive Barker

"Evil is not something superhuman; it's something less than human."
—Agatha Christie

"He that wrestles with us strengthens our nerves and sharpens our skill. Our antagonist is our helper."
—Edmund Burke

"An excellent man, like precious metal, is in every way invariable; a villain, like the beams of a balance, is always varying, upwards and downwards."
—John Locke

"I like to see the difference between good and evil as kind of like the foul line at a baseball game. It's very thin, it's made of something very flimsy like lime, and if you cross it, it really starts to blur where fair becomes foul and foul becomes fair."
—Harlan Coben

"I mean, without the antagonist, there would be no story! It'd be like: 'Once upon a time there was a girl who wanted to be loved, so she met a prince and got married and lived Happily Ever After, The End'? That's not a story; that's a bumper sticker."
—Shannon Hale

"My theory of characterization is basically this: Put some dirt on a hero, and put some sunshine on the villain, one brushstroke of beauty on the villain."
—Justin Cronin

"Evil doesn't attack, it seduces."
—Anne Perry

"As for an authentic villain, the real thing, the absolute, the artist, one rarely meets him even once in a lifetime. The ordinary bad hat is always in part a decent fellow."
—Sidonie-Gabrielle Colette

"Only a writer who has the sense of evil can make goodness readable."
—E.M. Forster

"I'll tell you the secret. When you begin with a character, you want to begin by creating a villain."
—Dorothy Allison

"It's rather disconcerting to sit around a table participating in a critique of someone else's work, only to realize the antagonist in the story is none other than yourself, and no one present thinks you're a very likable character."
—Michelle Richmond

"I don't write about good and evil with this enormous dichotomy. I write about people. I write about people doing the kinds of things that people do."
—Octavia E. Butler

"When something happens far back in the past, people often can't recall exact details. Blame depends upon point of view. There may be a villain, but reality is frustrating because it's often ambiguous."
—Hallie Ephron

"Harvard was also a little bit of a villain in my first book, *The Dante Club*. I guess there might be a way to make Harvard more of a sympathetic presence, but it's such a powerful institution that it more naturally lends itself toward not necessarily a negative but an obstructionist element in a story."
—Matthew Pearl

"The characters that have greys are the more interesting characters. The hero who sometimes crosses the line and the villain who sometimes doesn't are just much more interesting."
—Geoff Johns

"No man is clever enough to know all the evil he does."
—François de La Rochefoucauld

....

Supporting Cast

"No man is an island entire of itself; every man/is a piece of the continent, a part of the main .... " —*John Donne*

No man is an island—and neither is a hero an island. The best protagonists are surrounded by people: family, friends, neighbors, rivals, enemies, frenemies, colleagues, acquaintances, strangers, and more. This supporting cast of characters is your best friend as a writer; build yourself a company of players, and use them to create conflict and heighten the drama. Your secondary characters give your protagonist someone to play with, for, and against—someone to seduce or strike, fight or fix, marry or murder.

As the late great actor Spencer Tracy once said, "Acting, to me, is always reacting." Your protagonist needs to be reacting, acting, reacting, acting, reacting. Think of Spencer Tracy reacting to Katharine Hepburn, Kevin Spacey reacting to Robin Wright, Laurel reacting to Hardy, Tina Fey reacting to Amy Poehler, Tom Hanks reacting to Wilson, and Meryl Streep reacting to anything and anybody.

Unless your hero is stranded on Mars or cast away on a deserted island, your hero is part of a community, and that community is critical to the success of your story. Build that community, and as you do, consider the many functions supporting characters can provide:

- **MIRROR:** Supporting characters can act as mirrors for protagonists, reflecting their own positive and negative traits right back at them. Think of sisters Elinor and Marianne Dashwood in Jane Austen's *Sense and Sensibility*, each serving as a mirror to the other, as the author lets us know right there in the title of the novel.
- **MORAL SUPPORT:** These are the characters who serve as shoulders to cry on for the protagonist. In Candace Bushnell's *Sex and the City*, Carrie Bradshaw gets all kinds of moral support from her friends Miranda, Charlotte, and Samantha.
- **ALLY:** Every hero needs backup—the stronger and smarter, the better. Robert B. Parker gives his private detective Spenser the ultimate ally in Hawk, whose name says it all.

- **COLLEAGUE:** Your protagonist's workplace is rife with possibility for secondary characters, and in some genres, such as police procedurals, a cast of colleagues is *de rigueur*. Think of Ed McBain, who set the standard with his colorful cops of the 87th Precinct, Walt Longmire's associates in the Absaroka Sheriff's Department in Craig Johnson's Longmire series, and the tough and talented ladies of James Patterson's Women's Murder Club Series.
- **BAD INFLUENCE:** These characters are the unscrupulous pals who lead your protagonist down the wrong path. Think of Carlo Collodi's Pinocchio, who is persuaded to go to a land of perpetual recreation and amusement by the boy named Candlewick—a journey that results in Pinnochio's transformation into a donkey.
- **MENTOR:** If you're looking for a mentor, look no farther than Homer's *The Odyssey*, in which Telemachus receives assistance from Mentor, who is really the goddess Athena masquerading as a human, as the Greek gods were wont to do. Mentors run the gamut from Cinderella's fairy godmother to James Bond's M.
- **GURU:** Gurus are spiritual advisors who help keep their charges on the path of truth and beauty. Think Merlin, Obi-Wan Kenobi, and Yoda: "Powerful you have become; the dark side I sense in you." Indeed.
- **CORRUPTOR:** These characters are bad influences to the nth power—from Bud Fox's boss Gordon Gekko in Oliver Stone's *Wall Street* to war hero Michael Corleone's entire family in Mario Puzo's *The Godfather*.
- **WINGMAN:** Webster defines *wingman* as "a pilot or airplane that flies behind and outside the leader of a group of airplanes in order to provide support or protection—often used figuratively." Or in reference to singles bars. Pop culture definitions aside, every guy needs a wingman, which is why Miles has his Jack in Rex Pickett's *Sideways* (on which the acclaimed film was based), Sherlock Holmes has his Dr. Watson in Sir Arthur Conan Doyle's *The Adventures of Sherlock Holmes*, and Frodo Baggins has his Samwise Gamgee in J.R.R.Tolkien's *The Lord of the Rings*.

- **LOVER:** The protagonist's love interest may play a smaller or larger role in your story, but in any case the lover gives readers a chance to see another side of your protagonist. In Robert B. Parker's Spenser series, Spenser's psychologist girlfriend, Susan Silverman, gives Spenser a kind of emotional ballast that he might not otherwise achieve, given his occupation and code of honor.
- **COMIC RELIEF:** These are the supporting characters that make your protagonist and your readers laugh out loud, during good times and bad. Think of the Nurse, who provides comic relief in Shakespeare's tragedy *Romeo and Juliet*, or Timon and Pumbaa, who lighten things up in Disney's *The Lion King*.

Many of these roles are often combined, giving us wingmen who also serve as comic relief, lovers who also provide moral support, etc. Play with your supporting cast, and make them work on behalf of your protagonist and plot.

WHEN YOUR MAN IS AN ISLAND

If your hero *is* stranded on Mars, cast away on a deserted island, or otherwise alone in your story, you might want to rethink that. Otherwise, you will have your work cut out for you, as you'll have to create what will prove the equivalent of a one-man show without the benefit of Matt Damon or Tom Hanks.

Sure, Andy Weir did it in *The Martian* (the novel on which the Matt Damon film was based), but the resourceful author had setting (Mars) and science (how the heck will the astronaut/engineer/ botanist survive without food or water?) on his side. Weir also had a supporting cast, his hero Mark Watney's fellow astronauts, engineers, and scientists, both up in space and down on Earth.

If you try this at home, you'll have to be equally resourceful to pull it off.

"The only characters I ever don't like are ones that leave no impression on me. And I don't write characters that leave no impression on me." —*Lauren DeStefano*

TOO MANY CHARACTERS, TOO SOON!

Don't overcrowd your story opening with so many characters that your leading men and women get lost in the shuffle. In too many stories, the writer introduces far too many characters for the reader to keep track of, much less care about. Worse, most of these characters are usually not doing much; they're just making an entrance and taking up space on the story's stage.

People your story slowly, starting with your leads and your strongest supporting characters.

A good rule of thumb: no more than three to six characters in your opening pages. Begin with fewer characters, and give those characters a lot *more* to do.

Naming Names

Giving your characters good names can be a surprisingly tricky business. The right name gives readers an instant sense of who the character is, right from their introduction in your story.

But you'd be surprised at how many writers either don't think about it at all or overthink it—all to the detriment of the story. Here are some basic guidelines you should consider when naming your characters:

- **FIND NAMES THAT ARE EASY TO READ, PRONOUNCE, AND SPELL.** Readers will stumble over excessively long, oddly spelled, and onerously enunciated names, and every time they do, they'll fall right out of your story. If you've ever read Leo Tolstoy's *War and Peace*, you surely stumbled over all those countless and confusing Russian names—from Arakcheyev to Zhilinsky.
- **MIX IT UP.** Do not use names that are too similar to other characters' names in your story; avoid names of the same ethnicities, the same syllabic structures, the same sounds, and even the same

first letters. No Watsons, Hudsons, and Watersons; no Dons, Jims, and Bobs; no Dawns, Ronnas, and Connors; no Claires, Chloes, and Catherines. When names are too much alike, readers may find themselves stopping to figure out who's who all the time. Editors are as sensitive to this as readers, perhaps more so. Your character names should be as diverse as possible in every possible way; think of J.K. Rowling and her world of Hogwarts, populated with such perfectly and precisely named characters as Severus Snape, Rubeus Hagrid, Lord Voldemort, Ron Weasley, Draco Malfoy, Viktor Krum, Padma Patil, Albus Dumbledore, Nearly Headless Nick, Hermione Granger, and of course, the one and only Harry Potter.

- **CHOOSE A NAME IN KEEPING WITH THE SEX, BACKGROUND, AND TEMPERAMENT OF THE CHARACTER.** Margaret Mitchell famously called her *Gone with the Wind* heroine Patsy in early drafts of the story, a name we find laughable today. It's difficult to imagine a wimp named Patsy playing the role of the survivor extraordinaire, Scarlett O'Hara.

IMPROMPTU

If your story were a movie, who would you cast as your characters? Create a scrapbook of characters, either on paper in a standard scrapbook or in an electronic scrapbook. Who would play your hero? Your heroine? Your villain? Your supporting players? Make a page for each, and fill in their stats: birthdate, hometown, occupation, family, etc. Find photos of the actors and actresses you'd cast the roles in the film version of your story; seek out pictures of the clothes they'd wear, the homes they'd buy/rent, the vehicles in their driveways. Add maps, family trees, and any information that informs who and what they are. Don't forget to add images that represent the light and dark of their natures as well. Turn to these scrapbooks to help you create well-rounded characters that readers will remember—and to remind or inspire you whenever you feel stuck while writing your narrative.

The Writer's Guide to Beginnings

SETTING

"I [have] spent my life on the road, waking in a pleasant or not so pleasant hotel, and setting off every morning after breakfast hoping to discover something new and repeatable, something worth writing about." —*Paul Theroux*

Setting is a critical but often underrated and underutilized element of a good story. One of the most common mistakes writers make in opening their stories is failing to embrace setting—or worse, ignoring it altogether. Pulitzer Prize-winning writer Eudora Welty said it best when she advised that setting is so paramount to story that changing the setting would change the story itself, because fiction is so dependent on a sense of place. As Welty said, "Place is the crossroads of circumstance, the proving ground of: 'What happened? Who's here? Who's coming?'"

This is an elegant way of saying that you ignore setting at your own peril. Setting is one of the storyteller's most valuable tools, one to be employed from the very beginning of your story. The trick is to make your setting as specific as possible; specificity is the key to compelling storytelling in general and compelling setting in particular.

Let's take a look at writers who start straight off by grounding their stories in a very specific setting.

> In the late summer of that year we lived in a house in a village that looked across the river and the plain to the mountains. In the bed of the river there were pebbles and boulders, dry and white in the sun, and the water was clear and swiftly moving and blue in the channels. Troops went by the house and down the road and the dust they raised powdered the leaves of the trees. The trunks of the trees too were dusty and the leaves fell early that year and we saw the troops marching along the road and dust rising and leaves, stirred by the breeze, falling and the soldiers marching and afterward the road bare and white except for the leaves.
>
> —*A Farewell to Arms*, by Ernest Hemingway

Here we get pulled right into the story by the rhythm of Hemingway's prose and the uneasy beauty of the setting: a serene and lovely place, except for the marching troops, the rising dust, and the falling leaves. And we know we are in for a story about the inevitability of war and death, dust to dust, as it were.

> No live organism can continue for long to exist sanely under conditions of absolute reality; even larks and katydids are supposed, by some, to dream. Hill House, not sane, stood by itself against its hills, holding darkness within; it had stood so for eighty years and might stand for eighty more. Within, walls continued upright, bricks met neatly, floors were firm, and doors were sensibly shut; silence lay steadily against the wood and stone of Hill House, and whatever walked there, walked alone.
>
> —*The Haunting of Hill House*, by Shirley Jackson

In this chilling opening, Shirley Jackson uses setting as a character to set the tone and warn the reader that Hill House is alive with wickedness, inviting the reader in for a walk through that house, alone.

> When Sean Devine and Jimmy Marcus were kids, their fathers worked together at the Coleman Candy plant and carried the stench of warm chocolate back home with them. It became a permanent character of their clothes, the beds they slept in, the vinyl backs of their car seats. Sean's kitchen smelled like a Fudgsicle, his bathroom like a Coleman Chew-Chew bar. By the time they were eleven, Sean and Jimmy had developed a hatred of sweets so total that they took their coffee black for the rest of their lives and never ate dessert.
>
> —*Mystic River*, by Dennis Lehane

When the story is titled by its setting, as is Dennis Lehane's *Mystic River*, we know before we even open the book that place is paramount. In this opening, we enter a working-class neighborhood where even the sweetness corrupts—and meet two boys who will navigate this neighborhood, for better or worse.

> The night air was thick and damp. As I drove south along Lake Michigan, I could smell rotting alewives like a faint perfume on the heavy air. Little fires shone here and there from late-night barbecues in the park. On the water a host of green and red running lights showed

people seeking relief from the sultry air. On shore traffic was heavy, the city moving restlessly, trying to breathe. It was July in Chicago.

—*Indemnity Only*, by Sara Paretsky

In this first of Paretsky's celebrated V.I. Warshawski private-detective series, we feel the all-consuming heat of the city of Chicago, and we know the stage is set for violence.

It was my father who called the city the Mansion on the River.

He was talking about Charleston, South Carolina, and he was a native son, peacock proud of a town so pretty it makes your eyes ache with pleasure just to walk down its spellbinding, narrow streets. Charleston was my father's ministry, his hobbyhorse, his quiet obsession, and the great love of his life. His bloodstream lit up my own with a passion for the city that I've never lost nor ever will. I'm Charleston-born, and -bred. The city's two rivers, the Ashley and the Cooper, have flooded and shaped all the days of my life on this storied peninsula.

—*South of Broad*, by Pat Conroy

Pat Conroy made a career out of setting—whether it's the Citadel, Melrose Island, Rome, or Charleston. In this opening, we meet a native son who's been raised in the mythos of this Deep South gem, and we understand that gems can be as hard as they are lovely and myths are stories about fallen gods.

We didn't always live on Mango Street. Before that we lived on Loomis on the third floor, and before that we lived on Keeler. Before Keeler it was Paulina, and before that I can't remember. But what I remember most is moving a lot. Each time it seemed there'd be one more of us. By the time we got to Mango Street we were six—Mama, Papa, Carlos, Kiki, my sister Nenny and me.

The house on Mango Street is ours, and we don't have to pay rent to anybody, or share the yard with the people downstairs, or be careful not to make too much noise, and there isn't a landlord banging on the ceiling with a broom. But even so, it's not the house we thought we'd get.

—*The House on Mango Street*, by Sandra Cisneros

The House on Mango Street is a coming-of-age classic, and we know from the charm and poignancy of this opening that here is an immigrant heroine who will not be defined by where she lives, even as she embraces the people who live there with her.

Each of these settings grounds its story in a very specific place. Whether it's a European countryside torn apart by the Great War or a blue-collar Boston neighborhood reeking of chocolate, setting informs these stories from their opening lines. These stories could not be set anywhere else; setting is part and parcel of their plot and their power.

Specificity Counts

One of the most common failings of story openings is a lack of specificity, particularly when it comes to setting. Many writers set their scenes in places we've seen a million times before and miss a critical opportunity to reveal character, propel the plot, and explore themes in the process. There's a reason movie and television producers hire location scouts to seek out interesting and unique locations for their productions; they know how important setting is to a good story, and they want to set their action against a compelling background that shows the audience something different and captivating on the screen.

When I read a writer's story opening and realize the writer has not made the most of setting, I circle the nondescript nouns that clutter the prose. Three of the worst offenders: *rooms, houses, streets.* Those very nouns—*rooms, houses, streets*—are nondescript.

Let's take a look at the many options you might use instead.

- **ROOM:** accommodation, alcove, attic, cabin, cave, cell, chamber, cubbyhole, cubicle, den, dorm, flat, flop, foyer, hall, hideout, hole, garret, joint, lean-to, lobby, lounge, lodging, nest, niche, office, quarter, setup, shed, shelter, space, studio, suite, turf, warren, vault
- **HOUSE:** abode, apartment, barrack, box, brownstone, building, bullpen, bungalow, cabin, cape cod, casa, castle, cave, chateau, co-op, commorancy, condo, condominium, cottage, coop, crash pad, digs, domicile, dump, dwelling, edifice, estate, flat, flophouse, habitation, haunt, headquarters, hole–in-the-wall, home, homestead, hut, joint,

kennel, manor, mansion, pad, palace, pied-à-terre, pigpen, pigsty, quarters, ranch, residence, roost, sanctuary, shack, shanty, teepee, tent, trailer, villa

- **STREET**: artery, avenue, back alley, boulevard, byway, causeway, court, cul-de-sac, dead end, drag, drive, esplanade, freeway, highway, lane, parkway, passage, pavement, pike, place, road, roadway, rotary, route, roundabout, row, stroll, terrace, thoroughfare, toll road, track, trail, turf, way

JUMP-START

Comb through your work, and circle all the nouns and other words and phrases related to your setting. Swap out the bland and generic ones for more descriptive terms that help paint your setting in fine detail. Don't go overboard; you don't want your story to read like a thesaurus, but do see how the right telling detail can bring your scenes to life.

Change Your Setting; Change Your Story

Ask yourself this: If I changed my setting, would it change my story? If not, you have some work to do in regard to your setting. Learn from the masters here, and check out the best writers in your genre as well to see how they handle setting. You need to get setting right, and if you do, your story opening will be all the more compelling for it.

THE DIREWOLF SOLUTION

If you are writing science fiction, fantasy, or historical fiction, you face an especially tough challenge in regard to setting. You must drop your readers into a whole new world—another place, another time, another dimension. Here, again, the key to creating a believable alternate environment is specificity.

Show us what makes your world special and unique. Be specific. Specificity can help you transcend the tropes that have become clichés:

- Don't say *castle*; say "Castle Black." Just naming the castle makes all of the difference, and naming it Castle Black gives readers a hint of the dark mission of the Night's Watch.
- Don't say *city*; say "King's Landing." Now the reader knows that this is a capitol city, a seat of power, where kings rise … and fall.
- Don't say *dog*; say "direwolf." George R.R. Martin borrowed the term *dire wolf*, which Webster defines as a "large extinct wolflike mammal (*Canis dirus*) known from Pleistocene deposits of North America," to create his own magical species known as the direwolf, which beats the heck out of *dog* any day.

I use these examples from *A Game of Thrones* on purpose because Martin is always *very* specific—and he brings his world to life in living, breathing color—from dragons to direwolves. You must be, too.

....

"I wanted to write something in a voice that was unique to who I was. And I wanted something that was accessible to the person who works at Dunkin Donuts or who drives a bus, someone who comes home with their feet hurting like my father, someone who's busy and has too many children, like my mother."
—*Sandra Cisneros*

THE SOFTER SIDE OF STORY

Now that we've outlined the rules of voice, point of view, character, and setting, you not only know how to avoid making the mistakes that could sabotage your efforts to sell your story; you've learned how to use these elements to give your story the subtleties, layers, and nuances that will take your work to the next level.

These elements are the meat on the bones of plot and the muscle of drama. When you master these elements, you imbue your writing with the sophistication and polish that, from the opening pages, can distinguish your work as being among the most well-crafted—and that can make the difference with editors, agents, and readers.

For you to showcase these finer points of storytelling to your best advantage, you need that solid muscle of drama beneath your story—the muscles of action, conflict, dialogue, and theme. In the next chapter, we'll tackle the rules that can help you build the strong muscle you need to power up your story and keep it running at top speed.

"Writing has laws of perspective, of light and shade, just as painting does or music. If you are born knowing them, fine. If not, learn them. Then rearrange the rules to suit yourself."
—*Truman Capote*

CHAPTER SIX

THE BEGINNINGS RULEBOOK II

The Dignity of Greatness

"To get the truth, you want to get your
own heart to pound while you write."
—*Robert McKee*

○

"Action is the dignity of greatness."
—*José Marti*

ACTION

The most reliable way of opening your story is with action. Readers respond to proactive characters; they want to read about people who err on the side of action, rather than inertia. That's why you don't want to open your story with your character asleep, flat on her back, dreaming her life away. No dream is that good. I know I've said this before, but it bears repeating, and I'll keep on saying it until writers stop opening stories with dreams.

Even those of you who say that you write character-driven stories are not off the hook. As F. Scott Fitzgerald pointed out, "Action is character." Characters who don't act are boring and stuck and impotent. No one wants to read about boring, stuck, impotent people. We get enough of that in real life, and it frustrates us. We don't want those kinds of characters in our lives or in our fiction. In fact, one of the reasons we read fiction is because we identify with the heroine, who must act to achieve her happy ending or, failing that, to achieve wholeness. We look to fiction as entertainment, sure, but also as enlightenment: Here's how Dorothy makes it home to Kansas; here's how James Bond foils Goldfinger; here's how Elizabeth Bennet (and Bridget Jones) wins her Mr. Darcy; here's how Sherlock Holmes solves another impossible case; here's how Piper Kerman survives her year in prison. The best stories teach us through action, not sermons.

Action conquers fear, monotony, lethargy, and plot problems. Without action there is no plot, only dead prose. Writing good action isn't easy, but if you can do it, you can sell your work. That's why I'm always on the lookout for authors who write action well. So open with action, and grab your reader. It's just that simple—and that difficult.

Visualize Your Story

If your story were a film, what would you see on the screen? What would your hero actually be doing? How would you *show us* his peccadillos and problems, hopes and dreams, flaws and failures, virtues and victories?

One of the most affecting story openings is Anne Tyler's *The Accidental Tourist*. In this classic family drama, Macon and Sarah Leary are a middle-aged couple whose only child has died at the hands of a random shooter. We meet them as they are driving home in a rainstorm from a week at the beach. Sarah wants Macon to pull over until the rains stops. He says that everything is fine and keeps on driving, and she asks him for a divorce.

In the next scene, Sarah has moved out, and Macon is alone in their house. Macon takes advantage of her absence by devising a series of energy-saving systems designed to facilitate household chores, incorporating a number of eccentric home inventions.

> Breakfast: Breakfast was your most important meal. He hooked up the percolator and the electric skillet to the clock radio on his bedroom windowsill. Of course he was asking for food poisoning, letting two raw eggs wait all night at room temperature, but once he'd changed menus there was no problem. You had to be flexible about

these matters. He was awakened now by the smell of fresh coffee and hot buttered popcorn, and he could partake of both without getting out of bed. Oh, he was managing fine, just fine. All things considered.

—*The Accidental Tourist*, by Anne Tyler

Anne Tyler never tells us Macon is depressed, as any man might be in the wake of death and divorce. But in an accumulation of hilariously heartbreaking actions, she shows us a man drowning in grief—without actually using the word *depression*. This very short selection from *The Accidental Tourist* proves that action doesn't have to mean car chases and bomb explosions. Action means characters doing things, and here, Tyler shows us *what it looks like* when a devoted husband and father loses what matters most to him.

LIGHTS! CAMERA! ACTION WRITER!

One of the best shortcuts to writing good action is to take a screenwriting class. This will help you learn to: (1) think cinematically, (2) write in scenes, and (3) transform thought into action for your characters.

Research Your Story

If you're stymied by the thought of beginning your story with action, then do your research. The more you know about the time, place, and content that you aim to dramatize in your opening scenes, the better. And the more likely you are to discover a way into the story that you had not imagined before.

For her shattering masterpiece *Paradise*, Toni Morrison researched the all-black towns formed in Oklahoma after the Civil War by ex-slaves. She took that history and made it her own, creating "an all-black community, one chosen by its inhabitants, next to a raceless one, also chosen by its inhabitants." And then she let the drama rip, starting with the very first line.

They shoot the white girl first. With the rest they can take their time.

—*Paradise*, by Toni Morrison

The Writer's Guide to Beginnings

Morrison says that she wanted this opening sentence "to signal (1) the presence of race as hierarchy and (2) its collapse as reliable information." That devastating line of action did all that and more: It grabbed the reader by the throat and didn't let go.

Research can prove the springboard for your opening scene's action as well. When you get stuck, go back to the well and prime your story pump.

Enact Your Story

"I think of writing in theatrical terms, and generating raw prose on a blank page is roughly equivalent to performing on a bare stage in rehearsal. Do something. Take up space."
—*William Alexander*

Storytelling is an elaborate and stylized form of the "pretend" game we all played as children. If you're having trouble dramatizing your story opening, then step into the role of your protagonist. Act out what you mean to communicate in your beginning, the action you need to happen to get your story started.

In short, this exercise is why actors often make good writers. Take Hugh Laurie of *Jeeves and Wooster* and *House* fame, who acts, sings, plays the piano (among several instruments), and writes novels. Here are the first lines of his acclaimed thriller, lines obviously informed by his life as an actor.

> Imagine that you have to break someone's arm.
>
> Right or left, doesn't matter. The point is that you have to break it, because if you don't ... well, that doesn't matter either. Let's just say bad things will happen if you don't.
>
> Now, my question goes like this: do you break the arm quickly—snap, whoops, sorry, here let me help you with that improvised splint—or do you drag the whole business out for a good eight minutes, every now and then increasing the pressure in the tiniest of increments, until the pain becomes pink and green and hot and cold and altogether howlingly unbearable?
>
> —*The Gun Seller*, by Hugh Laurie

This beginning could be the ruminations of an actor considering how to approach a scene as easily as it could be what it truly is: the opening scene of a novel. When you're looking for the drama in your story, imagine you are Hugh Laurie or the actor of your choice and write away.

If you have any actor friends—and all writers should—invite them over and ask them to inhabit your characters. See what they come up with, and play around with their approaches to your story. Sometimes two or three or four drama queens are better than one.

Go Big—or Go Back

There is no such thing as too compelling a story opening. From *Jaws* to *Paradise*, *The Accidental Tourist* to *Pride and Prejudice*, the opening action should be big enough to jolt your characters and your readers right out of their complacency, upturn the world as they know it, and blast them right onto the path of transformation.

Which brings us to conflict.

IMPROMPTU

You're writing a story in which the lead role is to be played on screen by Angelina Jolie. List fifty ways to *show* us that she's depressed.

Now, do this same exercise once more. Only this time, do it for a male character to be played by Brad Pitt. When you're finished, compare versions.

NOTE: This is also a great exercise to do with your writing group.

WRITERS ON ACTION

Let's take a look at some of the best advice from accomplished authors on writing action, and examine how it might work for your own story.

"Never mistake motion for action."
—Ernest Hemingway

The Writer's Guide to Beginnings

"I have a graduate degree from Penn State. I studied at Penn State under a noted Hemingway scholar, Philip Young. I had an interest in thrillers, and it occurred to me that Hemingway wrote many action scenes: the war scenes in *A Farewell to Arms* and *For Whom the Bell Tolls* come to mind. But the scenes don't feel pulpy."
—David Morrell

"Suit the action to the word, the word to the action."
—William Shakespeare

"… the writer must be a participant in the scene … [like] a film director/producer who writes his own scripts, does his own camerawork, and somehow manages to film himself in action, as the protagonist or at least a main character."
—Hunter S. Thompson

"… believable action is based on authenticity, and accuracy is very important to me. I always spend time researching my novels, exploring the customs and attitudes of the county I'm using for their setting."
—Sidney Sheldon

"Good action films—not crap, but good action films—are really morality plays. They deal in modern, mythic culture."
—Sylvester Stallone

"There is a comfort zone of knowing where things are going and having characters in place, but the action gets more and more dramatic and is very challenging to describe."
—Jerry B. Jenkins

"Plot is a big pain in the ass. I work very, very hard on that, but I enjoy working on it because it has great rewards. … I think when you're working on the plot, you're talking about 'What does the character want?' All the plot is the structure of the main character towards the achievement of one goal."
—David Mamet

"All fiction is about people, unless it's about rabbits pretending to be people. It's all essentially characters in action, which means characters moving through time and changes taking place, and that's what we call 'the plot'."
—Margaret Atwood

"Drama is action, sir, action and not confounded philosophy."
—Luigi Pirandello

"The mark of a good action is that it appears inevitable in retrospect."
—Robert Louis Stevenson

"Narrative is linear, but action has breadth and depth as well as height and is solid."
—Thomas Carlyle

....

CONFLICT

"The greatest rules of dramatic writing are conflict, conflict, conflict." —*James Frey*

Conflict is the currency of drama and the driving force behind action, but action alone does not a story make. That's why video games make such terrible movies and, God help us, novelizations.

Merriam-Webster defines conflict in literature as "the opposition of persons or forces that gives rise to the dramatic action in a drama or fiction." The most compelling action is the result of the conflict between those people or forces. Let's take a look at the many kinds of conflict available to you as a storyteller and how you can use conflict to craft your story opening for maximum effect.

The Many Faces of Conflict

You probably learned about the four basic kinds of conflict—man vs. man, man vs. society, man vs. nature, man vs. self—in your high school English class, along with the rest of us. But writing now in the twenty-first century, we have even more options at our disposal than just these four tried-and-true types; modern literature scholars often also include man vs. fate/God, man vs. paranormal, and man vs. technology among the main types of conflicts. This is good news for us; as writers we need all the conflict we can get. All are plotting tools we can't live without—and the more tools in our writer's toolbox, the more opportunities for drama in our stories. Let's examine each type of conflict in turn.

Man vs. Man

Man vs. Man is the conflict that pits your protagonist against your antagonist. Think of the opening of every James Bond film, when Ian Fleming's one-of-a-kind spy 007 faces down the first of the story's many villains. Or the more subtle discussion amongst the March sisters that opens Louisa May Alcott's *Little Women,* where they debate the unfairness of a Christmas without presents or their beloved father.

> "Christmas won't be Christmas without any presents," grumbled Jo, lying on the rug.
>
> "It's so dreadful to be poor!" sighed Meg, looking down at her old dress.
>
> "I don't think it's fair for some girls to have plenty of pretty things, and other girls nothing at all," added little Amy, with an injured sniff.
>
> "We've got Father and Mother, and each other," said Beth contentedly from her corner.
>
> The four young faces on which the firelight shone brightened at the cheerful words, but darkened again as Jo said sadly, "We haven't got Father, and shall not have him for a long time." She didn't say "perhaps never," but each silently added it, thinking of Father far away, where the fighting was.

Man vs. Society

Man vs. Society is the quintessential story about fighting City Hall. Most dystopian stories fall into this category: Katniss Everdeen takes on the Capitol in Suzanne Collins's *The Hunger Games,* and her first act of defiance occurs in the very beginning, when she goes poaching in the forbidden woods, trades her illicit catch for bread and salt on the black market, and volunteers to take her little sister's place when her name is called at the reaping. We know right away in this first line that trouble is brewing.

> When I wake up, the other side of the bed is cold. My fingers stretch out, seeking Prim's warmth but finding only the rough canvas cover of the mattress. She must have had bad dreams and climbed in with our mother. Of course, she did. This is the day of the reaping.

Man vs. Nature

From the beginning of human time, the survival of our species has depended on our winning more conflicts with Mother Nature than we lose. Many stories open with her treachery: the cyclone that carries Dorothy to Oz, the storm at sea that shipwrecks the Swiss Family Robinson, the boot-destroying perils of the great outdoors that challenge Cheryl Strayed on the Pacific Crest Trail. Bad weather, wild animals, disease-spreading mosquitoes, venom-injecting snakes, and swarms of killer bees—Mother Nature at her worst—can make for very scary, literary storytelling. Consider the beginning of Ernest Hemingway's classic *The Old Man and the Sea*.

> He was an old man who fished alone in a skiff in the Gulf Stream and he had gone eighty-four days now without taking a fish.

Man vs. Self

Inner conflict—otherwise known as Man vs. Self—is the one kind of conflict that *all* good stories must offer readers. A character's inner life can be revealed directly only in the novel; film, television, and theater cannot let us into the very heads of our heroes to hear all of their unspoken thoughts (the limited device of voice-over not withstanding). So every good story must open with this kind of conflict, inevitably ramped up by the other kinds of conflict as well.

For most coming-of-age stories, inner conflict takes center stage, beginning with word one. Think of Holden Caulfield, that poster boy for adolescent angst, who begins his narration of J.D. Salinger's *A Catcher in the Rye* with this opening line.

> If you really want to hear about it, the first thing you'll probably want to know is where I was born, and what my lousy childhood was like, and how my parents were occupied and all before they had me, and all that David Copperfield kind of crap, but I don't feel like going into it, if you want to know the truth.

Man vs. Fate/God

In Man vs. Fate/God, the conflict is between the protagonist and his God, or his Fate. The heroes and heroines of classic mythology always suffer at the capricious and often cruel hands of the gods and goddesses. In Sophocles's *Oedipus Rex*, Oedipus does everything possible to avoid his fate but—spoiler alert!—ends up killing his father and marrying his mother anyway. Rick Riordan opens the first entry in his best-selling middle-grade series, *The Lightning Thief*, with his half-blood hero Percy Jackson taking on his pre-algebra teacher, Mrs. Dodds, a.k.a. Alecto, one of the Furies from Hades, and he wastes no time about it.

> I ACCIDENTALLY VAPORIZE MY PRE-ALGEBRA TEACHER
> **Look, I didn't want to be a half-blood.**
>
> If you're reading this because you think you might be one, my advice is: close this book right now. Believe whatever lie your mom or dad told you about your birth, and try to lead a normal life.

Man vs. Paranormal

Conflicts with the paranormal are very common in today's storytelling. Vampires and werewolves, ghosts and demons, UFOs and aliens—all these creatures, and more populate the stories with this type of conflict. In the opening lines of Stephenie Meyer's massive bestseller *Twilight*, heroine Isabella Swan narrates the tale of her own seduction.

> I'd never given much thought to how I would die—though I'd had reason enough in the last few months—but even if I had, I would not have imagined it like this.
>
> I stared without breathing across the long room, into the dark eyes of the hunter, and he looked pleasantly back at me.

Man vs. Technology

In the high-tech world we live in, the threats of technology loom as large as the benefits. Thus Man vs. Technology is the timeliest of conflicts and can come into play in stories as varied as James Cameron and Gale Anne Hurd's *The Terminator*, in which Sarah Connor and Kyle Reese are pitted against the cyborg, and Spike Jonze's *Her*, in which Theodore falls in love with his operating system. No one does Man vs. Technology conflicts better than Philip K. Dick, as evidenced by the opening lines of *Do Androids Dream of Electric Sheep?*, the sober novel upon which the cult film *Blade Runner* was (loosely) based.

> A merry little surge of electricity piped by automatic alarm from the mood organ beside his bed awakened Rick Deckard. Surprised—it always surprised him to find himself awake without prior notice—he rose from the bed, stood up in his multicolored pajamas, and stretched.

NOTE: Here Dick cleverly breaks the rule about not opening with a character sleeping. He gets away with it because his character is literally *shocked* awake.

The more kinds of conflict you can use in your story opening, the bigger the impact on your reader. Think of Shakespeare's *Hamlet*, in which so many types of conflict occur:

- **MAN VS. MAN:** Hamlet clashes with his uncle King Claudius, his mother Gertrude, and his beloved Ophelia, among others.
- **MAN VS. SOCIETY:** Hamlet rages against the power of the monarchy, represented by his treacherous uncle, who has killed Hamlet's father and married his mother, setting his dead brother's crown upon his own head.
- **MAN VS. NATURE:** Hamlet's beloved Ophelia, distraught by his rejection and her father's death at his hands, festoons herself with garlands of flowers and falls into the weeping brook, and drowns.
- **MAN VS. SELF:** Hamlet is the king of inner conflict, and his indecision and melancholy contribute to his fall—to be or not to be, indeed.
- **MAN VS. FATE/GOD:** Hamlet worries that the ghost claiming to be his father's spirit may instead be an agent of the devil, and he hesitates to kill Claudius while he is praying.
- **MAN VS. PARANORMAL:** Hamlet's encounters with his father's ghost disturb him and provoke his desire for revenge.
- **MAN VS. TECHNOLOGY:** Hamlet uses a number of tools that might qualify as technology in his era—a poisoned sword, forged documents, the "play within a play" reenactment of his father's murder,

among others. The poisoned sword results in multiple deaths, including Hamlet's.

JUMP-START

How might you arrange for your characters, like Hamlet, to experience each of these types of conflict? Brainstorm lists of possibilities for each kind of conflict; come up with at least ten for each type. Which combination would prove most effective for your story opening? Aim for at least three kinds of conflict in your story opening, one of them being the ubiquitous inner conflict.

"The story ... must be a conflict—and specifically, a conflict between the forces of good and evil within a single person."
—*Maxwell Anderson*

DIALOGUE

"All the information you need can be given in dialogue."
—*Elmore Leonard*

Readers love dialogue. Good dialogue is fun to read, moves quickly, and even looks good on the page. In fact, readers love dialogue so much that before they decide to buy a book, many readers flip through the pages to see how much dialogue is in the story. They can tell at a glance: The white space, indents, and quotation marks that characterize pages blessed by dialogue mean they're in for an engaging read, as opposed to long paragraphs of prose with no dialogue, which promise a denser reading experience.

The best dialogue enlivens a scene, brightens the page, and provides much opportunity to reveal character and propel the plot forward. As Chuck Wendig says, dialogue is the "Swiss Army knife of storytelling." What's not to like? The trick is to write good dialogue. Doing so will impress agents, editors, and readers, but writing bad dialogue will immediately expose you as an inexperienced writer who has not yet mastered the craft. Here are the dos and don'ts of writing dialogue.

Do Listen to How People Talk

As a writer, your role as eavesdropper cannot be overrated. You need to get a sense of the rhythm and syntax of your characters' speech and then enhance it. Your characters need to talk like real people, only better.

Think of David Mamet, whose characters talk like real people, only sharper, snarkier, and edgier. In his play *Glengarry Glen Ross*, Ricky Roma lambastes poor Williamson in a speech marked by venom and obscenity, the least of which follows.

> *You*, Williamson … I'm talking to *you*, shithead … You just cost me *six thousand dollars*. Six thousand dollars. And one Cadillac. That's right. What are you going to do about it?

Aaron Sorkin is another writer whose characters always talk like real people, only smarter, faster, and more articulate. Just look at a magnificent blip from the wicked-genius diatribe delivered by Jeff Daniels as news anchor Will McAvoy in Sorkin's *The Newsroom*, where Daniels goes off on a co-ed about how the United States is failing its citizens across the board and is thus no longer the greatest country on Earth.

> … none of this is the fault of a twenty-year-old college student, but you, nonetheless, are without a doubt, a member of the *worst*-period-*generation*-period-*ever*-period, so when you ask what makes us the greatest country in the world, I don't know what the fuck you're talking about! Yosemite?!

NOTE: This is a classic modern-day soliloquy; for the full speech, see https://www.youtube.com/watch?v=1zqOYBabXmA.

Judy Blume's characters talk like real people, only with more honesty, vulnerability, and poignancy, as in this snippet of a scene from her ever-popular novel *Are You There God? It's Me, Margaret.*

Nancy spoke to me as if she were my mother. "Margaret dear—you can't possibly miss Laura Danker. The big blonde with the big *you know whats!*"

"Oh, I noticed her right off," I said. "She's very pretty."

"Pretty!" Nancy snorted. "You be smart and stay away from her. She's got a bad reputation."

"What do you mean?" I asked.

"My brother said she goes behind the A&P with him and Moose."

"And," Janie added, "she's been wearing a bra since fourth grade and I'll bet she gets her period."

Don't Weigh Down Your Dialogue with Information Dumps

Many writers make the mistake of using dialogue to convey information and backstory.

> "Gee, Mary," said Harold. "I forgot that you are the incarnation of the Goddess Athena and that you only have six days to find the Owl of Knowledge before the world comes to a devastating end. What can I do to help?"
>
> "That's okay, Harold." Mary held up her palm in a blessing. "I can initiate you now into the Order of the Owl, and then you can guide me through the Enchanted Forest and over the Mountain of Wonder, but we will have to watch out for the goblins and elves and giant spiders and bobcats as my spells are useless in the fourth dimension, and you as a human are so vulnerable that you could die of thirst, hunger, venomous bites, or exposure."

Obviously, I just made this up, and it's truly terrible, but you get the gist. And honestly, a lot of the dialogue I see in opening pages is not much better—and just as burdened with backstory and info dumping.

Dialogue must do one of two things (or do both): (1) reveal character and/or (2) propel the plot forward. The best dialogue does both and is not simply a way to "disguise" info dumping and backstory plants. You're not fooling anyone when you burden your dialogue with backstory and info dumps, but you're certainly sabotaging your ability to keep your readers engaged.

BREAKING THE DIALOGUE RULES

Bestselling author Wally Lamb opens his novel *We Are Water* with dialogue that does reveal a lot of information and backstory, but he does it skillfully, with content rich in the story's themes of violence, race, and art.

> August 2009
> "I understand there was some controversy about the coroner's ruling concerning Josephus Jones's death. What do you think, Mr. Agnello? Did he die accidentally or was he murdered?"
>
> "Murdered? I can't really say for sure, Miss Arnofsky, but I have my suspicions. The black community was convinced that's what it was. Two Negro brothers living down at that cottage with a white woman? That would have been intolerable for some people back then."
>
> "White people, you mean."
>
> "Yes, that's right. When I got the job as director of the Statler Museum and moved my family to Three Rivers, I remember being surprised by the rumors that a chapter of the Ku Klux Klan was active here. And it's always seemed unlikely to me that Joe Jones would have tripped and fallen headfirst into a narrow well that he would have been very much aware of. A well that he would have drawn water from, after all. But if a crime had been committed, it was never investigated as such. So who's to say? The only thing I was sure of was that Joe was a uniquely talented painter."

Do Use Dialogue to Reveal Character

On the very first page of Dashiell Hammett's classic noir novel *The Maltese Falcon*, the author opens with private detective Sam Spade's secretary entering his office.

> He said to Effie Perine: "Yes, sweetheart?"
>
> She was a lanky sunburned girl whose tan dress of thin woolen stuff clung to her with an effect of dampness. Her eyes were brown and playful in a shiny boyish face. She finished shutting the door behind her, leaned against it, and said: "There's a girl wants to see you. Her name's Wonderly."

The Writer's Guide to Beginnings

"A customer?"

"I guess so. You'll want to see her anyway: she's a knockout."

"Shoo her in, darling," said Spade. "Shoo her in."

In these few opening lines, we learn a lot about our hero, Sam Spade. We learn he's not drowning in work, that he enjoys women of all kinds, and that he has a congenial and loyal, if sardonic, employee in Effie, who knows him well and likes him anyway. We learn that he's a pragmatist with an eye for the ladies who is not above flirting (or worse) with his attractive customers. We also get that any knockout named Wonderly is probably trouble. But Spade's ready to shoo her in nonetheless.

We already have a good sense of our hero, and that's a lot to accomplish in only a few lines.

Do Use Dialogue to Propel the Plot Forward

Dialogue is a great way to move your story forward right from word one and keep the readers reading. No one was better at this than dialogue master Elmore Leonard, as you'll see in this clever and funny opening of his bestseller *Freaky Deaky*.

Chris Mankowski's last day on the job, two in the afternoon, two hours to go, he got a call to dispose of a bomb.

What happened, a guy by the name of Booker, a twenty-five-year-old super-dude twice-convicted felon, was in his Jacuzzi when the phone rang. He yelled for his bodyguard Juicy Mouth to take it. "Hey, Juicy?" His bodyguard, his driver and his houseman were around somewhere. "Will somebody get the phone?" The phone kept ringing. The phone must have rung fifteen times before Booker got out of the Jacuzzi, put on his green satin robe that matched the emerald pinned to his left earlobe and picked up the phone. Booker said, "Who's this?" A woman's voice said, "You sitting down?" The phone was on a table next to a green leather wingback chair. Booker loved green. He said, "Baby, is that you?" It sounded like his woman, Moselle. Her voice said, "Are you sitting down? You have to be sitting down for when I tell you something." Booker said, "Baby, you sound different. What's wrong?" He sat down in the green leather chair, frowning, working his butt around to get comfortable. The woman's voice said, "Are you sitting down?" Booker said, "I *am*. I have sat the fuck down. Now you gonna talk to me, what?" Moselle's voice said, "I'm suppose to tell you that when you get up, honey, what's left of your ass is gonna go clear through the ceiling."

This is dialogue propelling the plot forward in a big way. And note how Leonard breaks the "never open with a phone call" rule of beginnings with such panache.

Do Make Your Dialogue Do Double Duty

The best dialogue both reveals character and propels the plot forward. Certainly in the scene from *The Maltese Falcon*, we know that everything is about to change when Sam Spade agrees to see this new customer, Miss Wonderly. That's plot in action. And in the scene from *Freaky Deaky*, we not only see the action unfolding before us; we also get a real feel for Booker, his bodyguard Juicy, his girlfriend Moselle, and even the guy called out to dispose of the bomb, Chris Mankowski.

Here's another example of plot and character revealed in a short snippet of dialogue, this one from the opening scene of Anita Shreve's *The Pilot's Wife*.

> "Mrs. Lyons?" he asked.
>
> And then she knew.
>
> It was in the way he said her name, the fact that he knew her name at all. It was in his eyes, a wary flicker. The quick breath he took.
>
> She snapped away from him and bent over at the waist. She put her hand to her chest.
>
> He reached his hand through the doorway and touched her at the small of her back.
>
> The touch made her flinch. She tried to straighten up but couldn't.
>
> "When?" she asked.
>
> He took a step into her house and closed the door.
>
> "Earlier this morning," he said.
>
> "Where?"
>
> "About ten miles off the coast of Ireland."
>
> "In the water?"

"No. In the air."

"Oh …. " She brought a hand to her mouth.

"It almost certainly was an explosion," he said quickly.

"You're sure it was Jack?"

He glanced away and then back again.

"Yes."

Here we see a woman open her door to the stranger who's come to tell her that her husband is dead. We see how perceptive she is, how observant, how she knows before he can tell her that the worst has happened. And we know that the event that took her husband was no accident and that she'll want to know the truth, no matter where it takes her. This is dialogue that works on many levels, revealing several aspects of the story, including plot, character, and foreshadowing of more terrible disclosures to come.

Do Capitalize on Subtext in Your Dialogue

Subtext is the true meaning of the words being spoken—what is left unsaid, in effect. We all know people for whom replying to the question "Are you alright?" with "I'm fine" rarely truly means "I'm fine." The subtext here is often more like "I'm angry," "I'm hurt," "I'm frightened," "I'm frustrated," or "I'm homicidal."

Similarly, we know people for whom a reply of "nothing" when asked, "What's wrong?" rarely means "nothing." The subtext here is often more like "I'm angry," "I'm hurt," "I'm frightened," "I'm frustrated," or "I'm homicidal."

Use subtext appropriately, and you can amp up the drama of your scene exponentially. In the old days of Hollywood, when censors would have forced any direct mention of sex to be edited out, writers perfected the art of subtext as innuendo. Lauren Bacall and Humphrey Bogart milked the subtext for all it was worth in this racy scene supposedly about racing in *The Big Sleep*.

> VIVIAN: Speaking of horses, I like to play them myself. But I like to see them work out a little first, see if they're front runners or come from behind, find out what their hole card is, what makes them run.

MARLOWE: Find out mine?

VIVIAN: I think so.

MARLOWE: Go ahead.

VIVIAN: I'd say you don't like to be rated. You like to get out in front, open up a little lead, take a little breather in the backstretch, and then come home free.

MARLOWE: You don't like to be rated yourself.

VIVIAN: I haven't met anyone yet that can do it. Any suggestions?

MARLOWE: Well, I can't tell till I've seen you over a distance of ground. You've got a touch of class, but I don't know how, how far you can go.

VIVIAN: A lot depends on who's in the saddle.

One of the most splendid examples of subtext in literature comes in F. Scott Fitzgerald's *The Great Gatsby* in the famous scene where Gatsby shows Daisy his shirts.

> "I've got a man in England who buys me clothes. He sends over a selection of things at the beginning of each season, spring and fall."
>
> He took out a pile of shirts and began throwing them, one by one, before us, shirts of sheer linen and thick silk and fine flannel, which lost their folds as they fell and covered the table in many-colored disarray. While we admired he brought more and the soft rich heap mounted higher—shirts with stripes and scrolls and plaids in coral and apple-green and lavender and faint orange, and monograms of Indian blue. Suddenly, with a strained sound, Daisy bent her head into the shirts and began to cry stormily.
>
> "They're such beautiful shirts," she sobbed, her voice muffled in the thick folds. "It makes me sad because I've never seen such—such beautiful shirts before."

Of course Daisy doesn't care about shirts; no rich girl ever cried over a shirt. She rejected the dynamic but poor Gatsby years before, and now he's drowning in the money that's paid for all those fine shirts. But Daisy is already married to the dull but rich Tom Buchanan.

Subtext is fun to read and very true to life. Readers love subtext because we spend our lives trying to figure out what people are really trying to say—or not say. So use subtext when you can; your readers will love you for it.

Don't Write in Dialect

Don't write in dialect, and don't spell dialogue phonetically. *Ever.* For the most part, it's considered outdated even in the right hands and potentially racist/sexist/xenophobic in the wrong hands. Never mind that it drives editors crazy because (1) it slows down readers, often taking them right out of the story, and (2) it's a pain in the butt to fix; they know they're the ones who'll have to fix it. So you'll lose the sale of your book right there.

I know you sometimes see this rule broken—see "Dialects: Don't Try This at Home" later in this chapter—but if you're a debut author, you break it at your peril. You'll invite criticism, rejection, and maybe worse if you do, and even should you succeed, it will most likely be in spite of the dialect, rather than because of it.

Do Use Word Choice and Sentence Structure to Indicate Speech Patterns

This is the preferred method of revealing ethnicity and place of origin today. Writers sometimes insist that they can't infuse the flavor of their characters' speech patterns into their dialogue without resorting to dialect, but they're wrong. And their stubbornness is often what can derail them on the road to publication.

There are writers who have made it work, but they are truly masters of the craft. Let's look at a few openings by writers known for tackling dialect, for better or worse.

You better not never tell nobody but God. It'd kill your mammy.

DEAR GOD,

I am fourteen years old. I am I have always been a good girl. Maybe you can give me a sign letting me know what is happening to me. Last spring after little Lucious come I heard them fussing. He was pulling on her arm. She say It too soon, Fonso, I ain't well. Finally he leave her alone. A week go by, he pulling on her arm again. She say Naw, I ain't gonna. Can't you see I'm already half dead, an all of these chilren.

—*The Color Purple*, by Alice Walker

"Jeeves," I said that evening. "I'm getting a check suit like that one of Mr. Byng's."

"Injudicious, sir," he said firmly. "It will not become you."

"What absolute rot! It's the soundest thing I've struck for years."

"Unsuitable for you, sir."

Well, the long and the short of it was that the confounded thing came home, and I put it on, and when I caught sight of myself in the glass I nearly swooned. Jeeves was perfectly right.

—*My Man Jeeves*, by P.G. Wodehouse

August 1962

Mae Mobley was born on a early Sunday morning in August, 1960. A church baby we like to call it. Taking care a white babies, that's what I do, along with all the cooking and the cleaning. I done raised seventeen kids in my lifetime. I know how to get them babies to sleep, stop crying, and go in the toilet bowl before they mamas even get out a bed in the morning.

—*The Help*, by Kathryn Stockett

"Oh, Miss Inez," Mrs. Reilly called in that accent that occurs south of New Jersey only in New Orleans, that Hoboken near the Gulf of Mexico. "Over here, babe."

"Hey, how you making?" Miss Inez asked. "How you feeling, darling?"

"Not so hot," Mrs. Reilly answered truthfully.

"Ain't that a shame." Miss Inez leaned over the glass case and forgot about her cakes. "I don't feel so hot myself. It's my feet."

"Lord, I wisht I was that lucky. I got arthuritis in my elbow."

The Writer's Guide to Beginnings

"Aw, no!" Miss Inez said with genuine sympathy. "My poor old poppa's got that. We make him go set himself in a hot tub fulla berling water."

"My boy's floating around in our tub all day long. I can't hardly get in my own bathroom no more."

"I thought he was married, precious."

"Ignatius? Eh, la la," Mrs. Reilly said sadly. "Sweetheart, you wanna gimme two dozen of them fancy mix?"

—*A Confederacy of Dunces*, by John Kennedy Toole

In these examples, the writers make good use of colloquialisms, speech patterns, and syntax to indicate dialect without overdoing it. But these are writers working at the top of their craft—and even then, they make risky choices. Toole was not published in his lifetime, and Kathryn Stockett was described as "a Southern-born white author who renders black maids' voices in thick, dated dialect" by no less than the *New York Times*.

So again, when it comes to dialect, remember: *Less is more.*

DIALECTS: DON'T TRY THIS AT HOME

Even in 1884, when Mark Twain first published *The Adventures of Huckleberry Finn*, he worried that readers might not appreciate or understand why he used so many different dialects in the story, including these of Huck, Jim, and Tom, respectively.

> You don't know about me without you have read a book by the name of *The Adventures of Tom Sawyer*; but that ain't no matter.

> Say, who is you? Whar is you? Dog my cats ef I didn' hear sumf'n. Well, I know what I's gwyne to do: I's gwyne to set down here and listen tell I hears it ag'in.

> Why, blame it all, we've got to do it. Don't I tell you it's in the books? Do you want to go to doing different from what's in the books, and get things all muddled up?

So the great writer prepared people for the dialects by including a note to readers in the book, before the story's opening.

The shadings have not been done in a haphazard fashion, or by guesswork; but painstakingly, and with the trustworthy guidance and support of personal familiarity with these several forms of speech.

I make this explanation for the reason that without it many readers would suppose that all these characters were trying to talk alike and not succeeding.

That was back in the nineteenth century, and still Twain figured he might be on shaky ground. So here in the twenty-first century, well, just don't try this at home.

....

Do Use Dialogue Tags Wisely

Nothing says amateur in dialogue faster than "creative" dialogue tags. Don't use dialogue tags like *queried*, *proclaimed*, *pondered*, *replied*, *grinned*, *screeched*, *expounded*, etc. Stick to *said*, or use action instead.

"Don't move," she exclaimed. (bad)

"Don't move," she said. (better)

"Don't move." She pointed a pearl-handled pistol straight at me. (best)

DITCH DIALOGUE TAGS ALTOGETHER

Craig Johnson never uses dialogue tags, preferring to only use action statements when he needs to identify the speaker. This takes enormous discipline, but it's effective, as this exchange in the opening pages of his Walt Longmire novel *Dry Bones* shows.

"Hey, Omar."
He started, just visibly, and spoke to us over his shoulder as he continued throwing pebbles into the water. "Walt. Vic."
"What are you doing?"
He glanced at us but then tossed another stone. "Trying to keep those snapping turtles off that body out there."
We tiptoed to the edge of the bank in an attempt to keep the water from seeping into our boots, and Vic and I joined Omar in his target practice, Vic showing her acumen by bouncing a flat

stone off the shell of small turtle that skittered and swam into the depths. "Any idea who it is?"

Omar leaned forward and lifted his Oakley Radarlock yellow-tinted shooting glasses to peer into the reflective surface of the water at the half-submerged body. "I'm thinking it's Danny."

Even in this short exchange, you can see how using action statements keeps Craig Johnson focused on the bigger picture while he's writing a scene—that is, how it looks, what's happening, where it's happening, and not just on what's being said.

We're not all Craig Johnsons. Writing an entire novel, much less a series of novels, without ever using dialogue tags requires vigilance and discipline. And it certainly forces you to weave other elements such as action, setting, character, and inner monologue into your conversations.

You don't have to go that far. But reminding yourself to mix up dialogue tags with action statements is good practice. Too many writers tend to fall into stripped-down exchanges that read more like scripts than novels when they write dialogue. They miss the opportunity to weave in those other fictive elements and fail to write fully realized scenes as a result.

JUMP-START

Take a look at the dialogue in your opening. How do you identify who's speaking? If you use any dialogue tags other than "said," swap those out for "said." Read it again, and compare it to your original. Now swap out all of your "said" dialogue tags for action statements. Compare that with your second draft. How did using "said" dialogue tags and action statements change the scene?

Do Not Break the Fourth Wall

Addressing the reader directly is called breaking the fourth wall. We see this in films, most famously in *Ferris Bueller's Day Off*, when Ferris Bueller talks to the audience, and in nineteenth-century novels, as when Jane addresses the reader in *Jane Eyre*.

Gentle reader, may you never feel what I then felt! May your eyes never shed such stormy, scalding, heart-wrung tears as poured from mine. May you never appeal to Heaven in prayers so hopeless and so agonized as in that hour left my lips: for never may you, like me, dread to be the instrument of evil to what you wholly love.

Matthew Broderick's beloved Bueller and Charlotte Bronte's Jane aside, this is a very risky business. When you break the fourth wall, you jolt the readers out of their fictive dream—sometimes never to return. Worse, you taunt the reader, promising good things to come, telling them they're not ready to hear this or that or to pay attention. Whenever you do this, you risk the reader saying, "I don't think so," and just closing the book. Readers don't like to be told what to do; they are waiting to be entertained by the story, not told when and how to think about that story.

That's not to mention that editors hate this, often dismissing it as an indulgence on the part of the author, and that alone will ruin it for some. So comb through your prose, and get rid of the sections where you break the fourth wall, wherever it appears. You may be reluctant to do that because it would mean losing what you may think (wrongly) are your best lines.

But do it; let the action stand on its own.

"Our eyes flow over dialogue like butter on the hood of a hot car. This is true when reading fiction. This is true when reading scripts. What does this tell you? It tells you to use a lot of dialogue." —*Chuck Wendig*

THEME

"For me, not knowing your theme until you're finished is like using a scalpel to turn a kangaroo into Miss Universe—there will be a lot of deep cuts, and there's a high chance it won't work." —*David G. Allen*

The Writer's Guide to Beginnings

Theme is what your story is really about, grounded in the emotions that drive us: the search for love, the desire for revenge, the lust for power, the need to belong, the impulse toward violence, and the instinct to nurture. The sooner your reader knows what your story is really about, the sooner they can relax into your narrative. Readers want stories that are about something, stories that enlighten as well as entertain.

Theme is where the enlightenment part comes in. Good writers know this, and they know what their stories are really about, and they tell the reader straight off in the opening lines.

> Happy families are all alike; every unhappy family is unhappy in its own way.
>
> —*Anna Karenina*, by Leo Tolstoy

> It was the best of times, it was the worst of times, it was the age of wisdom, it was the age of foolishness, it was the epoch of belief, it was the epoch of incredulity, it was the season of Light, it was the season of Darkness, it was the spring of hope, it was the winter of despair, we had everything before us, we had nothing before us, we were all going direct to Heaven, we were all going direct the other way—in short, the period was so far like the present period, that some of its noisiest authorities insisted on its being received, for good or for evil, in the superlative degree of comparison only.
>
> —*A Tale of Two Cities*, by Charles Dickens

> Be careful what you wish for.
>
> —*The Ice Queen*, by Alice Hoffman

> It is a truth universally acknowledged, that a single man in possession of a good fortune must be in want of a wife.
>
> —*Pride and Prejudice*, by Jane Austen

> Life changes fast. Life changes in the instant. You sit down to dinner and life as you know it ends.
>
> —*The Year of Magical Thinking*, by Joan Didion

When we read these beginnings, we are compelled to read on because we recognize the truths in their themes. We sense the scope of the stories to come—and we want to experience the journey for ourselves.

As we see in these opening lines, the themes are right there, setting readers up and preparing them for the explorations of family, revolution, wish-making, courtship, and the very nature of life itself.

Opening with theme requires knowing what your themes are. What are the themes—light and dark—that drive your stories? Here's a list of light and dark aspects of various themes that might apply to your work:

THEME	LIGHT	DARK
Love	Compassion	Hate
Power	Leadership	Tyranny
Desire	Lust	Obsession
Sex	Intimacy	Adultery
Loyalty	Fidelity	Betrayal
Truth	Honesty	Lies
Sensation	Pleasure	Pain
Trust	Confidence	Doubt
Admiration	Praise	Envy
Crime	Justice	Revenge
Family	Unity	Dysfunction
Courage	Bravery	Cowardice
Resiliency	Flexibility	Rigidity
Sacrifice	Offering	Self-Immolation
Generosity	Charity	Greed
Friendship	Solidarity	Rivalry
Self-Actualization	Growth	Stagnation
Coming of Age	Maturation	Immaturity
Faith	Belief	Skepticism
Survival	Life	Death
Peace	Détente	War
Good	Indifference	Evil
Money	Wealth	Poverty
Forgiveness	Redemption	Punishment
Nature	Wild	Unnatural
Technology	Science	Inhumanity

Make your own list of light and dark aspects of your themes. Ask yourself how those aspects drive the story you are telling and how you can weave those themes into your opening.

Look to Your Protagonist

If you're still not sure what your themes are, look to your hero. His desires, feelings, motivations, and actions are all related to the themes of your story. Consider how you can reveal your theme in your opening through your protagonist as the following writers have done in their opening lines.

> I was born twice: first, as a baby girl, on a remarkably smogless Detroit day in January of 1960; and then again, as a teenage boy, in an emergency room near Petoskey, Michigan, in August of 1974.
>
> —*Middlesex*, by Jeffrey Eugenides

Here the narrator makes it clear that gender identity will be one of the main themes in this sprawling novel, which also explores nature vs. nurture, the American dream, and more. Readers are captivated by this direct and dramatic opening line and read on for the details of this transformation.

> Lolita, light of my life, fire of my loins.
>
> —*Lolita*, by Vladimir Nabokov

This classic opening lament of obsession prepares the reader for the story to come, a disturbing story about a man whose illicit love for a teenage girl remains controversial to this day.

> In the time it takes for her to walk from the bathhouse at the seawall of Fortune's Rocks, where she has left her boots and has discreetly pulled off her stockings, to the waterline along which the sea continually licks the pink and silver sand, she learns about desire.
>
> —*Fortune's Rocks*, by Anita Shreve

This very sensual beginning gives credence to the assertion that "she learns about desire," and we read on to find out what the consequences of that desire will be—and we know there will be consequences.

> I told you last night that I might be gone sometime, and you said,
> Where, and I said, To be with the Good Lord, and you said, Why, and
> I said, Because I'm old, and you said, I don't think you're old.
>
> —*Gilead*, by Marilynne Robinson

In the opening line of Robinson's Pulitzer-Prize-winning tour-de-force, we meet elderly Congregationalist minister John Ames as he attempts to write the story of his life and family history in the town of Gilead for the benefit of his seven-year-old son. We see from this beginning that this will be a story about faith, life, and death and all the temptations in between, and we read on.

As with these stories, the key to determining your themes is your protagonist: What does he want? How does she feel about it? What is he willing to do to get it? What does she need to learn to deserve it? Answer these questions and explore your themes, and then weave them into your opening lines. Showing your readers what your story is really about will help you engage your readers and keep them reading.

THE BEGINNINGS RULEBOOK REVISITED

As we've seen, the rules that govern good story openings are not made to be broken unless you know what you're doing and you're sure the benefits outweigh the risks. The good news is that you should have a much better understanding of these rules and how to apply them to the beginning of your story so you can impress agents, editors, and readers with your storytelling. And when you do dare to break the rules, you'll know the risks and write accordingly.

We've examined the main elements of fiction—the tools you use to craft your story—through the looking glass of the opening line, the opening page, the opening scene. But where do you go from there? In chapter seven, we'll explore the rest of Act One—from premise to plot point—and its place within the story structure as a whole. We'll also discuss the structural implications of genre, how the conventions of a given genre can affect the structure of your story.

"The writer who develops a beautiful style but has nothing to say, represents a kind of arrested aesthetic development; he is like a pianist who acquires a brilliant technique by playing finger exercises but never gives a concert." —*Ayn Rand*

CHAPTER SEVEN

THE STRUCTURE OF REVELATION

The End of the Beginning

"All writing is that structure of revelation.
There's something you want to find out.
If you know everything up front in the beginning,
you really don't need to read further
if there's nothing else to find out."
—*Walter Mosley*

───────── ◯ ─────────

"Now this is not the end. It is not even the beginning of the end. But it is, perhaps, the end of the beginning."
—*Winston Churchill*

Right before I started writing this section of the book, I spent some time with the extraordinary writer Robert Olen Butler. I met the Pulitzer-Prize-winning author at the St. Augustine Author-Mentor Novel Workshop, which is run by our mutual pal and writer Michael Neff. St. Augustine is a lovely beach town with great restaurants; over the course of a wonderful dinner—several hours of fine wine and delicious seafood at Catch 27—we talked about books, writing, and the art of teaching writers to write.

Butler had spent the day meeting with writers and critiquing the first five hundred words of their novels, short stories, and memoirs. I'd been helping these writers prepare for their meetings with Butler, and many had expressed dismay that Butler was only considering the first five hundred words of their stories.

"That's not enough for him to know what my story is about," they each told me, more or less in the same words each time.

"Not true," I told them. "Five-hundred words fill two double-spaced manuscript pages, and that's more than many editors, agents, and readers give you before passing or proceeding."

They were unhappy to hear that. I told Butler, and he smiled. I smiled back. Because we both knew that if the first five hundred words aren't right, then the next five hundred words won't be either, nor will the five hundred words after that, and so on, for fifty- or seventy- or ninety-thousand words. The best stories are integrated units, from beginning to end. Achieving this integration is critical if your story is to hold together over some three-hundred pages.

For Butler, that integration requires knowing what your character wants and having that yearning—*yearning* is Butler's favorite word—infuse the very DNA of your story. We drank more wine, and Butler expounded on his "unified field theory of yearning," which is, plainly put, the idea that this integration is bound to the protagonist's yearning. (**NOTE**: For more on his unified field theory of yearning, read Butler's *From Where You Dream: The Process of Writing Fiction*, a must-have for all fiction writers.)

That's why, to make sure you have a good beginning, you need to make sure that you have a good middle and a good end as well. This doesn't mean that you need to know every detail of the work from page one to "The End," but it does mean that you need a sense of where the story is going, what you are trying to say, and how you are going to say it.

And what your hero is yearning for.

"Yearning seems to be at the heart of what fiction as an art form is all about.... This notion of yearning has its reflection in one of the most fundamental craft points in fiction: plot. Because plot is simply yearning challenged and thwarted."
—*Robert Olen Butler*

STORY STRUCTURE 101

In chapter two, we examined the three-act structure in terms of a story's beginning (act one), middle (act two), and end (act three). We also looked at the structure of your first scene. Now let's look at the structure of your story in terms of plot points, not simply as events, but as, to paraphrase Butler, the challenges and thwarters of your character's desires. This will allow you to break down Act One along with the rest of your story so that you can make sure that you build your story from your strong opening with equal strength and mastery to Plot Point One and right on to "The End."

Refining the Three-Act Structure

Let's start by refining our understanding of the three-act structure. Don't just think of the three-act structure as the beginning, middle, and end; think of the three-act structure as the setup (act one), main action (act two), and resolution (act three). Let's see how this looks for three classically structured stories that we all know and love.

Star Wars

SETUP/ACT ONE: Luke finds Princess Leia's message in the droid but refuses to help until his aunt and uncle are killed by Stormtroopers.

MAIN ACTION/ACT TWO: Luke and his pals rescue Princess Leia and plan the attack on the Death Star.

RESOLUTION/ACT THREE: Luke learns to trust the Force and destroys the Death Star.

What Luke wants (consciously): to become a Jedi Knight

What Luke wants (subconsciously): to find meaning in his life, to belong

Pride and Prejudice

SETUP/ACT ONE: Elizabeth Bennet meets the very rich, very eligible, and very proud Mr. Darcy—and hates him.

MAIN ACTION/ACT TWO: Mr. Darcy falls for Elizabeth despite her family and rank, but she rejects his badly delivered proposal in no uncertain terms.

RESOLUTION/ACT THREE: Mr. Darcy redeems himself by saving the Bennet sisters' reputation; Elizabeth realizes she has judged him too harshly, and they live happily ever after.

What Elizabeth wants (consciously): to marry a man of means whom she can respect and love

What Elizabeth wants (subconsciously): to merge with another without losing herself

The Maltese Falcon

SETUP/ACT ONE: Private detective Sam Spade's partner Miles Archer is murdered while working on their new case for the mysterious Miss Wonderly.

MAIN ACTION/ACT TWO: Sam investigates the case, chases the Maltese Falcon, and falls for Wonderly a.k.a. Brigid O'Shaughnessy.

RESOLUTION/ACT THREE: Sam Spade solves the case, confronts the murderer, and brings Brigid to justice.

What Sam Spade wants (consciously): to find Miles's murderer

What Sam Spade wants (subconsciously): to be a man of honor

In chapter two, you broke down your first scene into its beginning, middle, and end. Now it's time to break down your entire work into its beginning, middle, and end. Start by thinking in terms of setup, main action, and resolution, as shown in the aforementioned examples.

If you're having trouble, consider these broad genre templates, which you can customize for your own story:

Love Story/Romance

SETUP/BEGINNING: Boy meets girl.

MAIN ACTION/MIDDLE: Boy loses girl.

RESOLUTION/END: Boy gets girl back.

Protagonist's Conscious Desire: To meet Mr./Ms. Right

Protagonist's Subconscious Desire: To merge with his/her soulmate

Crime: Mystery/Thriller/Police Procedural

SETUP/BEGINNING: Someone gets murdered.

MAIN ACTION/MIDDLE: The cops/detective/amateur sleuth investigates the murder.

RESOLUTION/END: The murderer is brought to justice.

Protagonist's Conscious Desire: To solve the crime

Protagonist's Subconscious Desire: To be an instrument of justice

Hero's Journey: YA/Coming of Age/Self-Actualization

SETUP/BEGINNING: The hero/heroine longs for adventure, and new acquaintances and events conspire to make that happen.

MAIN ACTION/MIDDLE: With the help of the new friends and mentor, the hero/heroine undergoes a series of transformative experiences.

RESOLUTION/END: Armed with this newfound knowledge and experience, the hero/heroine triumphs against overwhelming odds and is changed for the better.

Protagonist's Conscious Desire: To be a grown-up

Protagonist's Subconscious Desire: To live a meaningful life

Mission Story: SF/Fantasy/War Story/Military Thriller

SETUP/BEGINNING: Our hero(es) is confronted with the challenge of the mission.

MAIN ACTION/MIDDLE: Our hero(es) plans out, trains for, and undertakes the mission.

RESOLUTION/END: Our hero(es) must go above and beyond to overcome the enemy, and the mission is won.

Protagonist's Conscious Desire: To complete the mission

Protagonist's Subconscious Desire: To champion a worthy cause

These templates can help you determine the setup, main action, and resolution of your own story, as well as the conscious and subconscious desires of your protagonist. Play around with these templates; adapt and combine them as you will. The important thing is to identify the yearnings of your hero and the broad strokes of the plot and work from there.

When you deconstruct a story this way, it's easy to see why the beginning is so important. Not only must the beginning grab your readers by the throat and keep them reading, the beginning also needs to reveal your heroine's desires and set up the rest of the story.

If the beginning doesn't work, the rest of the story doesn't work either. Act One blasts the story into the head space—and heart space—

of the reader. Your opening scenes are the rocket boosters that thrust your story shuttle up and away.

THE POINT OF PLOT POINTS

The term *plot point* is one you've probably heard before. It's just a fancy way of referring to the big scenes of your story, the ones that form the framework for the work itself. You frame your story with these scenes, just as you frame a house before you add the walls and the roof.

Without this framework, your story will not stand up but instead will fall in on itself, unable to support the weight of the characters and conflict with which you have burdened it. See the following chart for a graphic representation of this three-act structure, complete with plot points.

To fashion the most effective framework for your story, you simply need to build on the setup, main action, and resolution you've already designed.

Let's look at those same three classic stories we examined before; only this time we'll build their three-act structures to include the plot points.

Act One: Setup

BEGINNING: This is how the story opens, generally just before the Inciting Incident. (Or, in many stories, it can be the Inciting Incident itself.) In *Star Wars*, Princess Leia is running from the Stormtroopers. In *Pride and Prejudice*, news of the rich bachelor Mr. Bingley coming to town reaches Mrs. Bennet, and she redoubles her efforts to marry off her daughters well, starting with Jane and Elizabeth. *The Maltese Falcon* opens with Miss Wonderly arriving at Sam Spade's office and hiring him to find her little sister.

INCITING INCIDENT: This is the scene that jumpstarts the action of your story. For *Star Wars*, the Inciting Incident is when Princess Leia is captured and places the message and the plans in R2-D2. In *Pride and Prejudice*, Elizabeth meets Mr. Darcy at a local ball, where he declines to dance with her, saying she is not handsome enough to tempt

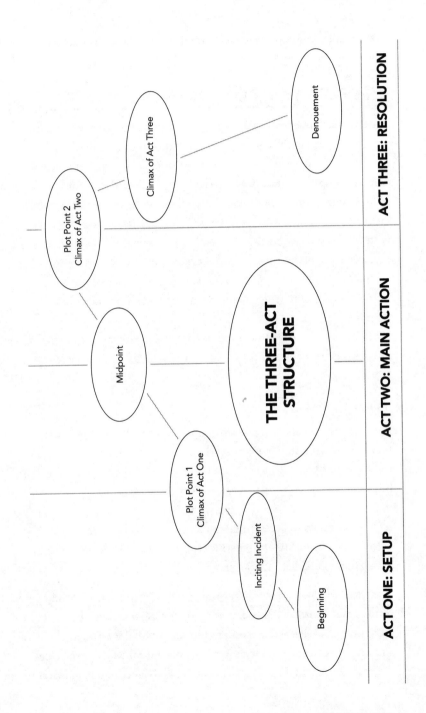

THE THREE-ACT
STRUCTURE

ACT ONE: SETUP

Beginning

Inciting Incident

Plot Point 1
Climax of Act One

ACT TWO: MAIN ACTION

Midpoint

Plot Point 2
Climax of Act Two

ACT THREE: RESOLUTION

Climax of Act Three

Denouement

The Writer's Guide to Beginnings

him. In *The Maltese Falcon*, Sam Spade's partner Miles Archer is murdered while on Miss Wonderly's case, and Sam is honor-bound to find his killer.

PLOT POINT #1: The first Plot Point is the big scene that takes the story in a new direction, setting up the action to come in Act Two. In *Star Wars*, Plot Point #1 is the murder of Luke's aunt and uncle, which changes everything for him and convinces him to join Obi-Wan and become a Jedi Knight. In *Pride and Prejudice*, Plot Point #1 happens when Darcy persuades Bingley to abandon his courting of Elizabeth's sister Jane and the Bingleys and Darcy leave Netherfield, taking the Bennet girls' best prospects with them. In *The Maltese Falcon*, Plot Point #1 certainly takes the story in an entirely new direction, as it introduces the titular Maltese falcon and Joel Cairo offers Sam Spade five thousand dollars to find it. **NOTE:** Five grand was some serious money back in 1929. The search for this "MacGuffin of all MacGuffins" drives much of the action for the rest of the story.

MAKE A MACGUFFIN

MacGuffins are the objects, goals, events, or even characters in a story that help propel the plot, pitting characters in a struggle to capture it, control it, conceal it, or destroy it. Think of Bilbo's ring in *Lord of the Rings*, the broomstick in *The Wonderful Wizard of Oz*, or even Helen of Troy, "the face that launched a thousand ships" in *The Iliad*.

Do you have a MacGuffin in your story? If not, brainstorm ideas for MacGuffins. List the ways in which each possible MacGuffin might help you drive the action of your plot.

Act Two: Main Action

MIDPOINT: This is the big scene that you plant right in the middle of the story, building from Plot Point #1 to a significant reversal or twist. The Midpoint is a dangerous place in a story, as it's the place where readers are most likely to quit on you and go watch HBO. That's why you need something big to happen here, to keep readers engrossed in the plot and to avoid what the Hollywood people fear most—that telltale swishing in the seats that announce how bored the audience is at that most critical time in the viewing of a film. So make sure that you give your audience a scene to stay put for. In *Star Wars*, the Midpoint comes as Luke, Han et al attempt to rescue Princess Leia and get caught in the trash compactor from hell, the one with the terrible beastie lurking inside. In *Pride and Prejudice*, the Midpoint comes when Darcy proposes to Elizabeth in the least romantic way possible and in turn she rejects him in the most devastating terms. At the Midpoint in *The Maltese Falcon*, Spade passes out after being drugged and kicked in the head and comes to, determined to find out the real story behind the falcon.

PLOT POINT #2: This is the second big event in the story that takes it in a different direction, just as Plot Point #1 does. In *Star Wars*, Plot Point #2 happens when Obi-Wan takes on Darth Vader in a fight to the death, allowing Luke et al to escape unharmed. This has huge ramifications for everyone but especially our hero Luke, who loses his mentor just when he needs him the most. In *Pride and Prejudice*, Plot Point #2 has Lydia running off with the wicked Wickham, thereby threatening the all-important reputation of the Bennet girls, Elizabeth included, which could forever ruin their chances of making good marriages. In *The Maltese Falcon*, Plot Point #2 occurs when a bleeding man bursts into Spade's office carrying a wrapped parcel containing the fabled Maltese falcon and promptly dies.

Act Three: Resolution

CLIMAX: The Climax is the biggest event in the story, the one that resolves the main action of the story. In *Star Wars*, the Climax forces Luke to trust the Force and apply the wisdom and skill he learned from his beloved mentor Obi-Wan in order to destroy the Death Star. In *Pride and Prejudice*, the Climax comes when Elizabeth finds out that Mr. Darcy has saved the good Bennet name by arranging for Lydia and

Wickham to be married, realizes she has misjudged him, and happily accepts his (second) proposal. In *The Maltese Falcon*, the Climax comes when Sam Spade confronts Brigid O'Shaughnessy, confesses his love for her, and turns her in to the police anyway.

DENOUEMENT: This is the wrap-up that ties up all the loose ends of the story and sets the scene for the sequel, should there be one in the works. In *Star Wars*, Luke comes home to a hero's welcome, but we know that however sweet this victory, there will be more challenges ahead. The empire will strike back. In *Pride and Prejudice*, the Denouement describes the marriage of Elizabeth and Mr. Darcy, as well as that of Jane and Mr. Bingley and the ramifications of those happy unions throughout their circle of friends and family. In *The Maltese Falcon*, the Denouement sees Sam Spade back at the office, and when Iva shows up, he tells Effie to show his dead partner's wife in to see him.

In *Star Wars*, Luke gets what he wants on both the conscious and subconscious levels: He destroys the Death Star, becomes a Jedi Knight, embraces the light side of the Force, and takes his place among the community of revolutionaries. In *Pride and Prejudice*, Elizabeth Bennet gets what she wants on both the conscious and subconscious levels as well: She makes a successful marriage by anyone's standards, including her mother's, and even better, marries a man she truly loves and respects. She looks forward to a marriage of equals—at least as much as can be expected in the nineteenth century. In *The Maltese Falcon*, Sam Spade does get what he wants: He finds his partner's killer and stays true to the code of honor that decrees that "when a man's partner is killed, he's supposed to do something about it." In the process, he loses the woman he loves.

When you're planning the plot points of your story, keep the desires of your protagonist in mind. In the end, does your hero get what he wants? And does getting what he consciously wants also give him what he wants subconsciously or not?

These are the questions that you and your plot need to answer.

JUMP-START

Break down your story into its main plot points:

- Beginning
- Inciting Incident
- Plot Point #1
- Midpoint
- Plot Point #2
- Climax
- Denouement

Create one storyline in which your heroine gets what she wants on both the conscious and the subconscious levels and another in which she does not.

Ask yourself:

- Which story is more appealing?
- Which is more dramatic?
- Which is more emotionally satisfying for you?
- Which is more emotionally satisfying for your readers?

"I guarantee you that no modern story scheme, even plotlessness, will give a reader genuine satisfaction unless one of those old-fashioned plots is smuggled in somewhere. I don't praise plots as accurate representations of life but as ways to keep readers reading." —*Kurt Vonnegut, Jr.*

ACT ONE, SCENE BY SCENE

The next step is to plot the first act of your story scene by scene, from the Beginning to Plot Point #1. That typically translates to between ten and fifteen scenes, but that can vary, depending on the length of the work and the nature of the story, as we'll see in the following chart, which lists the Act One scenes for *The Maltese Falcon*.

ACT ONE	
Beginning	Miss Wonderly hires Sam Spade and Miles Archer to find her baby sister.
Scene 2	Spade gets a phone call, and he hails a cab.
Inciting Incident	Spade finds the cops at the crime scene where Miles's body has been found.
Scene 4	Spade calls his secretary, Effie, and asks her to tell Miles's wife about his murder.
Scene 5	The cops drop by to interrogate Spade about Thursby, who has also been murdered.
Scene 6	Miles's widow Iva is waiting for Spade at his office. Iva kisses him; he sends her home.
Scene 7	Effie tells Spade that Iva had just gotten home when she went to tell her about Miles.
Scene 8	Spade goes to the St. Mark, but Wonderly has checked out.
Scene 9	At the office, Effie tells Spade that Wonderly said to meet her at the Coronet.
Scene 10	Wonderly, a.k.a. Brigid O'Shaughnessy, tells Spade she's scared and needs protection from the police.
Scene 11	Spade goes to visit Wise the attorney.
Plot Point #1	Joel Cairo offers Spade $5,000 to find the Maltese falcon.

Now that you have a clearer view of your story's three-act structure, you can drill down to the scene level and plot out your entire first act. In a 90,000-word novel or memoir, the first act is your first 90 pages, or 22,500 words. (In a 120-page screenplay, the first act is your first 30 pages.) **NOTE:** This is a flexible number; you should let your own story and the conventions of your genre have the last word.

You know your Beginning, Inciting Incident, and Plot Point #1. Now all you need to do is connect the dots with the scenes that fall in between these plot points. You can use the chart below for this purpose.

"A novel is a tricky thing to map." —*Reif Larsen*

ACT ONE	
Beginning	
Scene 2	
Scene 3	
Scene 4	
Inciting Incident	
Scene 6	
Scene 7	
Scene 8	
Scene 9	
Scene 10	
Scene 11	
Scene 12	
Scene 13	
Scene 14	
Scene 15	
Plot Point #1	

"There are only three kinds of scenes: negotiations, seductions, and fights." —*Mike Nichols*

THE 90,000-WORD SWEET SPOT

Right now, when it comes to word count, it's all about 90,000 words. Virtually every book I try to shop by a debut author that's any longer than that—regardless of category—receives the same response from editors: "It's just too long." "No more than 90,000 words" seems to be the editor's mantra these days. So I've asked several of my clients to shorten their novels and memoirs and am happy to say that we've won contracts when I shopped the shortened versions, often to the same editors who complained about the length of the original stories.

So when you plot your beginning, you need to plan with that 90,000-word sweet spot in mind. The following is a neat trick I came up with that's proved useful for my clients and that may work for you as well.

Here's how 90,000 words (which is 360 pages at 250 words per page) breaks down by act:

- Act One: 90 pages (22,500 words)
- Act Two: 180 pages (45,000 words)
- Act Three: 90 pages (22,500 words)

With that in mind, write out your basic storyline in major plot points only: *Beginning, Inciting Incident, Plot Point #1, Midpoint, Plot Point #2, Climax, Denouement*. Remember that these page counts and word counts are approximate and will vary according to the dictates of your story—but not too much. Too much variance might be a grand experiment, but odds are it's a grand experiment that fails.

If you've already written your first draft and you're over the 90,000-word sweet spot, then use the word counts by act as a general guideline, and cut anything you can cut to the word counts outlined above. Anything that does not get you from plot point to plot point *must go*.

If you haven't yet finished your first draft, these act-by-act word counts will serve as your guidelines as you pound out the first draft.

PLANTING SUBPLOTS IN ACT ONE

Now that you've identified the major plot points of your story, you have some idea what your subplots will be. In *Star Wars*, the subplots are mostly relationship-based: Han and Luke, Luke and Princess Leia, Han and Princess Leia, Luke and Darth Vader, Obi-Wan and Darth Vader, Luke and Obi-Wan, and R2-D2 and C-3PO. In *Pride and Prejudice*, many of the subplots revolve around the other romantic entanglements besides Elizabeth and Mr. Darcy: all those sisters, all those subplots! In *The Maltese Falcon*, the subplots center around Sam's relationships with women, namely Effie, Iva, and Brigid, his relationships with cops, lawyers, and the DA, and the relationships and rivalries among the various suspects, including Brigid, Gutman, Cairo, Wilmer, and Sam Spade himself.

For your subplots to prove effective, you need to introduce some (if not all of them) in Act One. This lends another layer of complexity to the challenge of writing a strong beginning to your story. We'll take a harder look at introducing subplots in our genre-by-genre examination, as they vary according to category. But in the meantime, you should take note of the subplots that might help elevate your story to the next level. Start with your secondary characters since they often provide fertile ground for subplots. Here's a list of the basic subplot types for you to consider for your story, as they relate to your protagonist:

- love interest(s)
- exes
- relationship with BFF
- relationship with family
- relationship with boss
- relationship with colleagues
- relationship with antagonist(s)

As you build your scenes in Act One, remember to weave in your subplot threads and introduce the characters who will people your subplots—from family and friends to suspects and strangers.

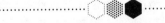

PIVOT YOUR PLOT POINT #1

Coming up with a powerful scene for Plot Point #1 is very important. Often the genre may dictate the nature of the scene, many of which are often firsts: the first kiss in a romance, the first murder in a mystery, or the first skirmish in a war story. But even so, you should brainstorm ways to differentiate your first kiss, first murder, or first skirmish from those we've seen a million times before. Make your take on the conventional plot point stand out.

The Writer's Guide to Beginnings

ACT ONE POINTERS

There are structural approaches for Act One that you may be tempted to try. Sometimes these approaches work and elevate your story; other times they fall flat.

Let's examine these strategies one by one so that you may evaluate which might serve your story well and how you might make the most of each approach while avoiding their potential pitfalls.

The Prologue

"... what's past is prologue ..." —William Shakespeare

The prologue is ubiquitous. Why? It's because writers mostly love them, even though readers mostly hate them. I know that you're probably saying that you read stories with prologues all the time. Well, so do I. Some of my favorite novels begin with prologues, and I love them anyway. Sometimes I even *write* prologues but not that often because I know that the very word "prologue" is enough to alienate readers, editors, and agents.

For the record, readers often skip prologues, just as they skip introductions, forewords, and prefaces. I say this with great authority because once upon a time, I was an acquisitions editor, and I always let my authors write all the introductions, prefaces, and forewords they wanted for their nonfiction books—because I knew readers would never read them. Readers are smart; they know that whatever comes before chapter one in a nonfiction book is (often) just a self-indulgent rant, a nostalgic trip down memory lane, or otherwise nonsensical notes that have more to do with the ego that wrote the book than the book itself (the introductions to my own books notwithstanding, she said with a smile).

But both as an editor and as an agent, I have been much tougher on novelists and memoirists who wanted to begin their stories with prologues. Readers know they can open most nonfiction books to any page in the middle, end, or beginning and start reading; they can jump around to the content that interests them, skimming what they like and skipping what they don't. But fiction and memoir are different. Here, the prologue should be a scene from the past that informs the story to come. For example: In a mystery, a prologue is often a murder scene that occurs years before the action of the story, a murder that comes back to haunt the characters in the present.

If the scene you have in mind for the prologue doesn't inform the story to come, then you don't need it. Ditch it. Too many writers have prologues that are just backstory and do not *truly* inform the story to come.

That's why readers approach prologues with caution; they know that half the time the prologues are just a waste of space and that the real story doesn't start until chapter one—*after* the prologue. They've been burned before, so many will simply skip it. Others will try it but will only keep reading if (1) it's a compelling scene and (2) they can sense its relevance to the story to come. Remember the backstory caveat: What you needed to know to write the story is not what the reader needs to read it. (Never underestimate your readers. They're as smart as you are, if not smarter.)

That said, begin your story with a prologue if you must. But if you do, write your prologue such that readers will actually read them. Here are some ways to help you do that.

"Avoid prologues. They can be annoying, especially a prologue following an introduction that comes after a foreword."
—*Elmore Leonard*

A Rose by Any Other Name Is Still a Prologue

The very word prologue is enough to put readers off. The best way to get around this problem is to simply *not* call your prologue a prologue. Call it something else. The easiest way is to use a time/place reference instead of the word "prologue," e.g., "Paris, 1945," "Six Years Earlier," or "3077 B.C."

This time/place reference grounds the scene in the past and cues the readers that what happened at that time is important to the story they are about to read.

You can also employ any number of devices to indicate time, place, or other information you might need to communicate to the reader.

Some of these devices may take the place of prologues altogether; others may serve as openers for prologues.

- **NEWS CLIPPINGS** can open your story, providing information and/or backstory in a more palatable manner that does not slow the story down (provided they are short enough), serving as context for your prologue or eliminating the need for one completely.
- **MAPS** are particularly useful in SF/fantasy and historical fiction, not only helping to ground the reader in the time and place of your story before it even begins but also giving agents and editors notice that you have done your homework in terms of setting and/or world-building, critical aspects of these genres. If you do include a map, make sure that it's a well-rendered one—amateur art screams, well, "Amateur!"
- **DIARY ENTRIES AND LETTERS** can also deliver information and/or backstory in a compelling manner, provided that you actually deliver it in a compelling manner. These devices can become clichés in unskillful hands, so make sure that if you use one you do it in a creative and novel way. (See the following section on organizing principles.)

We'll take a harder look at such devices as we explore the concept of organizing principles.

A LITTLE ITALIC GOES A LONG WAY

When you write a prologue, use a different format to set it apart graphically from the rest of the text. Italics, breaks, and other graphic elements alert readers that this part of the text is special.

NOTE: If you use italics, try to keep the italics section to one page, two at the most. Reading italics can irritate the eyes, and readers may quit reading due to the strain, without really even knowing why.

The Organizing Principle

Your story may be a good candidate for an organizing principle. This is different from the plot; plot is what happens in your story, the list of scenes dramatizing the events of your story. You lay an organizing principle over the plot; it's a way of organizing, sorting, and enhancing the themes, motifs, and imagery of your story. A well-chosen organizing principle can even serve as a strong differentiator for your story, helping to set it apart from the competition.

Think of it this way: Making a story is like baking a cake. You combine the essential ingredients—scenes—to create the batter of plot. Now you can choose to organize that batter in a number of ways: You can make cupcakes, sheet cake, a cake roll, or a double-layer cake. No matter which you choose, the batter remains the same; it's the shape or vessel that holds the batter that changes, according to the organizing principle you choose.

Say you're writing a love story. As we've seen, the basic plot for love stories is: Boy gets girl; boy loses girl; boy gets girl back (or not). Adding an organizing principle to the telling of a love story can help create a unique recasting of this same plot:

- In the *New York Times* best-selling rock 'n' roll romance *Nick & Norah's Infinite Playlist,* co-authors Rachel Cohn and David Levithan incorporate two organizing principles: (1) alternating his-and-her first-person points of view and (2) the metaphor of music. These two work together to introduce readers to Nick and Norah and give them a front-row seat at the ongoing concert of their relationship. Readers fall in love with these characters, the music, and the novel, thanks to these strongly conceived and executed organizing principles. And yes, this is the novel that inspired the swell film of the same name; read the book, watch the movie, and then compare notes.
- In the romantic comedy *(500) Days of Summer,* writers Scott Neustadter and Michael H. Weber tell the story of a couple's relationship over the course of 500 days, numbering each scene. This organizing principle of numbered scenes permits the writers to jump around in the actual

chronology of the plot without losing the audience. If you haven't seen this film, you should see it, if only to admire its clever organizing principle in action, which turns a nonlinear narrative into very effective and even poignant storytelling. Moreover, this organizing principle gives the usual romantic-comedy treatment a very new twist, a twist that is largely responsible for its success.

- In the magical-realism classic *Like Water for Chocolate: A Novel in Monthly Installments with Recipes, Romances, and Home Remedies*, author Laura Esquivel lays the groundwork for her organizing principle right there in the subtitle, preparing readers for a journey of the heart like no other. She milks her food-as-life theme for all it's worth, using recipes as chapter openers and infusing her prose with imagery of food, cooking, and fire. This story is a wonderful read, and all that imagery translates beautifully to the screen in the film adaption of the work.

- In the sad, sweet, hilarious, and ultimately irresistible *PS, I Love You*, author Cecelia Ahern uses an organizing principle as a plot device. The story is about a young widow named Holly whose beloved childhood sweetheart, Gerry, dies of a brain tumor. His last gift to her is a series of notes, one for each month of the year following his death. These notes form a blueprint of sorts, listing a number of goals for her to accomplish as she makes a new life without him. The notes are a recurring device throughout the story, driving the plot while also organizing it. (And, yes, they made a movie version of this one, too. See a pattern here?)

- In the blockbuster *Gone Girl*, which is at its heart a love story gone very, very wrong, Gillian Flynn tells the story of a married couple from alternating his-and-her first-person points of view, which, as we've seen with *Nick & Norah's Infinite Playlist*, is an organizing principle in and of itself. Flynn also uses the device of a diary to tell the wife's side of the story. Devices used as running elements throughout the entire story become organizing principles. In *Gone Girl*, the diary device helps remind readers whose point of view they're reading at any given time (always a challenge with multiple first-person point of view), but also, in Flynn's masterful hands, it becomes a slick sleight of hand that contributes to the story's suspense. (If you haven't read this book, you need to read it for craft alone—and no, seeing the movie is *not* the same thing; you need to see the words on the page to understand how she pulls off this magic trick.) Both of these strategies help make the story unique.

> "All love stories are tales of beginnings. When we talk about falling in love, we go to the beginning to pinpoint the moment of freefall." —*Meghan O'Rourke*

Everyone loves a good organizing principle—agents, editors, and readers themselves. Organizing principles can also help you add layers of meaning, milk your metaphor, enhance the imagery, enhance the setting, and deepen the story's themes. Most important, the best organizing principles run throughout your story from beginning to end, giving you the opportunity to set your story apart in agents', editors', and readers' minds from the very first lines. This gives you a real edge when it comes time to shop your story to agents, editors, and publishers.

Getting Creative with Organizing Principles

When it comes to organizing principles, the possibilities are endless. Here's an admittedly incomplete list of successful stories that employ a creative and clever organizing principle:

- *Julie & Julia: 365 Days, 524 Recipes, 1 Tiny Apartment,* by Julie Powell, a memoir in which Powell sets out to make all the recipes in Julia Child's *Mastering the Art of French Cooking* over the course of one year and blogs about it
- *Wild: From Lost to Found on the Pacific Crest Trail,* by Cheryl Strayed, a memoir in which Strayed goes on a long journey—in travel memoirs there's always a journey—through the wilderness to reclaim herself

- *The Secret Life of Bees*, by Sue Monk Kidd, a novel in which Kidd begins chapters with snippets from various texts on beekeeping (note that even the title speaks to the metaphor of her novel)
- *My Horizontal Life*, by Chelsea Handler, a memoir in which Handler reveals her sexual history, presenting her life as a series of one-night stands
- *The Jane Austen Book Club*, by Karen J. Fowler, a novel in which a group of women—and one man—gather monthly to discuss the novels of Jane Austen, whose themes, plot points, and preoccupations mirror the romantic lives of the characters
- *And Then There Were None* (a.k.a. *Ten Little Indians*), by Agatha Christie, a mystery in which the characters invited to a rich man's island disappear one by one, a murderous organizing principle, even for this genre, but one so compelling that the book became an instant classic
- *The World According to Garp*, by John Irving, a best-selling literary novel in which the life of the hero, Garp, is told from his extraordinary conception to his messianic death, the organizing principle being the entire life cycle, as illuminated in the very last line (which I will leave to you to discover, if you have not yet read this moving story)
- *Raiders of the Lost Ark*, by George Lucas (story) and Lawrence Kasdan (screenplay), the remarkable adventure based on the Saturday serials of the thirties, forties, and fifties, in which the hero, Indiana Jones faces one cliffhanger after another—from deadly spiders and slithering snakes to angry natives and nefarious Nazis
- *Star Wars*, by George Lucas, the epic space-opera film in which Luke Skywalker goes from farm boy to Jedi Knight in a transformation inspired by famed mythologist Joseph Campbell's "hero's journey"
- *Mrs. Dalloway*, by Virginia Woolf, the luminous novel in which Clarissa Dalloway lives one day in her life, based on Aristotle's assertion in *Poetics* that the action of a story should take place in twenty-four hours to achieve a unity of time

The best organizing principles are inextricably connected to a story's plot, settings, and themes in subtle and not-so-subtle ways, starting right in the story's opening. Let's take a look at what that may actually look like on paper, with three wonderful stories whose organizing principles set them apart from the competition and proved a big part of their success.

Bridget Jones's Diary, by Helen Fielding

In this hilarious international bestseller, each chapter opens with a diary entry in which the heroine recounts her day in terms of pounds gained, cigarettes smoked, and alcohol imbibed. Here's the diary entry from its first chapter.

> Sunday 1 January
>
> *129 lbs. (but post-Christmas), alcohol units 14 (but effectively covers 2 days as 4 hours of party was on New Year's Day), cigarettes 22, calories 5424.*
>
> Food consumed today:
>
> 2 pkts Emmenthal cheese slices
>
> 14 cold new potatoes
>
> 2 Bloody Marys (count as food as contain Worcester sauce and tomatoes)
>
> ⅓ Ciabatta loaf with Brie
>
> coriander leaves—½ packet
>
> 12 Milk Try (best to get rid of all Christmas confectionery in one go and make fresh start tomorrow)
>
> 13 cocktail sticks securing cheese and pineapple
>
> Portion Una Alconbury's turkey curry, peas and bananas
>
> Portion Una Alconbury's Raspberry Surprise made with Bourbon biscuits, tinned raspberries, eight gallons of whipped cream, decorated with glacé cherries and angelica.

The Know-It-All, by A.J. Jacobs

In this moving memoir, Jacobs weaves the story of his and his wife's struggle with infertility with his obsessive goal of reading the entire Encyclopaedia Britannica—all 44 million words of it. Jacobs starts at the beginning, with the As, in this story organized alphabetically.

a-ak

That's the first word in the *Encyclopaedia Britannica*. "A-ak." Followed by this write-up: "Ancient East Asian music. See gagaku."

That's the entire article. Four words and then: "See gagaku."

What a tease! Right at the start, the crafty *Britannica* has presented me with a dilemma. Should I flip ahead volume 6 and find out what's up with this gagaku, or should I stick with the plan, and move onto the second word in *AA* section? I decide to plow ahead with the *AAs*. Why ruin the suspense? If anyone brings up "a-ak" in conversation, I'll just bluff. I'll say, "Oh, I love gagaku!" or, "Did you hear that Madonna's going to record an a-ak track on her next CD?"

Where'd You Go, Bernadette, by Maria Semple

This delightful novel uses all manner of devices for its organizing principle. In fact, I often recommend this novel to my clients and writing students because reading it is virtually a crash course in how to use devices in novel and fun ways. Semple ostensibly writes the novel from the first-person point of view of young heroine Bee, whose mother disappears right before Christmas. Semple obviously took the "if you're writing from a first-person point of view, stick to that one point of view only for your entire story" very seriously (as well she should—and so should you). But this resourceful author was not about to let that limit her ability to write the story, so she used devices to bring other voices into the story. The following list of devices from this novel, which may or may not be complete, includes:

- report cards
- emails
- FBI official correspondence
- letters
- school notes
- grammar-school reports
- invitations
- signs
- blog posts

- book excerpts
- press releases
- articles
- Christmas poems
- transcripts
- IM messages
- police reports
- authorization requests
- presentations
- psychiatric examinations
- songs
- hymns
- faxes
- ship captain's reports
- forensic reports

I kid you not. Let's take a look at the first device she uses in the story, which appears in the first chapter:

MONDAY, NOVEMBER 15
Galer Street School is a place where compassion, academics, and global connectitude join together to create civic-minded citizens of a sustainable and diverse planet.

Student: Bee Branch
Grade: Eight
Teacher: Levy

KEY
S Surpasses Excellence
A Achieves Excellence
W Working towards Excellence

Geometry	S
Biology	S
World Religion	S
Music	S
Creative Writing	S
Ceramics	S

Language Arts   S
Expressive Movement   S

COMMENTS: Bee is a pure delight. Her love of learning is infectious, as are her kindness and humor. Bee is unafraid to ask questions. Her goal is always deep understanding of a given topic, not merely getting a good grade. The other students look to Bee for help in their studies, and she is always quick to respond with a smile. Bee exhibits extraordinary concentration when working alone; when working in a group, she is a quiet and confident leader. Of special note is what an accomplished flutist Bee continues to be. The year is only a third over, but already I am mourning the day Bee graduates from Galer Street and heads out into the world. I understand she is applying to boarding schools back east. I envy the teachers who get to meet Bee for the first time, and to discover for themselves what a lovely young woman she is.

All of these examples reflect how entertaining and enlightening a good organizing principle can be. They add a fun and fierce element that can add a layer of complexity to your story, boost its appeal to readers, and set it apart from the competition. In short, I've found as an agent that a strong organizing principle can help sell projects that might otherwise not find a home in today's tough marketplace—maybe yours.

JUMP-START

Read one of the stories I've used as a good example here. Identify the various organizing principles and devices used in that story. Do the same for your favorite stories. How do the writers pull it off? How might you pull it off in your story? Brainstorm a long list.

BEGINNINGS BY GENRE

Every genre has its idiosyncrasies and conventions, and you need to understand them to ensure that your story opening hits the marks of the genre and avoids the clichés and tropes that will doom your efforts to publish your work. Let's look at each genre in turn, and identify the dos and don'ts of each.

Women's Fiction

"I say, 'I write romance, women's fiction, chick lit.' I think it all fits very comfortably under the same umbrella. Basically, I write books for women—books about relationships: books that make you laugh and sometimes make you cry a little."
—*Susan Elizabeth Phillips*

- Do give us a likable and resourceful heroine readers can relate to.
- Do give your heroine a yearning for something bigger than herself.
- Do focus your story on the relationships your heroine has with her parents, her children, her siblings, her friends, her colleagues, and her rivals—as well as her love interest(s).
- Do consider planning your story around weddings, funerals, reunions, anniversaries, holidays, baby showers, graduations, and other rite-of-passage events of women's lives.
- Do choose a setting that readers would love to visit.
- Do tell your story in a strong voice.
- Do weave in women's themes—the bigger, the better.
- Do use an organizing principle if you can.
- Do use devices, metaphor, and imagery to layer your work.
- Don't use tired tropes like the unhappy housewife, the bitter divorcée, the evil ex, the evil in-laws, etc.
- Don't open with your character alone, thinking.
- Don't slow your story down with backstory or info dumping.

"I've been typed as historical fiction, historical women's fiction, historical mystery, historical chick lit, historical romance—all for the same book." —*Lauren Willig*

Literary Fiction

"That's what fiction is for. It's for getting at the truth when the truth isn't sufficient for the truth." —*Tim O'Brien*

- Do give us a protagonist with a yearning for something.
- Do thwart that yearning again and again.
- Do make something happen.
- Do give us well-rounded, complex, and complicated characters.
- Do steep your story in setting.
- Do tell your story in a strong voice.
- Do weave in theme—the bigger, the better.
- Do use an organizing principle if you can.
- Do use metaphor and imagery to layer your work.
- Do pay attention to the language.
- Don't leave your characters alone too long doing nothing or just navel-gazing.
- Don't sacrifice story for pretty words.

"... good fiction's job [is] to comfort the disturbed and disturb the comfortable." —*David Foster Wallace*

Romance

"A romance novel focuses exclusively on two people falling in love. It can't be about a woman caring for her aging mother or something like that. It can have that element, but it has to be primarily about the male-female relationship." —*Kristin Hannah*

- Do give us a hero that any self-respecting heroine or reader can fall in love with.
- Do give us a likable, attractive, and strong heroine readers can relate to.
- Do arrange for a meet cute we haven't seen before.
- Do set your story in a romantic place.
- Do use an organizing principle if you can.

- Do give your hero and/or heroine a secret that will be revealed.
- Do make us believe that this couple must be together or they'll be unhappy forever.
- Do surround your couple with family, friends, frenemies, and rivals.
- Don't use tired tropes like evil exes, manipulative mothers-in-law, BFFs turned lovers, charming bad boys, student/teacher romances, amnesia plots, or the country-mouse/city-mouse theme.

"The lust and attraction are often a given in a romance novel— I want to dig into the elements of true friendship that form a foundation for a solid, gonna-last-forever romantic relationship."
—*Suzanne Brockmann*

Crime Fiction

"Mysteries and thrillers are not the same things, though they are literary siblings. Roughly put, I would say the distinction is that mysteries emphasize motive and psychology, whereas thrillers rely more heavily on action and plot." —*Jon Meacham*

- Do give us a proactive protagonist who can drive the action, solve the crime, and save the day.
- Do ground your story in setting.
- Do give your amateur sleuth an interesting occupation.
- Do introduce your suspects in Act One.
- Do plant your clues and red herrings early and often.
- Do get out of the courtroom if you're writing a legal thriller.
- Do surround your protagonist with a strong supporting cast.
- Do set your cozy in a community that readers will love.
- Do drop the first body as soon as possible, chapter one, if not page one.
- Don't use tired tropes like alcoholic cops, stupid criminals, phone calls in the middle of the night, etc.
- Don't let up on the conflict or the pacing, especially in a thriller.

"In suspense novels, even subplots about relationships have to have conflict." —*Jeffery Deaver*

Science Fiction

"To write good SF today ... you must push further and harder, reach down deeper into your own mind until you break through into the strange and terrible country wherein live your own dreams." —*Gardner Dozois*

- Do give us a protagonist worthy and able to save the universe.
- Do get the science right.
- Do get out of the spaceship.
- Do give us strong, well-drawn female characters who defy the space-babe stereotype.
- Do give us aliens worth reading about—no more tentacles, please.
- Don't give us all-powerful computers.
- Don't use tired tropes like warp drives, hyperdrives, interstellar empires/federations, pulse weapons, etc.
- Don't overburden your story with endless explanations of the science.
- Don't give us a *deus ex machina* ending.
- Do resolve the main action of the story, even if you're planning on writing a series.

"If it has horses and swords in it, it's a fantasy, unless it also has a rocketship in it, in which case it becomes science fiction. The only thing that'll turn a story with a rocketship in it back into fantasy is the Holy Grail." —*Debra Doyle*

Fantasy

"Fantasy doesn't have to be fantastic. American writers in particular find this much harder to grasp. You need to have your feet on the ground as much as your head in the clouds. The cute dragon that sits on your shoulder also craps all down your back, but this makes it more interesting because it gives it an added dimension." —*Terry Pratchett*

- Do give us a worthy, well-rounded—not perfect!—protagonist.
- Do build a world we haven't seen a million times before—that is, *not* rehashed J.R.R. Tolkien or George R.R. Martin.
- Do consider creating a map of your world.
- Do give us strong, well-drawn female characters who defy the princess/warrior/witch stereotypes.
- Do surround your protagonist with a strong supporting cast.
- Do use names for people, places, and things that are easy to read and spell and won't trip up the reader.
- Don't open with dreams and visions.
- Don't use tired tropes like faeries, dragons, elves, *Dungeons & Dragons* magic, telepathy, etc.
- Don't overburden your opening with backstory and/or flowery description.
- Do resolve the main action of the story, even if you're planning on writing a series.

"Fantasy is hardly an escape from reality. It's a way of understanding it." —*Lloyd Alexander*

Horror

"[Horror fiction] shows us that the control we believe we have is purely illusory and that every moment we teeter on chaos and oblivion." —*Clive Barker*

- Do give us a brave and *intelligent* protagonist.
- Do give us a well-rounded villain who's not just a one-trick psychotic pony.
- Do give us monsters we have *not* seen before.
- Do give us strong, well-drawn female characters who defy the weak and whiny stereotypes.
- Do give us settings we have *not* seen before.
- Do keep the suspense and the terror coming.
- Do use humor for comic relief.

- Don't be gross just for the sake of being gross.
- Don't use tired tropes like scary basements, noises in the attic, and multiple-personality disorder.
- Don't overburden your reader with backstory and/or description.

"Any writer of horror needs to at least have a good, solid love of the genre. Also, good horror writers need to have a slightly twisted sense of humor. Without humor, horror just isn't as good." —*Alistair Cross*

Historical Fiction

"It's really important in any historical fiction, I think, to anchor the story in its time. And you do that by weaving in those details, by, believe it or not, by the plumbing." —*Jacqueline Winspear*

- Do get the history right.
- Do consider using maps, family trees, news clippings, and other devices to deliver information the reader needs.
- Do create a protagonist readers can admire and relate to despite the difference in time periods.
- Do give us strong, well-drawn female characters who defy the limitations placed on women at the time.
- Do write dialogue that evokes the time period but is still easy for modern readers to understand.
- Do use a prose style that evokes the era but is still accessible.
- Do show us something we haven't seen before or didn't know about the era and its people.
- Do render your setting so well that it becomes a character.
- Do people your story with real people and/or events based on or inspired by true events.
- Do tie your story to present-day anniversaries, holidays, etc., if you can.
- Do use themes that are as relevant today as they were then.
- Do incorporate a strong bridge to the present if you can.
- Don't overburden your story with endless historical research and description.

"Concentrate your narrative energy on the point of change. This is especially important for historical fiction. When your character is new to a place or things alter around them, that's the point to step back and fill in the details of their world." —*Hilary Mantel*

Young Adult/Children's

"As Jane Austen might have put it: It is a truth universally acknowledged that young protagonists in search of adventure must ditch their parents." —*Philip Pullman*

- Do give us a likable and resourceful protagonist.
- Do make sure your teenagers sound like teenagers and your children sound like children.
- Do make something happen fast, or your readers will bail on your story.
- Do open with conflict, and keep the action coming.
- Do keep your protagonist on the move.
- Do play against gender stereotypes.
- Do weave in coming-of-age themes.
- Do surround your protagonist with a strong supporting multicultural cast.
- Do use names for people, places, and things that are easy to read and spell and won't trip up the reader.
- Don't use tired tropes like evil parents, playground bullies, lame teachers, dystopian settings, etc.
- Don't overburden your opening with backstory and/or info dumping.
- Don't underestimate your young readers.

"Children's books are harder to write. It's tougher to keep a child interested because a child doesn't have the concentration of an adult. A child knows the television is in the next room. It's tough to hold a child, but it's a lovely thing to try to do." —*Roald Dahl*

Memoir

"I'm very detail-oriented. I think that's why people enjoy my memoirs—because I tend to remember everything."
—*Jen Lancaster*

- Do write your memoir in a strong voice.
- Do choose your timeframe carefully, and condense it as much as possible.
- Do be as hard on yourself—if not harder—as you are on the others you write about in your memoir.
- Do make sure that you dramatize your story and write it in fully realized scenes.
- Do ground your memoir in the settings of your life.
- Do use an organizing principle if you can.
- Do use devices, metaphor, and imagery to layer your work.
- Don't open with your character alone, thinking.
- Don't slow your reader down with backstory or info dumping.

"In the worst memoirs, you can feel the author justifying himself—forgiving himself—in every paragraph. In the best memoirs, the author is tougher on him- or herself than his or her readers will ever be." —*Darin Strauss*

JUMP-START

Run down the list of caveats for each genre, starting with your own. Which might apply to your story? What do you need to work on?

Also consider the dos and don'ts for the other genres, and identify which of those could be strengthening or sabotaging your own work.

THE END OF THE BEGINNING

We've taken a hard look at your entire first act in this section, and now you're ready to finish your story. When you do, you'll need to rewrite, revise, refine, and polish, polish, polish your work, starting with the opening.

The opening is the part of your story that agents and editors usually ask for—the first ten or fifty or one-hundred pages. Whether or not they ask to see more depends on the strength of your submission.

In chapter eight, we'll look at the best way to polish your work in preparation for approaching agents and editors and submitting pages to them for review—with an eye on publication.

CHAPTER EIGHT

FINE-TUNING YOUR BEGINNING

Bulletproof Your Beginning

"Bring all your intelligence to bear on your beginning."
—*Elizabeth Bowen*

"If you start with a bang, you won't end with a whimper." —*T.S. Eliot*

You've written your story now—from word one to Plot Point #1 and beyond. But are you ready for prime time? Before you start showing your work to publishing professionals, you need to bulletproof that work, especially the beginning, because it's the beginning that agents and editors typically ask to see: the first page, the first ten pages, the first fifty pages, the first one-hundred pages. And even should you prove lucky enough to be asked to submit your entire manuscript, the beginning is what people will read first—and last, if it doesn't work.

If you think talk of bulletproofing is overkill, think again. The submission process is a painful one for many writers, and the only defense against the slings and arrows of rejection is a story so polished and professional that the only reasonable response to reading it is "Yes," as in "Yes, I'd love to represent this" or "Yes, I'd love to publish this," or "Yes, I'd like to buy this in hardcover and read it at home tonight."

Getting to "yes" is what this final section of *The Writer's Guide to Beginnings* is all about.

READING FOR STORY QUESTIONS

As I said in chapter one, lack of narrative thrust is the most common reason I pass on manuscripts. All other things being equal, I cannot sell a story short on narrative thrust. *No narrative thrust equals no sale.*

Before you let anyone see your work, you need to test your story for narrative thrust. This is the most important revision you need to do. Sure, you'll revise for clarity, language, precision, and more later, but before you worry about line editing and copy editing, you need to make sure that you're revving up that engine of narrative thrust, hitting the first page running, and speeding along until your story ends.

There is a test for narrative thrust, and you can perform it on your manuscript yourself.

It's all a matter of story questions: the *who, what, where, when, why,* and *how* questions that readers ask themselves as they read and keep on reading. Good storytellers pepper their prose with story questions—and not just the mystery and thriller writers but writers of all genres, including literary fiction.

"Books aren't written; they're rewritten—including your own. It is one of the hardest things to accept, especially after the seventh rewrite hasn't quite done it ..." —*Michael Crichton*

The Three Kinds of Story Questions

There are three kinds of story questions, and a strong beginning boasts all three.

- The *macro* story question is the big question that drives the entire plot, the one related to the main action of your story: Will Cinderella wed her Prince Charming? Will Luke Skywalker become a Jedi Knight and destroy the Death Star? How will Dorothy find her way back home?
- The *meso* story questions are the ones that drive each scene, starting with the first one: Will Cinderella's stepmother let her go to the ball once she's finished her chores? Will Dorothy survive the cyclone?

Will Princess Leia upload the Death Star plans into R2-D2 before she's captured?

- And the *micro* questions are the questions scattered throughout the narrative at every opportunity: Why did Cinderella's father marry such a witch? Why are her stepsisters so hateful? Will Cinderella ever get to leave the house? Where's that cyclone taking Dorothy? What happens in the eye of a cyclone, anyway? Will the house just fall out of the sky? Will Princess Leia escape the Stormtroopers? Will C-3PO and R2-D2 get away with the plans? What will the Empire do with Princess Leia?

JUMP-START

Watch one of your favorite television shows/movies in your genre. As you watch, verbalize the story questions that occur to you as the show/movie progresses. You can use a tape recorder or your smartphone to record the story questions as you watch, or you can write them down. If you choose to watch a TV show, pay particular attention to the story questions that arise right before the commercials; TV writers are trained to pose strong story questions before the breaks to make sure that viewers come back when the breaks are over.

NOTE: This is a good exercise to do with your writers' group. And fun, too!

"The way to write a thriller is to ask a question at the beginning and answer it at the end." —*Lee Child*

A CASE STUDY (PART II): *SPARE THESE STONES*

"A good novel begins with a small question and ends with a bigger one." —*Paula Fox*

The more story questions you pose and the more compelling they are, the greater the narrative thrust of your story will be. Remember the scene from my novel *Spare These Stones* that we deconstructed in terms of action, backstory, character, and description? Now let's look at that same scene in terms of story questions.

Spare These Stones [*title in keeping with the genre*]
By Paula Munier

"Good friend for Jesus' sake forbeare,
To dig the dust enclosed here.
Blessed be the man that spares these stones,
And cursed be he that moves my bones."
　　　—William Shakespeare (epitaph) [*Are bones to be found shortly?*]

The woods were blessedly cool, even in July [*Where's the woods? Why does she hate being hot?*]. The northern hardwoods of the Southern Green Mountains were in full summer leafing, towering birches and beeches and maples draping the forest in shade. After several years in the desolate white heat of the Afghanistan desert [*Is that why she hates heat? What was she doing there? Was she a soldier? Did she get hurt?*], Elvis and I loved the gelid greens and blues and silvers of the trees [*Who's Elvis? Who names anybody Elvis?*]. We welcomed the soft sweep of moss and lichens and pine needles beneath our feet, the warble of wrens and the skittering of squirrels, the crisp scent of mountain air breathed in and out, in and out, in and out [*Why does she love the woods so much? Does she have PTSD?*].

This was our happy place [*Why?*]. The place where we could leave the hot, whirling sands of war behind us [*What happened to them there?*]. After that last deployment, the one where I got shot and Elvis got depressed, we'd both been sent home [*Where did she get shot? Was it his fault? Is Elvis still depressed?*]. It took me a year to track down the Belgian shepherd—think German shepherd, only sleeker and smarter—and another three months to talk the private contractor into letting me adopt him [*Elvis is a dog? Smarter than German shepherds? Really? She adopted him?*]. But in the end, Elvis and I prevailed—and entered retirement together [*She's retired? Now what does she do?*]. Two former military police—one thirty-three-year-old two-legged female Vermonter with an exit wound scar blighting her once perfect ass and one handsome six-year-old four-legged male Malinois with canine PTSD—reclaiming our minds and bodies and souls in the backwoods, one hike at a time [*Military police? Shot in the butt? Dogs get PTSD? Who knew?*]. U.S. Army Sergeant Annie Carr and Military Working Dog Elvis reporting for permanent R&R [*Military Working Dog? What did Elvis do?*].

Today was the Fourth of July [*Ironic, huh?*]. The holiday I once loved most [*But not anymore? Why?*]. But now Elvis and I spent every Independence Day independent of the trappings of civilization [*Why?*]. We didn't like fireworks much anymore. Sounded too much like Afghanistan on a bad day [*What happens on a bad day?*]. Elvis and I worked explosives there; he'd sniff them out, and I'd call in the EOD team [*Bomb-sniffing dog?*]. On good days, it was just that simple. On bad days, it was all noise and blood and death [*What all did they see and experience over there?*].

Here in the Lye Brook Wilderness, all the sounds we heard were made by nature, not by man [*How remote is this place?*], save for the crunch of my old boots on the overgrown path and the *whoosh!* of Elvis as he bounded ahead of me, blazing the trail with no thought of IEDs. At least I hoped Elvis had no thought of IEDs here [*Is that why he has PTSD?*].

Deep in the timberland there was no past, no future. Only now [*Now what?*]. The terrain grew rougher, steeper, tougher [*Are they both in good physical shape?*]. I adjusted my pack, which at only 20 pounds barely registered on my body [*Twenty pounds?*], once burdened by nearly 100 pounds of gear [*How could she carry all that?*], including body armor, flak, weaponry, and an IV for Elvis if he got dehydrated in the desert [*How often did that happen?*].

All I carried now was a leash, lunch, and drinking water for me and Elvis, compass, hiking GPS, flashlight, lighter, power pack, sunscreen, bug spray, first-aid kit, duct tape, and extra batteries [*That's all?*]. My keys, wallet, and smartphone were distributed among the many pockets in my cargo pants, along with my Swiss Army knife, dog treats, and Elvis's "rabbit," the indispensable squeaky Kong toy critical to his training and his joie de vivre [*Should I get my dog a Kong?*]. One squeak and I had his full attention every time [*One squeak?*]. He lived for these squeaks, which signaled successful completion of the task at hand—from sit, down, and stay to alerting to explosive devices [*What else can this dog do?*].

Not that Elvis was working now. He was just playing, diving into the scrub, scampering over downed trees, racing up the rocky trail only to circle back to check my progress [*Is he always this good?*]. A downpour the night before had left muddy puddles in its wake, and my boots were streaked with dirt. As was Elvis, his fawn fur stippled with dark splotches of sludge [*Will he get a bath when they get home?*].

I kept my eyes on the slick, stone-ridden path, and my mind off my future, which loomed ahead of me with no clear goal in sight [*What will she do now? What is she living on? Why can't she decide what to do?*]. Unlike this trail we hiked, which led along the bed of a former logging railroad, rising before me along a steady 20 percent incline for some two-and-a-half miles up to Lye Brook Falls [*How long will this hike take?*]. The falls were among the tallest in Vermont, cascading down 160 feet.

We'd hiked about two-thirds of the way so far [*Aren't they getting tired? Does the dog need a drink?*]. I'd brought Elvis up here before; we both liked the trail, as much for its solitude as its scenery, provided you set off early enough [*Doesn't she like any people at all? Are they always alone?*]. We began at dawn, and so often had the trail to ourselves, even on glorious summer mornings like this [*Does she have insomnia? Where is everyone?*]. Of course, this being the Fourth, most New Englanders were not hiking the wilderness, they were celebrating with family and friends at town parades and neighborhood barbecues and bonfires on the beach, a national fracas of hot dogs and beer and fireworks Elvis and I were content to miss [*Is she completely anti-social now? Why?*].

Elvis plunged through a swollen stream and disappeared into a thicket of small spruce. I saw no reason to follow him; I preferred my feet dry. I tramped on, dodging the worst of the mud and careful not to slip on the wet stones [*How slippery is it? What happens if she falls? Who would find her? Would the dog go fetch someone?*].

After about half a mile, Elvis had still not returned [*Where's the dog? What happened to him?*]. This was more than unusual; it was unprecedented [*Why is she so worried? Should I be worried too?*]. Elvis's job had always been to walk in front of me, scouting ahead and alerting to danger [*Where's the danger here?*]. The only dangers here were the ubiquitous clouds of biting black flies—and the occasional bear [*Black flies? Biting? Bears? Don't bears bite too?*].

I whistled and waited [*Is Elvis trained to come when she whistles?*]. Elvis darted out of the scrub onto the path [*Where'd he been?*]. He skidded to a stop right in front of me and jangled his head [*Why?*]. In his mouth he held what looked like one of his rabbits [*What's in his mouth?*]. But it wasn't a doggie squeaky toy [*What is it?*].

"Drop it." I held out my hand [*Will he put it in her hand?*].

Elvis obliged, releasing the canary-yellow object into my open palm, his bright eyes on me and his new plaything [*What is it?*]. I held it up and examined it in the light filtering through the trees [*What is it?*].

"I think it's a baby teether," I told Elvis [*Baby teether? What baby?*]. About 5 inches long, the teether was shaped like a plastic daisy with a thick stem, the better for a baby's grip, and a flower-shaped lion's head blooming at the top. Apart from Elvis's drool, the little lion toy was clean, so it wasn't something that had been abandoned in the woods for long [*Drool? How did it get there? Where is the baby?*]. I bent over towards Elvis, holding the teether out to him. "Where did you get this" [*What will Elvis do?*]?

Elvis pushed at my hand with a cold nose and whined [*What does that mean when he does that? What is he trying to tell her?*]. With another quick yelp, he leapt back into the underbrush [*Now what? Will she follow?*]. I tucked the baby toy into one of my cargo pockets and followed the dog, as he obviously meant me to do. I cursed under my breath as I sank into a marshy patch, mud seeping into the tops of my boots as I stomped through the mire after Elvis [*What's in that mud?*]. Sometimes Elvis behaved erratically as a result of his PTSD [*How erratically?*]. Most of the time, I could anticipate his triggers: slamming doors, thunderstorms, fireworks [*How? Do all loud noises scare him? Does he have flashbacks like some soldiers do?*]. But at other times, his triggers eluded me [*Why?*] and were known only to Elvis: scents, sounds, and situations that went unnoticed by my human senses and were only ascertained by his superior canine senses [*How superior is his sense of smell?*]. But baby toys had never been among them [*Where'd it come from?*].

Elvis led the way to a stream that paralleled the trail, a rushing of water over a bed of rocks. He jumped, clearing the 6-foot wide current easily [*Can all dogs jump that far? Can she jump that far?*]. I splashed after him, not willing to risk breaking a leg or twisting an ankle in a poorly landed leap [*How deep is the water? Isn't it cold?*]. The cold water came up to my knees, and I was grateful it was July, or the water would have been even colder. Elvis waited for me, his ears perked and his dark eyes on me [*What does he know that we don't?*].

I clambered out of the brook and stumbled over the stones into a thick copse of young birch trees. There Elvis sat down on his haunches in the middle of a large blowdown area littered with tree limbs [*What's the dog doing? What does it mean?*].

"What you got there, buddy?" I squatted down next to him [*Shouldn't she be careful? What's this got to do with the teether?*]. Elvis looked at me, dark eyes lively, ready for his reward—his own toy or a treat or both [*Why does he think he gets a reward?*].

But he could not earn his reward until I could figure out what he'd found [*If she doesn't know, who does?*]. Like all military working dogs, Elvis was trained as a patrol dog, to guard checkpoints and gates, detecting intruders, secure bases, apprehend suspects, and attack on command [*How smart is this dog?*]. But beyond that, MWDs were specialists; they were trained to sniff out drugs or cadavers or explosives. Elvis was an explosive-detection dog, trained to find weapons and to detect a number of explosive odors [*What kind of explosives? What kind of odors? Is there a bomb in the woods?*]. When he alerted to a scent, that scent was typically gunmetal, detonating cord, smokeless powder, dynamite, nitroglycerin, TNT, or RDX, a chemical compound often found in plastic explosives [*Then why did the teether pique his interest? How smart is this dog?*].

Elvis looked at me as if to say, "Okay, my job here is done. Where's my rabbit" [*Where's his rabbit? Is she going to give the dog a break or what?*]?

I looked at the ground in front of his paws [*Why? What's there?*]. The forest floor was thick with detritus—dead leaves and twigs and pine needles—as well as mushrooms and moss and ferns and what looked like poison oak. No evidence of trespass here [*Trespass?*]. No

The Writer's Guide to Beginnings

evidence of explosives [*What did Elvis smell?*]. And no evidence of a baby to go with the baby toy, either [*Where's that baby?*].

On the other hand, Elvis had an excellent track record—and the best nose of any dog I'd met, either in training or in Afghanistan [*The best nose? Then it's still possible that there is danger nearby? How smart is this dog, really?*]. He'd never been wrong before [*Never? What does this mean here and now?*]. What were the odds he was wrong now?

"Good boy," I said, scratching that favorite spot between his pointed ears. I slipped a treat out of my pocket and held it in my open palm, and Elvis licked it up [*What kind of treat?*].

"Stay," I said [*Why?*].

Why Elvis would alert to a scent here in the Vermont woods was unclear to me [*Why indeed?*]. If we were on a mission, we'd call in the Explosive Ordnance Disposal (EOD) team, responsible for bomb disposal [*So what will she do instead?*]. We never touched anything; the EOD guys took it from there [*How dangerous was it?*]. But here in the Lye Brook Wilderness, half a world away from the Middle East, I wasn't sure what to do. There was no EOD team trailing us; we weren't wearing flak or body armor [*Does she need it? What about the dog?*]. I wasn't even sure Elvis had alerted to explosives [*Why not? Is it the PTSD?*]. Who would plant explosives in a national forest [*Who indeed?*]?

Or maybe they were just fireworks [*Fireworks?*]. It was the Fourth of July, after all. Apart from sparklers, fireworks were illegal in Vermont [*Really?*]. Even supervised public fireworks displays required a permit [*Really?*]. But who would bother to bury fireworks in the woods—and even if someone had done so, you'd think they would have dug up them up by now for the holiday [*Who buries fireworks in the woods?*].

I slipped my pack off my shoulders and retrieved the duct tape [*what will she do with the duct tape?*]. I used the duct tape to rope off a crescent around Elvis and the target area, using birch saplings as posts [*Why is she doing this? Is it dangerous? Will she get blown up?*].

I pulled my cell phone out of my pocket and turned it on [*Who's she calling? Will her cell phone work in the woods?*]. No bars [*Is there any service close by?*]. No dial tone [*Where will she have to go to be able to make a call?*]. Coverage was spotty [*Now what?*]. One bar [*Can she make the call now? Is that enough?*]. Dial tone [*Will she get through? Are there any cops in the woods?*]. Quickly I dialed 911 and hoped that I'd get through [*But what if she doesn't?*]. But the connection died just as quickly [*What will she do now?*].

Elvis and I would have to head for higher ground and a stronger signal [*Will that really work?*].

"Come on, Elvis." I headed over to the edge of the clearing, Elvis bounding ahead of me, disappearing into the brush [*Where is the dog going now?*]. That's when I heard it [*Heard what?*]. A thin cry [*From what?*]. Followed by another. And another, growing in volume with each wail [*Is it a baby? The baby who lost the teether?*]. Sounded like my mother's cat Alice back in Quincy, meowing for breakfast [*Cat or baby?*].

But I knew that was no cat [*What is it then?*].

Elvis bellowed, accompanied by a burst of bawling [*Why is Elvis so alarmed? Where is that baby?*]. I broke through the leatherleaf and bog laurel and came into a small glade [*Where is the child?*]. There in the middle sat a squalling baby in a blue backpack-style infant carrier [*Is the baby alright? Where's the mother?*].

A baby girl, if her pink cap and long-sleeved onesie were any indication. A red-faced, cherub-cheeked baby girl, her chubby arms and legs flailing against an assault of black flies [*Flies? Is she going to do something about those flies?*].

I hurried over and fell to my knees in front of the pack, swatting away at the swarm [*How do you get rid of black flies? What effect will their bites have on the infant?*]. The baby appeared to be about six months old, but that was hardly an educated guess [*What does she know about babies?*]. Everything I knew about babies was based on my sister's toddler Tommy, whose infancy I'd mostly missed [*Because she was in the military? How much has she given up for her country?*].

This baby seemed okay, but her little neck and face and fingers were dotted with angry red marks left by the mean bites of black flies [*Will they make the baby sick?*]. I reached for my pack and the bug spray but then thought better of it [*Why? Why won't she get rid of the black flies?*]. Nothing with DEET in it could be much good for babies [*How bad is DEET for anybody?*].

The Writer's Guide to Beginnings

She kept on screaming, and Elvis kept barking [*Is the baby okay? Why doesn't she pick the baby up?*].

"Quiet," I ordered, but only the dog obeyed [*Is this the perfect dog or what?*]. I looked around, but there was no mom in sight [*Where is the mother? Father? Who left this baby out here in the woods? Why? Who would do such a thing?*]. So I unbuckled the straps on the carrier and pulled the child out of it [*Is she okay?*]. She lifted her small head up at me, and I stared into round sky-blue eyes rimmed in tears. I took her in my arms and stood up. I held her against my chest, then backed up to a tree to steady myself as I pulled the ends of my hoodie together and zipped it up around her as protection against the flies [*Will that work?*]. I bounced her up and down until her sobs subsided [*Is she okay?*]. Within minutes she was asleep [*Is she just exhausted or what?*].

"Now, what?" I looked at Elvis, but he just stood there looking back at me, head cocked, ears up, waiting for our next move. Whatever that might be [*What is she going to do?*].

One of the rules of the universe should be: Wherever there's a baby, there's a mother close by [*Where is that mother? Was the baby abducted?*]. But I'd seen plenty of babies without mothers over in Afghanistan [*What else did she see over there?*]. I just didn't expect to come across one here at home, in the Lye Brook Wilderness [*Isn't it safe anywhere?*].

"Where's your mother?" I asked the sleeping child [*Where's your mother, indeed?*].

Maybe she'd gone off behind some bushes to pee [*Really?*].

"Hello," I called. "Hello" [*Is anyone there?*].

No answer. I kept on calling and bouncing [*Now what?*]. The baby gurgled into my shoulder. Maybe her mother had fallen or hurt herself somehow [*How will she find her?*]. I walked around the clearing, eyes on the ground [*What's she looking for?*]. The leaves and detritus on the forest floor were disturbed around the backpack, but then both Elvis and I had been there [*So what does that mean?*].

I could see the trail we'd left behind as we'd barreled into the clearing from the south. But leading out in the opposite direction, I saw broken branches and rustled leaves and faint boot prints tamped in the mud [*Maybe the mother's boot prints?*]. Elvis and I followed the trail out of the glade into a denser area of forest thick with maples and beeches in full leaf. We hiked for several minutes through the wood.

The traces ended abruptly at a rollicking stream some 10 yards wide [*So should she cross the stream?*]. Too far to see across, too far to jump, and too far to ford across holding a baby [*How's the baby?*].

I yelled again. Elvis barked. We both listened for the sounds of humans, but all I heard were the sounds of the water and the trees and the creatures that truly belonged here [*Where is whoever left the baby behind? Foul play?*]. The baby stirred against my chest. She'd be hungry soon and tired and cold and wet and all those things that made babies uncomfortable [*How will she keep the baby comfortable?*]. Not to mention those mean black-fly bites [*What will be the long-term effect of those bites? Does the baby need to see a doctor?*]. I was torn: I wanted to find her mother or whoever brought her out here [*What happened to them?*]. But I knew the baby needed more care than I could provide deep in the woods [*What will she do? Shouldn't the baby come first?*].

"We're going back," I told Elvis, and together we retraced our steps to the baby carrier. I carefully unzipped my hoodie and strapped the dozing child into the carrier [*What's she doing that for?*]. Then I slipped off my small pack—thank God I was traveling light—and hooked it to the baby backpack [*Why?*]. I squatted down on my haunches and pulled the infant carrier onto my shoulders and pulled myself up to my feet. The fit was good. Not as heavy as my pack in Afghanistan but not exactly light, either [*How strong is she?*]. And my pack in Afghanistan didn't squirm [*How will she manage?*].

"She's waking up," I told Elvis. "Let's go home" [*Home where?*].

We walked back to the Lye Brook Falls Trail, where I hoped my cell phone would work [*Will it work?*]. I wasn't exactly comfortable taking the baby, not knowing where her mother was [*But what else can she do?*]. But I couldn't leave her there, as someone else had obviously done [*Who leaves a baby in the woods?*]. How anyone could do such a thing was beyond me. But I'd seen firsthand that people were capable of all manner of cruelty [*What has she seen? Does it still haunt her?*]. I just tried not to think about it these days [*How can she not think about it?*].

Elvis set the pace, leading the way home [*Where is he going?*]. You never had to tell him twice to go where his bowl and bed were. I stepped carefully to avoid jostling my precious cargo, who apparently was napping again [*What might the baby be suffering from?*].

If my cell didn't work, we'd hike down to the trailhead [*Is that the beginning of the trail?*]. The sun was climbing in the sky now, so there should have been more people out on the trail [*Will they meet someone who can help?*]. We passed the area I'd roped off with duct tape, and I thought about taking it down [*Why?*]. But Elvis had alerted for explosives there, or maybe that's where he found the baby teether [*Are there explosives there? Was the dog confused?*]. I didn't know why he'd designated that spot. Maybe he was just confused, his PTSD kicking in [*Is that possible? What does canine PTSD look like?*]. But PTSD or no PTSD, I would never bet against Elvis and his nose [*Is his nose that good?*]. I left the tape alone and kept on walking. Elvis vaulted ahead, leading our way out of the forest.

When we reached the trail, I marked the spot where we'd gone into the woods with tape [*Why?*]. I figured the authorities would want to know where we found the baby [*Will they search the woods?*]. They could follow our path quite easily since we'd left a stream of muddy tracks and broken twigs and brush in our wake [*What will they find?*].

I pulled my phone from my pocket. Two bars [*Is that enough?*]. Worth a shot. I dialed 911 and held my breath [*Will the call go through now?*]. The call rang through on the third try [*What will she say?*]. I spoke to the dispatcher and had just enough time to say that I'd found a baby alone in the Lye Brook Wilderness when we got cut off [*Now what?*]. She called me back and told me she'd informed the authorities and that I should stay put until the game warden arrived [*Is the game warden enough? How long will that take?*].

"Roger that," I said, and promptly lost service again [*What will happen now?*]. I sighed, pocketed my phone, and sat down next to Elvis. I shrugged off the baby carrier and tented my hoodie over it to keep away the bugs [*Will that be enough?*]. The baby slept on.

A cloud of black flies settled on me and Elvis [*How can she get rid of them?*]. Swatting them away with one hand, I pulled the bug spray out of my pack with the other. Time to reapply, for me and Elvis.

We could have a long wait ahead of us, and the black flies seemed to know it [*How long will they have to wait? Will they all be okay? What will happen when the police arrive?*].

As you can see, this exercise is very revealing. You can see where the story lags. You can see where the story questions are compelling, less compelling, least compelling—and, by the same token, compelling, more compelling, most compelling.

And I can see it, too.

After combing through my opening scene for story questions, I realized that I still had work to do. I had to establish who my heroine and Elvis were more quickly, and I had to tighten up the action and beef up the conflict. I even considered switching from first-person to third-person-limited point of view, which would give me more flexibility.

In the end, I trimmed this opening scene by around 1000 words. Take a look, and as you read this revised version, think of all the ways you can trim your own opening.

Spare These Stones
By Paula Munier

"Good friend for Jesus' sake forbeare,
To dig the dust enclosed here.
Blessed be the man that spares these stones,
And cursed be he that moves my bones."
—William Shakespeare (epitaph)

Every morning Mercy Carr rose at dawn and hiked five miles through the Vermont woods in search of peace. Her way of banishing the ghosts of war that haunted her and Elvis, the bomb-sniffing dog that had saved her life more than once. At least during the daylight hours.

But today the wilderness held a hush that unnerved Mercy, the same sort of hush that Sergeant Martinez always called a disturbance in the Force when they went out on patrol. Bad things usually followed.

Elvis didn't seem to notice. He raced ahead of her and plunged through a swollen stream, disappearing into a thicket of small spruce. Mercy considered following him, but like all soldiers she preferred her feet dry. She figured he'd circle back to her shortly, as he'd been trained to do.

They'd hiked nearly a third of the way up to Lye Brook Falls. The trail led along the bed of a former logging railroad, rising along a steady 20 percent incline for some 2-and-a-half miles up to the falls. The woods were blessedly cool and empty of people so early in the day. Towering birches, beeches, and maples in full leafing draped the forest in shade. A downpour the night before had left muddy puddles in its wake, and Mercy's boots were streaked with dirt. She tramped on, dodging the worst of the mud and taking care not to slip on the wet rocks, her eyes on the slick stone-ridden path and her mind off her future, which loomed ahead of her with no clear goal in sight.

After that last deployment, the one where she got shot and Elvis got depressed, they'd both been sent home. Still, it took Mercy six months and a lot of string-pulling to talk the private defense contractor into letting her adopt Elvis. In the end she prevailed, and they entered retirement together. Two former military police—one thirty-three-year-old two-legged female Vermonter with an exit wound scar blighting her once perfect ass and one handsome six-year-old four-legged male Malinois with canine PTSD—reclaiming themselves in the backwoods one hike at a time.

The terrain grew rougher, steeper, tougher. Mercy adjusted her pack, which at less than 15 pounds barely registered on her body, once burdened by nearly 100 pounds of gear.

In Afghanistan Elvis's job had been to walk in front of her, scouting ahead and alerting to danger. The only dangers here in the Southern Green Mountains were the ubiquitous clouds of biting black flies— and the occasional bear. Still, after about a quarter of a mile, Mercy paused to listen for the sound of a happy dog diving into the scrub, scampering over downed trees, racing up the rocky trail—but all she heard was the rush of the nearby brook, the warble of winter wrens, and the skittering of red squirrels.

Enough, Mercy thought. She whistled and waited.

The Belgian shepherd darted out of the scrub onto the path, his fawn fur stippled with dark splotches of sludge, his black muzzle muddy. Even dirty he was a pretty dog, a standard-bearer of his breed, far sleeker and smarter than any German shepherd, if you asked Mercy.

Elvis skidded to a stop right in front of her and jangled his head. In his mouth he held what looked like one of his squeaky toys.

"Drop it." Mercy held out her hand.

Elvis obliged, releasing the canary-yellow object into her open palm, his bright eyes on Mercy and his new plaything. She held it up and examined it in the light filtering through the trees.

"I think it's a baby teether," she told Elvis. About 5 inches long, the teether was shaped like a plastic daisy with a thick stem, the better for a baby's grip, and a flower-shaped lion's head blooming at the top. Apart from Elvis's drool, the little lion toy was clean, so it wasn't something that had been abandoned in the woods for long. She bent over towards Elvis, holding the teether out to him. "Where did you get this?"

Elvis pushed at her hand with a cold nose and whined. With another quick yelp he leapt back into the underbrush. Mercy tucked the baby toy into one of her cargo pockets and followed the dog, as he obviously meant her to do. She cursed under her breath as she sank into a marshy patch, mud seeping into the tops of her boots as she stomped through the mire after him.

Sometimes Elvis behaved erratically. Most of the time, Mercy could anticipate his triggers—slamming doors, thunderstorms, fireworks. But at other times, the triggers eluded her; they were scents, sounds, and situations known only to Elvis. But baby teethers had never been among them.

Elvis barreled through the tangle of bracken and brushwood to a stream that paralleled the trail, a fast tumbling of water over a bed of rocks. He jumped, clearing the 6-foot wide current easily. Mercy splashed after him, not willing to risk breaking a leg or twisting an ankle in a poorly landed leap. The cold water came up to her knees. Elvis waited for Mercy, his ears perked and his dark eyes on her.

Mercy clambered out of the brook and stumbled over the stones into a thick copse of young birch trees. There Elvis dropped down on his haunches in the middle of a large blowdown area littered with tree limbs. This was his alert position, the posture he assumed when he sniffed out weapons or explosives. IEDs were his specialty.

"What you got there, buddy?" Mercy squatted down next to him. Elvis looked at her as if to say, "Okay, my job here is done. Where's my reward?"

But Mercy wasn't sure if he'd earned it. She examined the ground in front of his paws. The forest floor was thick with detritus—dead leaves and twigs and pine needles—as well as mushrooms and moss and ferns and what looked like poison oak. No evidence of trespass here. No evidence of explosives. He wasn't trained to alert for babies—not that there was any evidence of a baby here, either.

On the other hand, Elvis had an excellent track record—and the best nose of any dog Mercy had ever met, either in training or in Afghanistan. He'd rarely been wrong before. What were the odds he was wrong now?

"Good boy," Mercy said, scratching that favorite spot between his pointed ears. She slipped a treat out of her pocket and held it in her open palm, and Elvis licked it up.

If they'd been on a mission, she would have called in the EOD team responsible for bomb disposal. She and Elvis never touched anything; the EOD guys took it from there. But here there was no EOD team trailing them; they weren't wearing flak or body armor. Mercy wasn't even sure Elvis had alerted to explosives. Who would plant explosives in a national forest?

Or maybe they were just fireworks. It was the Fourth of July, after all. Apart from sparklers, fireworks were illegal in Vermont. Even supervised public fireworks displays required a permit. But who would bother to bury fireworks in the woods—and even if someone had done so, surely they would have dug them up by now.

Mercy rose to her feet, and stood in the middle of the blowdown, wondering what to do. Elvis leaped ahead of her and darted into the brush. She headed out after him.

And that's when she heard it. A thin cry. Followed by another. And another, growing in volume with each wail. Sounded like her mother's cat Alice back in Quincy, meowing for breakfast.

Elvis bellowed, accompanied by a burst of bawling. Mercy broke through the leatherleaf and bog laurel and came into a small glade. There in the middle sat a squalling baby in a blue backpack-style infant carrier.

A baby girl, if her pink cap and Hello Kitty long-sleeved onesie were any indication. A red-faced, cherub-cheeked baby girl, chubby arms and legs flailing against an assault of black flies.

Mercy hurried over and fell to her knees in front of the pack, swatting away at the swarm. The baby appeared to be about six months old, but that was hardly an educated guess. Everything she knew about babies was based on her sister's toddler Tommy, whose infancy she'd mostly missed, and the injured infants she'd seen in theater.

This baby seemed okay, but her little neck and face and fingers were dotted with angry red marks left by the mean bites of black flies. Mercy reached for her pack and the bug spray but then thought better of it. Nothing with DEET in it could be any good for babies.

The baby kept on screaming, and the dog kept on barking.

"Quiet," Mercy ordered, but only the dog obeyed. She looked around, but there was no mom in sight.

The baby continued to cry, an escalation of shrieks.

"Okay, okay." Mercy unbuckled the straps on the carrier and pulled the child out of the carrier. The baby lifted up her small head, and Mercy stared into round, slate-grey eyes rimmed in tears. Mercy took her in her arms and stood up. She held the little girl against her chest, then backed up to a tree to steady herself as she pulled the ends of her hoodie together under the baby's bottom and zipped it up around her as protection against the flies. Mercy bounced her up and down until her sobs subsided. Within minutes she was asleep.

"Now what?" Mercy looked at Elvis, but he just stood there looking back at her, head cocked, ears up, waiting for their next move.

One of the rules of the universe should be: Wherever there's a baby, there's a mother close by. But Mercy had seen plenty of babies without mothers.

"Where's your mother?" Mercy asked the sleeping child. Maybe she'd gone off behind some bushes to pee. "Hello," Mercy called. "Hello."

No answer.

The last time she'd held a baby over there, the child had died in her arms. An IED they'd somehow missed.

"Hello." Mercy kept on calling and bouncing. The baby gurgled into her shoulder. Maybe her mother had fallen or hurt herself somehow. Mercy walked around the clearing, eyes on the ground.

Mercy could see the trail they'd left behind as she and Elvis barreled into the glade from the south. But leading out in the opposite direction, she saw broken branches and rustled leaves and faint boot prints tamped in the mud. Mercy was a good tracker; Sergeant Martinez used to say she was part dog. Which part, she'd ask. Their little joke.

Mercy and Elvis followed the markings into a denser area of forest thick with maples and beeches in full leaf and hiked through the wood. The traces ended abruptly at a stream some 10 yards wide. Too far to see across, too far to jump across, and too far to ford across holding a baby.

Mercy yelled again. Elvis barked. She listened for the sounds of humans, but all she heard were the sounds of the water and the trees and the creatures that truly belonged here. The baby stirred against her chest. She'd be hungry soon and tired and cold and wet. And those nasty black-fly bites had to hurt. Mercy was torn; she wanted to find the mother or whoever brought the little girl out here. But she knew the baby needed more care than she could provide deep in the woods. And she'd need it sooner rather than later.

"We're going back." Together she and the dog retraced their steps to the baby carrier. Mercy carefully unzipped her hoodie and strapped the dozing child into the carrier. She slipped off her own small pack, tying it to the big one with the baby. She hoisted the carrier up onto her shoulders. The fit was good. Not nearly as heavy as what she carried in Afghanistan but not exactly light, either. And what she carried in Afghanistan didn't squirm.

"She's waking up," Mercy told Elvis. "Home."

Mercy never had to tell Elvis twice to go where his bowl and bed were. He set the pace, blazing back the way they came. Mercy stepped carefully to avoid jostling her precious cargo. They headed for the Lye Brook Falls Trail, where she hoped her cell phone would work and she could contact the authorities.

Mercy wasn't exactly comfortable taking the baby, not knowing where her mother was. But she couldn't leave the child there, as someone else had obviously done. How or why anyone would do such a thing was beyond her. Mercy knew that people were capable of all manner of cruelty. She just tried not to think about it these days.

They came to the blowdown where she'd first heard the child. Elvis trotted over to the very same place where he'd alerted before and dropped into his alert position.

"Again?" Mercy didn't know why Elvis seemed fixated on this spot. Maybe he detected explosives there, or maybe that was where he found the baby teether. Maybe he was just confused, his PTSD kicking in. But PTSD or no PTSD, she couldn't bet against Elvis and his nose.

Mercy unhooked her small pack from the baby carrier and pulled out the duct tape and her Swiss Army knife, the two tools she never left home without. She used the duct tape to rope off a crescent around the area Elvis had targeted, using birch saplings as posts.

"Better safe than sorry," she told Elvis.

Elvis vaulted ahead, steering them out of the forest. When they reached the trail, Mercy taped the spot where they'd gone into the woods. Then she pulled her cell phone out of her pocket and turned it on. No bars. No dial tone. Coverage was spotty up here. They'd have to trek down to the trailhead for a stronger signal.

"Back to civilization," Mercy said with a sigh.

The dog took the lead. As they began their descent, a cloud of black flies fell upon on them. The baby woke up with a start, and the wailing began again. Mercy swatted away at the miserable flying beasts, quickening her pace. Elvis stayed up front but close by.

They had a long walk ahead of them, and the black flies seemed to know it.

You'll notice that in this revised version, I follow the same advice I've given you: Trim the backstory, lose the info dumping, avoid phone calls, murder your darlings, and more.

You should do the same for your story—and not just the first scene but all of your scenes. This is the handiest tool for revision you can use and the most critical. The whole point of story questions is to keep the reader reading, which is the same point of the beginning itself.

"Rewriting is re-dreaming." —*Robert Olen Butler*

YOUR MACRO, MESO, & MICRO STORY QUESTIONS

Whether you're writing your first draft or revising your story for the tenth time, you need to keep your macro, meso, and micro story questions in mind. First, write out your macro story question, which is usually just a matter of reformatting the big story idea into a question. For example, with *The Martian*, the big story idea is, as we've seen, "*Cast Away* on Mars." Rework that idea as a macro story question, and it looks something like this: Will the astronaut marooned on Mars survive?

Now narrow down your story idea to one big question: Will my protagonist find true love/win the war/bring the perpetrator to justice?

Be specific and dramatic. Write down that single macro question, and post it where you can see it as you work on your story. This will help you remember what your story is really about.

When you make your scene list, identify the meso story question for each scene. This will help you remember what the scene is all about and what you need to accomplish in that scene.

And when you go through each scene as you revise, as we did here with the scene from *Spare These Stones*, make sure that your micro story questions are in place. This will help you remember that every story question is a narrative magnet, pulling the reader through your story—word by word, line by line, and scene by scene.

JUMP-START

Pacing is the thing editors complain most about and the thing authors must most often address, even after they've won a publishing contract. Here's a revision trick to make sure your pacing is on track: Get a pen and paper, and set your timer for fifteen minutes. Take the first thirty pages of your story, and cut it by 10 percent. Now do it again, and cut another 10 percent. Do it as fast as you can. Now read it again, and see how much better the pacing is. What did you delete? Why?

NOTE: This is a good exercise to do with your writers' group as well. Exchange openings, and edit each other's work. Then compare the edits you made to the edits your writer friend made. Which edits worked better? Why?

ACT ONE CHECKLIST

When you go over your story opening, ask yourself the following questions:

- Is your title compelling and in keeping with your genre?
- What actually happens?
- Why will the reader care about/relate to the characters?
- How do you want the reader to feel? What have you done to evoke that feeling?
- Have you used all the elements of fiction at your disposal—setting, plot, character, theme, etc.?
- Have you chosen the right POV?
- Are you writing in an engaging voice?
- Is your Inciting Incident strong enough? Plot Point #1?
- Does the dialogue ring true?
- Are you using several types of conflict?
- Are the story questions strong enough to keep the reader turning the pages?
- Is it clear what kind of story you're telling?
- What makes this beginning different from others of its ilk?
- Is it well-written and well-edited?

Once you're certain that your story opening keeps readers reading, you need to polish, polish, polish the prose itself.

THE REVISION BOOKSHELF

"Vigorous writing is concise. A sentence should contain no unnecessary words, a paragraph no unnecessary sentences, for the same reason that a drawing should have no unnecessary lines and a machine no unnecessary parts."
—William Strunk, Jr.

Putting your best prose forward is made easier when you have these classic primers on your writer's bookshelf:

- *The Elements of Style*, by William Strunk, Jr., E. B. White, and Roger Angell
- *Garner's Modern American Usage*, by Bryan A. Garner
- *On Writing Well*, by William Zinsser
- *The Artful Edit*, by Susan Bell
- *Reading Like a Writer*, by Francine Prose
- *The Chicago Manual of Style*, by the University of Chicago Press
- *Self-Editing for Fiction Writers*, by Renni Browne and Dave King
- *Eats, Shoots & Leaves*, by Lynne Truss
- *The Subversive Copy Editor*, by Carol Fisher Saller
- *Woe Is I*, by Patricia T. O'Conner
- *How to Write a Sentence: And How to Read One*, by Stanley Fish

YOUR COPY-READY PRE-FLIGHT CHECK

"I believe the road to hell is paved with adverbs ..."
—*Stephen King*

Do you remember the story *The Princess and the Pea*? In the Hans Christian Andersen fairy tale, a prince in search of a real princess to make his wife is beset by apparent fakes. When a young woman claiming to be a princess shows up at the castle gates in a rainstorm, looking like a drowned rat, the Queen devises a princess test. She places a pea on the bedstead, piles twenty mattresses on top of it, and puts twenty eiderdown featherbeds on top of the mattresses. She then sends the young woman to bed. In the morning, the sly Queen asks the girl if she slept well. "Oh," said the young woman. "No. I scarcely slept at all. Heaven knows what's in that bed. I lay on something so hard that I'm black and blue all over. It was simply terrible." This proves she is a real Princess because only a princess would be so sensitive. So with the Queen's blessing, the Prince and the real Princess are married and live happily ever after.

Well, agents and editors are the real princesses of the publishing world. We are as sensitive to language as that princess was to a pea, and copy that reads badly leaves us just as black and blue. I can tell you—from personal experience—that we've all lost sleep over it.

Remember: When you submit your work to publishing professionals, you're showing your work to people who make a living by being uber-sensitive to language. We know our grammar, our spelling, and our punctuation, and when we see spelling mistakes, grammatical errors, typos, redundancies, inconsistencies, and awkward sentences, it's like hearing fingernails scraping a chalkboard. We find it physically painful.

"Never throw up on an editor." —*Ellen Datlow*

If you think I'm exaggerating, think again. Would you try to sell your house without mopping the floors? Show your dog without grooming it? Interview for a job in stained sweats?

Neatness counts—in publishing as in life. Your copy needs to be as clean, clear, and concise as possible.

How clean is your copy? You must develop a good eye for precise prose. You need to be able to catch the problems that afflict your prose and fix them so they don't mark you as a fake princess right there on your first page. Here's a checklist that you can use to sharpen your editing skills and polish your manuscript.

- **WHEN IN DOUBT, DELETE.** Otherwise known as "Murder your darlings." Whenever you write a line of which you are inordinately proud, you should delete it or rewrite it. No one likes a show-off, and rather than showing off, you should aim for Elmore Leonard's high standard: "If it sounds like writing, I rewrite it."
- **TRUST YOUR CRITICAL INSTINCTS.** As you edit your story, whenever you find yourself thinking, *I'm not sure that works*, listen to yourself. Don't give in to the temptation to excuse it and say, "Oh, I'm sure that it's fine." It's not. Rework it, or delete it.
- **READ YOUR WORK OUT LOUD.** Reading your work out loud—every word of it—is the most reliable way to hear what is working and what is not working. Whenever you stumble or have to catch your breath, you'll know that's a section that needs reworking. As Dave Wolverton says, "Pay attention to the sound of words."

- **PAY ATTENTION TO YOUR CHARACTERS' NAMES.** As we've seen, the best character names are: (1) easy to read, pronounce, and spell (so the reader doesn't stumble over them), (2) not too similar to other characters' names in your story (so the reader doesn't have to figure out who's who all the time), and (3) are in keeping with the sex, background, and temperament of the character.
- **LOSE THE DIALECT.** Don't alienate agents and editors with phonetically spelled dialect. Use word choice and sentence structure to indicate regional speech patterns.
- **SOFTEN THE HYPERBOLIC LANGUAGE.** The more dramatic the action, the more important it is to let the action stand on its own. Don't milk it with hyperbolic language, or your compelling drama will deteriorate into melodrama. This will diminish your story as well as your authority as the storyteller.
- **STICK TO AMERICAN ENGLISH.** If your aim is to secure a contract with a U.S. publisher/agent/editor, you need to use American grammar, spelling, and punctuation.
- **CHECK THE READING LEVEL.** Running a reading level test on your story will help you ensure that your prose is engaging and easy to read. Look for readability statistics under the Review tab in Microsoft Word's Spelling and Grammar tool (and you should be writing your story in Microsoft Word since that's the standard for submission). Make sure that you've checked the "show readability statistics" box in the options under Spelling and Grammar. Then when you run the Spelling and Grammar tool, the Flesch-Kincaid reading level will show up under readability statistics. This level refers to the grade level of reading proficiency needed to comprehend a given work. The average newspaper in the United States is written at a sixth-grade reading level, so if yours comes in at anything much above that, you need to simplify your prose. Aim for a reading level between sixth and eighth grade.
- **CHECK YOUR DIALOGUE TAGS.** As we've seen, you should simply stick to *said*, or use action statements. Delete any "creative" dialogue tags.

- **CUT THE CLICHÉS.** Overused phrasings—"smooth as silk," "common as dirt," "sweet as sugar"—trivialize your prose and subvert your style.
- **REPLACE WEAK VERBS WITH STRONG VERBS.** Dump as many of the forms of the verb "to be" as you can, and then discard all the other overused verbs cluttering up your prose. Find stronger verbs, and you'll strengthen your sentences and story. Why say *talk* when you can say *whisper, communicate, inform, debate, sing, pronounce, murmur, mutter, mumble, express, clarify, vocalize, verbalize, chat, chatter, gab, yak, discuss, articulate, converse, enunciate, tell, gossip,* or *confess*?
- **AXE THE ADVERBS.** Strong verbs eliminate the need for adverbs altogether. Your prose will be all the cleaner for it.
- **INFUSE YOUR LANGUAGE WITH THE POWER OF THE SENSES.** The best writing evokes all the senses and allows your readers to see, hear, touch, smell, and taste the world in which your story takes place.

JUMP-START

Just as you should exchange pages with a writer friend to check the pacing of your story, you should also exchange pages with a writer friend to check the clarity and precision of your prose. Edit each other's stories on hard copy with red pens. Go over each other's edits, and compare notes. Note what you learn about your work, your friend's work, and your respective editing skills.

"I like to edit my sentences as I write them. I rearrange a sentence many times before moving on to the next one. For me, that editing process feels like a form of play, like a puzzle that needs solving, and it's one of the most satisfying parts of writing."
—*Karen Thompson Walker*

THE PROFESSIONAL EDITOR

Many writers hire copy editors and/or line editors to edit their manuscripts. And there's no shame in that; not everyone can edit themselves. And a fresh pair of eyes can be a godsend, provided that pair of eyes knows what to look for. But before you spend good money on an edit, you need to know exactly what you're paying for.

First, let's define our terms. Line edit and copyedit are not interchangeable terms. Copy editing addresses spelling, grammar, redundancies, repetitions, inconsistencies, and fact-checking. Line editing is all this and more—the more being reworking and even rewriting awkward sentences to address flow, clarity, and more. Most copy editors and line editors do both, and the lines blur depending on the editor and the manuscript. A heavy copy edit and a light line edit are about the same thing.

You can hire either a line editor or a copy editor to edit your entire manuscript, or you can ask the editor to do fifty or one-hundred pages—editing on hard copy so you can see what they do—and then input the changes yourself. This way, you'll learn how to do it yourself.

To make sure you get a good editor whose advice will be worth your investment, ask for referrals from published authors, agents, or acquisitions editors. Your genre association is also a good resource.

BEGINNING AGAIN

"He has the deed half done who has made a beginning." —*Horace*

When you're ready to show your work, you'll need to do your due diligence before you submit pages for review to story contests, writers conferences, literary agencies, publishing houses, and the like. First, check the websites of the organizations you'd like to approach for their submission guidelines. All have different requirements. For example: At our agency, Talcott Notch Literary Services, we ask writers like you to cut and paste the first ten pages of the story right into the query e-mail. If we like what we see, we'll usually request the first fifty or one-hundred pages next.

Generally speaking, you should be prepared to submit the first page, the first ten pages, the first fifty pages, and/or the first one-hundred pages. **NOTE:** While you may eventually be asked to send the entire manuscript, that won't happen if you don't make it past these benchmarks.

With that understanding, here are the checklists you should consult before sending off your beginning to publishing professionals.

First Page Checklist

"Make everybody fall out of the plane first, and then explain who they were and why they were in the plane to begin with."
—*Nancy Ann Dibble*

- Does something significant happen—such as the Inciting Incident?
- Do we get a sense of the main action of the story?
- Is the genre of your story clear?
- Do you introduce your protagonist in a proactive way?
- Is your character alone and if so, why? How do you make that compelling?
- Is your protagonist likable and/or admirable?
- What emotion do you aim to evoke in the reader?
- Have you burdened your opening with backstory, description, inner monologue, and/or info dumping?
- Are you telling the story in a strong voice?
- Do you ground your story in setting?
- Have you used a device to help differentiate your story?
- Do you raise enough story questions—micro and meso (if not macro yet)?
- Is your copy clean, clear, and concise?

"Good writing is rewriting." —*Truman Capote*

First-Ten-Pages Checklist

"No tears in the writer, no tears in the reader." —*Robert Frost*

- Does your opening set up, foreshadow, or introduce your big story idea?
- Do we know what your protagonist consciously and subsconsciously yearns for ? If not, why not?
- Are you using chapter openers to help establish the tone, mood, and theme?
- Is your Inciting Incident in the first chapter? If not, why not?
- Are you weaving all the elements of fiction into your story tapestry: setting, character, action, conflict, dialogue, theme, and tone?
- Is the meso question of the scene(s) clear and compelling? Does the opening scene(s) have a clear beginning, middle, and end?
- Have you planted a solid story question every fifty to one hundred words?
- Have you introduced your worthy antagonist? If not, why not?
- Have you referred to characters the reader has not met? If so, why?
- Have you introduced too many characters for the reader to keep track of so soon? If so, how will you fix that?
- Is your copy clean, clear, and concise?

First-Fifty-Pages Checklist

"I try to create sympathy for my characters, then turn the monsters loose." —*Stephen King*

- Have you hit the Inciting Incident? If not, why are you running so late? What do you need to cut to get there sooner?
- Is the main action clear? If not, why not?
- Have you burdened your story with any flashbacks? If so, how can you address what is often a terrible miscalculation?
- Have you left your protagonist alone too long thinking/brooding/navel-gazing?
- Have we fallen completely in love with your protagonist?
- Are we intrigued by an antagonist we love to hate?
- Are you on track for Plot Point #1?

- Have you peppered each page with micro story questions?
- Have you begun and ended each chapter with a strong meso story question?
- Is your copy clean, clear, and concise?

First-One-Hundred-Pages Checklist

"Be a sadist. No matter how sweet and innocent your leading characters, make awful things happen to them—in order that the reader may see what they are made of." —*Kurt Vonnegut*

- Have you introduced your subplots, significant secondary characters (love interests and suspects)?
- Have you hit Plot Point #1 yet? If not, why are you running so late? What do you need to cut to get there sooner?
- Are you telling your story primarily in scenes, rather than exposition?
- When it comes to drama, have you gone big (rather than middling)?
- Have you set the events in motion that will lead to the Midpoint, Plot Point #2, and Climax of your story? If not, why not?
- Have you milked the conflict in each scene?
- Have you milked the emotional impact of each scene?
- Have you reread your story opening just for action to ensure that enough is happening? If not, why not?
- Are you incorporating an organizing principle to add another layer of complexity to your story?
- Is your copy clean, clear, and concise?

IF YOU'RE WRITING A MEMOIR ...

At a recent writers conference, I was on a panel with about twenty agents. When the subject of memoir came up, more than half said that they preferred to shop memoir with a book proposal, rather than a full manuscript—myself included. This is because memoir is nonfiction, and with nonfiction, considerations such as author

The Writer's Guide to Beginnings

platform and marketing plans can be as important to the buying decision as the story itself. (Certainly my agent sold my own memoir, *Fixing Freddie: A True Story About a Boy, a Mom, and a Very, Very Bad Beagle*, on the basis of a book proposal.)

So if you are writing a memoir, then you should be prepared to put together a book proposal, even if you've already finished the entire work. A book proposal is a sales document that typically includes a description of the work, chapter-by-chapter outline, selling points, competitive titles, marketing plan, and author bio and platform, as well as the first fifty to one-hundred pages. For more on writing a good book proposal, see *How to Write a Book Proposal*, by Michael Larsen.

....

With these checklists in mind, give your beginning one more final polish—and let your story opening shine!

YOUR BEST BEGINNING

"For a true writer, each book should be a new beginning where he tries again for something that is beyond attainment. He should always try for something that has never been done or that others have tried and failed. Then sometimes, with great luck, he will succeed." —*Ernest Hemingway*

Every story is only as good as its beginning. During the course of this book we've explored all the nuances of writing good story openings, subtle and not so subtle. Arm yourself with these tips, tools, and techniques, and you'll write beginnings that rock your readers right into your story, from page one to "The End."

You're off to a great start. Now keep it coming, and keep those readers reading.

Now go start that story because you can't finish what you never begin.

And may the next story that keeps you up all night be your own.

"A good beginning makes a good end."
—*Traditional English Proverb*

ACKNOWLEDGMENTS

---◯---

My first thanks must go to the many writers who've participated in my Scene One: First Ten Pages Boot Camps, which inspired this book. My writing it was Phil Sexton's idea, and he talked me into it. So, thank you, Phil—and all of my friends at *Writers Digest*, including my editor Cris Freese, designer Alexis Estoye, Rachel Randall, Alex Rixey, Chuck Sambuchino, Kevin Quinn, Aaron Bauer, Michael Hanna, and Julie Oblander.

I must also thank my sister agents at Talcott Notch Literary, including Rachael Dugas, Saba Sulaiman, and our fearless leader Gina Panettieri, to whom this book is dedicated with my greatest thanks.

My great gratitude to William Martin, *New York Times* best-selling author, dear friend and mentor, who challenges me to raise the bar—and his generous foreword certainly raised the bar for this book.

Never-ending thanks to my parents for giving my life story a great beginning, my children, for providing the sweetest plot points, and Michael, for rewriting our second act.

A shout-out to my wonderful clients, the many editors and publishers with whom I work, my beloved Scribe Tribe, Hallie Ephron and

Hank Phillippi Ryan, Michael Neff of the Algonkian New York Pitch Conference, and all of the wonderful authors whose commitment to craft inspires me every day.

And a final heartfelt thanks to all of the writers who've shared their time and work with me over the years and to you, my readers.

I wish you great beginnings and many happy returns.

ABOUT THE AUTHOR

───────────◯───────────

Paula Munier, Senior Literary Agent and Content Strategist at Talcott Notch Literary Services, boasts broad experience creating and marketing exceptional content in all formats across all markets for such media giants as WGBH, Disney, Fidelity, Gannett, Greenspun Media Group, F+W Media, and Quayside. She began her career as a journalist, and along the way added editor, acquisitions specialist, digital content manager, and publishing executive to her repertoire. Her specialties include crime fiction, women's fiction, historical fiction, literary fiction, high-concept SF/fantasy, and YA/children's, memoir, humor, pop culture, health & wellness, cooking, self-help, pop psych, New Age, inspirational, technology, science, and writing. Paula is very involved with the mystery community, having served four terms as President of the New England chapter of Mystery Writers of America as well as on the MWA board.

Paula has also served on the New England Crime Bake committee for ten years and counting. And she's an active member of Sisters in Crime and SCBWI. A well-published journalist, author, copywriter, and ghostwriter, Paula has penned countless new stories, articles, essays, collateral, and blogs, as well as authoring/co-authoring more than a dozen books, including *Writing with Quiet Hands, Plot Perfect, Fixing Freddie,* and *5-Minute Mindfulness.*

INDEX

The Writer's Guide to Beginnings

Index